What Teachers Need to Know

David D. Dill
and Associates

What Teachers Need to Know

The Knowledge, Skills, and Values Essential to Good Teaching

Jossey-Bass Publishers
San Francisco • Oxford • 1990

WHAT TEACHERS NEED TO KNOW
The Knowledge, Skills, and Values Essential to Good Teaching
by David D. Dill and Associates

Library of Congress Cataloging-in-Publication Data

What teachers need to know : the knowledge, skills, and values essential to good teaching / [edited by] David D. Dill and Associates.
p. cm. — (A joint publication in the Jossey-Bass education series and the Jossey-Bass higher education series)
Includes bibliographical references.
ISBN 1-55542-226-8 (alk. paper)
1. Teaching—Congresses. 2. Teachers—Training of—United States—Congresses. I. Dill, David D., date. II. Series: Jossey-Bass education series. III. Series: Jossey-Bass higher education series.
LB1025.2.W46 1990
371.1'02—dc20 89-48337
CIP

Manufactured in the United States of America

The paper in this book meets the guidelines for permanence and durability of the Committee on Production Guidelines for Book Longevity of the Council on Library Resources.

JACKET DESIGN BY WILLI BAUM

FIRST EDITION
First printing: February 1990
Second printing: July 1990

Code 9020

A joint publication in
The Jossey-Bass Education Series
and
The Jossey-Bass Higher Education Series

Contents

To Martha Jennifer Givando Dill,
Teacher

Preface

Fundamental to the role of teacher is the capacity to identify and select the most important ideas and skills in a particular field. Whether a tutor is choosing a problem for a bewildered algebra student, or a high school teacher is outlining an essay for a composition course, or the curriculum committee of a medical school is redefining the content that must be included in the first-year program for all medical students, the challenge is similar. Each individual or group must decide what knowledge is most important for his, her, or their purposes. Therefore, it is not surprising that reformers in education should discover that the issue most central to what our students should know is what our teachers should know.

One distinguishing characteristic of the education reform movement of the 1980s is the assumption that a knowledge base for the teaching profession now can be defined—a knowledge base that can be used in designing future teacher education programs (Carnegie Task Force, 1986; Holmes Group, 1986). In response to the reports of the Carnegie Task Force (1986) and the Holmes Group (1986) and to the practical problems of developing the innovative Lyndhurst master of arts in teaching program for secondary school teachers, the University of North Carolina, Chapel Hill, hosted an invitational conference on the knowledge most worth having in teacher education. The goal of the conference was to begin a public discussion of the intellectual, practical, and normative knowledge essential to the education of future middle school and secondary school teachers. The conference planning committee invited some of the most distinguished researchers and scholars in the areas of effective teaching, student learning, clinical education, and values in teaching and in the content areas of English, mathematics, and science to offer their knowledge and wisdom on this topic. We also invited several nationally respected commentators on the profession of teaching to add their special insights and their sense of the larger context to the discussion of the knowledge most worth having.

We asked each participant to provide a paper addressing a simple question: What are the knowledge, skills, and values essential for the preparation of middle school and secondary school teachers? The audience for each paper included experienced public and private school teachers, school of education faculty members, faculty members in the arts and sciences and in professional school programs, school administrators, legislators, and public policy makers. We subjected each paper to extensive commentary and questioning, after which we edited and revised it for use as a chapter in this volume. The result is unusual. *What Teachers Need to Know* represents the distilled knowledge and experience of some of our most respected American educators, written in a style crafted for public discourse, on an enduring question central to the future of the teaching profession.

Our topic is an important one. Focus on the substance of teacher education programs has increased greatly since the publication of *A Nation at Risk* (National Commission for Excellence in Education, 1983) initiated the current wave of educational reform. The publication of *A Nation Prepared: Teachers for the 21st Century* by the Carnegie Task Force (1986) called for the creation of a national board of assessment for teaching—a call that immediately aroused interest in defining and operationalizing knowledge about teaching. The Carnegie Forum commissioned a number of studies to identify the judgments and standards that must undergird such a certification process, and these results are now beginning to appear (Shulman, 1987). Similarly, the Holmes Group, consisting of deans of education from the nation's leading universities, was launched in 1986 in an effort to stimulate reform of teacher education within research universities. Increasingly, however, the Holmes Group (1989, p. 5) agenda has come to focus on schools of education and the core knowledge they teach: "The central intellectual challenge facing Holmes Group institutions is the rethinking and rearrangement of the education curriculum into comprehensive, coherent programs that faculty collaboratively design and teach. . . . The credibility of the Holmes reforms rests here. The current political climate emphasizes liberal arts rigor and better supervised and supported clinical experiences and induction, but not professional education studies. Thus Holmesian program development must identify and organize a body of knowledge about learning and teaching substantial enough to occupy more than a semester or so of college coursework. Teaching's claim to professionalism and the education school's claim to a central role in teacher preparation requires such a demonstration." Because of this concern, a major focus for the Holmes Group has been the formation of a national curriculum committee to recommend teacher preparation curricula for Holmes Group member institutions.

Contribution of This Book

Stimulated by these efforts, an unusually large number of major publications have appeared recently focusing on the knowledge base of teacher education and on the mission of schools of education (Clifford and Guthrie, 1988; Galambos, 1986; Houston, forthcoming; Raths and Katz, 1986; Reynolds, 1989; Wittrock, 1986). Reasonably one might ask, what is the particular contribution of this volume to this ongoing discussion?

One way to approach this question is to place the content of this book within the emerging framework defining the knowledge base of teaching. Shulman (1987, p. 1) suggests that our understanding of the knowledge essential for teaching is shaped by our conceptions of what teaching is: "A teacher knows something not understood by others, presumably the students. The teacher can transform understanding, performance skills, or desired attitudes or values into pedagogical representations and actions. These are ways of talking, showing, enacting, or otherwise representing ideas so that the unknowing can come to know, those without understanding can comprehend and discern, and the unskilled can become adept. Thus, teaching necessarily begins with a teacher's understanding of what is to be learned and how it is to be taught. It proceeds through a series of activities during which the students are provided specific instruction and opportunities for learning, though the learning itself ultimately remains the responsibility of the students. Teaching ends with new comprehension by both the teacher and the student."

Given this core conception of teaching, Shulman (p. 4) then suggests the categories of knowledge that underlie the understanding teachers need to promote comprehension among students:

- content knowledge
- general pedagogical knowledge, with special reference to those broad principles and strategies of classroom management and organization that appear to transcend subject matter
- curriculum knowledge, with particular grasp of the materials and programs that serve as "tools of the trade" for teachers
- pedagogical content knowledge—that special amalgam of content and pedagogy that is uniquely the province of teachers, their own special form of professional understanding
- knowledge of learners and their characteristics
- knowledge of educational contexts, ranging

from the workings of the group or classroom, to the governance and financing of school districts, to the character of communities and cultures
- knowledge of educational ends, purposes, and values and their philosophical and historical grounds

This book directly or indirectly addresses all of the topics Shulman outlines. But we give particular weight to general pedagogical knowledge; knowledge of learners and their characteristics; content knowledge; and knowledge of educational ends, purposes, and values. In particular, the discussion of content knowledge is unusual in that distinguished faculty members in arts and sciences authored the chapters in this area. These scholars have thought long and hard about what knowledge in their subject matter disciplines is essential for teachers and about whether existing majors in the relevant arts and sciences are sufficient or appropriate for those preparing to be professional teachers.

A second unusual component of this collection is its careful appraisal of the values essential for the professional education of teachers. The preparation of teachers has been distinctive from its beginnings in the late nineteenth century for including, along with the science and art of teaching, the humanistic bases of teaching through courses in educational philosophy and history (Clifford and Guthrie, 1988). In the postwar period, this focus on history and philosophy was diluted as schools of education imported the social sciences and reorganized these subjects into the so-called social foundations of education. More recently, the humanistic content of professional education has been further diminished as the traditional concern with the purposes of education, which characterized the earlier teaching in philosophy and history, has been transmuted into the more utilitarian emphasis on policy analysis.

In contrast to the diminishing tradition of humanistic education in schools of education, other professional schools have been giving increasing attention to the role of ethics and values in professional education. In the late 1970s, the Hastings Center (1980) conducted a national study on the status, problems, and possibilities of the teaching of ethics in higher education. The center produced reports on the teaching of ethics in legal education, journalism, medical education, business management, engineering, and public policy. Despite the tradition of teaching educational philosophy in schools of education, the field of education was conspicuously absent from the Hastings report; the survey found little evidence of ethics teaching or materials development in professional schools of education. This absence of attention to ethics and values in teacher education, compared with the relatively greater attention paid to it in the fields of medicine, business, and law, may be traceable to the diminution of the humanities in education in the face of the supposedly more scientific social sciences. Or it may stem from the tradition of teaching educational philosophy courses in schools of education—courses influenced by traditional philosophy courses in arts and science departments. Or it may have been caused by academic sensitivities regarding separation of church and state and the potentially controversial role teachers play in the socialization of the young. Whatever the reason, the issues of discerning which values are essential to teaching, how to stimulate the moral imagination of teachers, and what role professional ethics should play in teacher education only recently have surfaced as important questions in teacher education (Sizer, 1984; Strom, 1989). Within this volume, we have attempted to consider not only the necessary knowledge and skills but also the moral dimension of teaching. Therefore, this collection suggests what values are essential for teacher education and how teacher education curricula might incorporate them.

One final contribution of this book is to suggest the implications of these ideas for current efforts to reform both the public schools and the schools of education in major universities. Efforts to professionalize teaching—through, for example, the identification of master teachers, the development of merit systems, and the enhancement of the actual conditions for teaching—assume a clear consensus on what effective teachers know and do, but such agreement likely does not exist. School board members, school administrators, and teachers will find in this collection a remarkably accessible discussion of the knowledge base for teaching in the middle schools and secondary schools—a discussion that can inform their explorations and innovations.

The definition of the knowledge base for teacher education has similar significant consequences for the design of teacher education programs and for the future development of schools of education as professional schools. But unlike professional programs in medicine, law, and business, teacher education programs require the direct involvement of arts and sciences faculty who contribute content knowledge to the educational process. Furthermore, because the content of teacher education programs is more directly affected than are other such programs by public policies influencing state certification requirements, policy makers outside academic institutions generally play a more significant role in the design of teacher education programs than they do in the professional programs in other fields. For all of these reasons, we have purposefully written this book to appeal to the school of education faculty members, the arts and sciences faculty members, and the clinical faculty from the public schools who will be party to the development, design, and teaching of future teacher education programs.

Unlike the valuable academic reviews of relevant research on teaching (Houston, forthcoming; Reynolds, 1989; Wittrock, 1986), which are designed to provide scholars with the critical models and references in each specialty, we address this book to the interested, educated individual who will influence or play some cooperative role in teacher education programs. We anticipate that this book will be of substantial interest to the many interdisciplinary and interorganizational groups engaged in the development of teacher education programs in major universities. They will find here a basis for discussion and debate. We also believe that the book will be uncommonly accessible and informative to university administrators and policy makers with a genuine interest in and concern for professional programs for teachers and the future of schools of education. Finally, we anticipate that faculty members in teacher education, and in education generally, will discover arguments here with which they may not agree but which they certainly can respect.

Overview of the Chapters

What Teachers Need to Know is organized into four parts. As a means of providing coherence and relationship, we introduce each part with a brief essay that relates the accompanying chapters to the theme of the book. These introductory essays raise substantive questions and issues as a perspective for the curious reader.

In the introduction, Ernest L. Boyer touches on the key themes of the book through a recollection of his most influential teachers. This chapter describes, in vividly human terms, the knowledge, values, and skills of the most effective teachers.

In Part One, Thomas L. Good (Chapter One) discusses the role of teaching research in school reforms, classroom practice, and teacher education. This chapter systematically reviews recent research on classroom instruction, critiquing our current knowledge base for teaching. In Chapter Two, Irving E. Sigel addresses the essential knowledge teachers require of learning and of the learner. Completing Part One, Carolyn M. Evertson confirms in Chapter Three that teacher education requires not only essential knowledge but also essential skills. Her chapter reviews mechanisms for learning the knowledge and skills essential to teaching.

In Part Two, Richard Lloyd-Jones, Peter J. Hilton, and Harold J. Morowitz, each a well-regarded scholar, offer their insights on the knowledge essential for the teacher in their respective fields of English, mathematics, and science. In their chapters (Chapters Four, Five, and Six), they offer suggestions for the academic curriculum appropriate to teacher preparation in each of these content areas.

Part Three turns to the moral dimension of teaching. Mortimer J. Adler distills his extraordinary experience as philosopher, educator, and teacher into a chapter (Chapter Seven) that defines the essential good in teaching. In Chapter Eight, David H. Smith examines the moral dimension of teaching from the perspective of a scholar on medical ethics. He argues that the essential values extend beyond the teacher to the school setting itself. Finally, in Chapter Nine, Warren A. Nord assays the issue of values in teaching, relates it to contemporary debates over values in public education, and then proposes specific changes in the teacher education curriculum to address the values most worth having.

Part Four examines implications for the reform of educational settings. Albert Shanker suggests in Chapter Ten how reforms in the preparation of teachers must influence the school settings in which teachers work, and he discusses needed accommodations in the profession of teaching itself. David D. Dill concludes the volume (Chapter Eleven) with suggestions on how the essential knowledge of teaching as defined in this collection may influence the mission and structure of schools of education in major universities.

Any attempt to definitively outline the essential knowledge, skills, and values in a discipline or field is by nature provocative. But it is also fundamental that committed scholars, researchers, and experienced practitioners in any substantive field must pause at key points to pursue the fundamental and unifying question: What is the knowledge most worth having?

Acknowledgments

The development of this volume would not have been possible without the creative and unstinting support of Christopher C. Fordham III. I would also like to thank the contributors for their patience and persistence in revising and developing their drafts for this collection. I am particularly appreciative of the dedicated contributions of Patricia K. Fullagar and Tyndall Harris in helping prepare this manuscript for publication and for the support of Alan Pinkelton in typing portions of the manuscript. Thanks also are due Blanche Arons for her editorial assistance and an anonymous reviewer for Jossey-Bass whose insightful comments were of genuine assistance in shaping the final draft. I also extend a special acknowledgment to the Lyndhurst Foundation for its generous support of the original conference. Finally, I would like to extend my warmest thanks to all those teachers, faculty members, and other educators whose positive criticism and enthusiastic support convinced us to share the knowledge, skills, and values we present in this volume.

Chapel Hill, North Carolina David D. Dill
December 1989

References

Carnegie Task Force on Teaching as a Profession. *A Nation Prepared: Teachers for the 21st Century.* Washington, D.C.: Carnegie Forum on Education and the Economy, 1986.

Clifford, G. J., and Guthrie, J. W. *Ed School.* Chicago: University of Chicago Press, 1988.

Galambos, E. C. (ed.). *Improving Teacher Education.* New Directions for Teaching and Learning, no. 27. San Francisco: Jossey-Bass, 1986.

Hastings Center. *The Teaching of Ethics in Higher Education.* Hastings-on-Hudson, N.Y.: Hastings Center, 1980.

Holmes Group. *Tomorrow's Teachers: A Report of the Holmes Group.* East Lansing: Michigan State University, 1986.

Holmes Group. *Work in Progress: The Holmes Group One Year On.* East Lansing: Michigan State University, 1989.

Houston, W. R. (ed.). *Handbook of Research on Teacher Education.* New York: Macmillan, forthcoming.

National Commission for Excellence in Education. *A Nation at Risk.* Washington, D.C.: National Institute of Education, 1983.

Raths, J. D., and Katz, L. G. (eds.). *Advances in Teacher Education.* Norwood, N.J.: Ablex, 1986.

Reynolds, M. C. (ed.). *Knowledge Base for the Beginning Teacher.* Elmsford, N.Y.: Pergamon Press, 1989.

Shulman, L. S. "Knowledge and Teaching: Foundations of the New Reform." *Harvard Educational Review,* 1987, *57,* 1-22.

Sizer, T. R. *Horace's Compromise.* Boston: Houghton Mifflin, 1984.

Strom, S. M. "The Ethical Dimension of Teaching." In M. C. Reynolds (ed.), *Knowledge Base for the Beginning Teacher.* Elmsford, N.Y.: Pergamon Press, 1989.

Wittrock, M. C. (ed.). *Handbook of Research on Teaching.* (3rd ed.) New York: Macmillan, 1986.

The Authors

David D. Dill is professor of education and assistant to the chancellor for planning at the University of North Carolina, Chapel Hill. He received his B.A. degree (1963) from Oberlin College in English and history, his M.Ed. degree (1967) from the University of Chicago, and his Ph.D. degree (1971) from the University of Michigan in higher education. He has been a faculty member at North Carolina since 1974. He also served as a research associate in 1981–82 at the R&D Management Research Center, University of Manchester.

Dill is the author of *Case Studies in University Governance* (1970) and currently serves as editor of *Planning for Higher Education* and as associate editor of *Higher Education: Handbook of Theory and Research.* He has been active in the American Educational Research Association, the Association for the Study of Higher Education, and the Society for College and University Planning. His numerous book chapters and articles, as well as his research grants, have focused on the organization and administration of higher education and on the management of research and development (R&D) organizations. He has consulted with universities and R&D laboratories in the United States and Europe.

Mortimer J. Adler is director of the Institute for Philosophical Research, chairman of the board of editors of *Encyclopaedia Britannica,* and University Professor at the University of North Carolina, Chapel Hill. He received his Ph.D. degree (1928) from Columbia University in psychology. He holds honorary degrees from the University of North Dakota, Brigham Young University, Marquette University, Moravian College, Manhattan College, Shimer College, and Washington College.

During the last decade, Adler has devoted much of his time to the Paideia Project, which in the summer of 1981 called for a major reform of public school education and provided a blueprint for its structure. On behalf of the Paideia Group, Adler wrote *The Paideia Proposal* (1982), *Paideia Problems and Possibilities* (1983), and, with members of the group, *The Paideia Program* (1984). His other books include *How to Speak/How to Listen* (1983), *A Guidebook to Learning* (1986), and *Reforming Education* (1989).

Ernest L. Boyer is president of the Carnegie Foundation for the Advancement of Teaching; senior fellow at the Woodrow Wilson School, Princeton University; and education columnist for the *London Times.* He received his B.A. degree (1950) from Greenville College in history and political science and both his M.A. and Ph.D. degrees in 1955 from the University of Southern California in language and psychology. He holds honorary degrees from 100 U.S. colleges and universities. Boyer is former United States commissioner of education and former chancellor of the State University of New York. Boyer authored two major Carnegie Foundation studies: *High School* and *College.* He has been named to national commissions by three presidents and was awarded a Fulbright fellowship in 1984.

Carolyn M. Evertson is professor of education at Peabody College, Vanderbilt University. She received her B.S. degree (1958) in elementary education and her Ph.D. degree (1972) in educational psychology, both from the University of Texas, Austin. The author of numerous books and articles on classroom organization and management, Evertson has been a consultant on teacher training and professional development to universities, state governments, and regional educational laboratories across the country.

Thomas L. Good is professor of curriculum and instruction at the University of Missouri and research associate at the university's Center for Research in Social Behavior. He received his A.B. degree (1965) from the University of Illinois in political science and both his M.S. degree (1967) in higher education and his Ph.D. degree (1968) in educational psychology from Indiana University. His work in instructional behavior includes studies of teacher expectations, teacher management, and instructional issues. Good is editor of *Elementary School Journal* and an advisory editor for the *Journal of Educational Psychology*. He prepared two position papers for the National Commission for Excellence in Education.

Peter J. Hilton is Distinguished Professor of Mathematics at the State University of New York, Binghamton. He received his M.A. degree (1950) from Oxford University and his Ph.D. degree (1952) from Cambridge University, both in algebraic topology. He holds honorary degrees from Northern Michigan University, the Memorial University of Newfoundland, and the Autonomous University of Barcelona. He has published extensively on topics in topology and algebra and on mathematics education. Hilton is past secretary of the International Commission on Mathematical Instruction and was the honoree of a 1983 international conference on algebraic topology held to mark his sixtieth birthday.

Richard Lloyd-Jones is professor and former chair of the Department of English at the University of Iowa, where he has taught writing and composition for over thirty years. He received his B.A. degree (1949) from the University of New Mexico in English and philosophy and his M.A. degree (1950) from the University of North Carolina, Chapel Hill, and his Ph.D. degree (1956) from the University of Iowa, both in English. His teaching activity has covered business, technical, expository, and creative writing, as well as rhetoric. Lloyd-Jones was associate director of the Iowa/NEH Institute on Writing from 1978 to 1983 and has served as president of the National Council of Teachers in English.

Harold J. Morowitz is Robinson Professor of Biology and Natural Philosophy at George Mason University. He received his B.S. degree (1947) in physics and philosophy, his M.S. degree (1950) in physics, and his Ph.D. degree (1951) in biophysics, all from Yale University. Morowitz writes a monthly column for *Hospital Practice* and has a longstanding interest in science education. His most recent book is *Cosmic Joy and Local Pain: Musings of a Mystical Scientist* (1987). He is a member of the Sigma Xi committee on science, mathematics, and engineering education.

Warren A. Nord is director of the program in the humanities and human values and lecturer in the Department of Philosophy at the University of North Carolina, Chapel Hill. He received his B.A. degree (1967) from the University of Minnesota and his Ph.D. degree (1978) from the University of North Carolina, Chapel Hill, both in philosophy. Nord has published articles on the humanities, adult education, and issues in moral education. He is currently at work on a book on the relationship between religion and public education.

Albert Shanker has been president of the American Federation of Teachers since 1974 and is vice-president of the AFL-CIO. He received his B.A. degree (1949) from the University of Illinois in philosophy. He holds honorary degrees from Rhode Island College, the University of Rochester, the Graduate Center at the City University of New York, the State University of New York, and Adelphi University. "Where We Stand," Shanker's weekly column on education, labor, political, and human rights issues, appears in *The Sunday New York Times* and some sixty other newspapers across the country. He is a frequent contributor to national magazines and education journals and is often seen on national news and public affairs programs, such as *Meet the Press* and *Face the Nation.* He is also a member of the National Academy of Education, the board of the National Endowment for Democracy, and the Tri-Lateral Commission.

Irving E. Sigel is a Distinguished Research Scientist at Educational Testing Service. He received his B.A. degree (1943) in psychology and his M.A. degree (1948) and his Ph.D. degree (1951) in human development, all from the University of Chicago. Sigel is editor of the *Journal of Applied Developmental Psychology* and series editor of *Advances in Applied Development Psychology.* His published work on cognitive growth and family learning spans more than thirty years of research.

David H. Smith is director of the Poynter Center for the Study of Ethics and American Institutions and professor of religious studies at Indiana University. He received his B.A. degree (1961) from Carleton College in philosophy, his B.D. degree (1964) from Yale Divinity School, and his Ph.D. degree (1967) from Princeton University in philosophy. Smith is a fellow of the Institute for Society, Ethics, and the Life Sciences and has convened several projects on the teaching of ethics. He has directed numerous seminars and conferences on bioethics for health professionals, college teachers, and religious leaders.

What Teachers Need to Know

Introduction: Giving Dignity to the Teaching Profession

Ernest L. Boyer

For over 300 years, America has had a love affair with education. Our first college was born when the little colony on Massachusetts Bay was only six years old. In 1647, that same colony passed a law requiring every town and village of fifty or more souls (adult males who owned land) to hire a schoolteacher at public expense to teach all children to read and to write. George Washington affirmed that knowledge is the surest basis of public happiness. Thomas Jefferson drew up a plan for universal public education, and John Jay described knowledge as the "soul" of the Republic. And during the Civil War, President Lincoln signed the historic Morrill Act, which launched colleges from Maine to California. Our forebears understood that education was far too important to be left to chance. Yet, while Americans have always had a love affair with education, we have, at the same time, been enormously ambivalent about teachers.

Professor Dan Lortie (1975, p. 10) of the University of Chicago captured this ambivalence best when he wrote, "Teaching in this country is both honored and disdained. It's praised as dedicated service and it's lampooned as easy work." Lortie went on to say that teaching, from its inception, has occupied a special but shadowed place. He concluded by observing, "Our real regard for those who teach has never matched our professed regard."

Several years ago, while writing a report on high schools (Boyer, 1983), I heard a fascinating story, about a late-nineteenth century Nebraska school, that colorfully described our lack of real regard for teachers. One hundred years ago, at this one-room school on the prairie, the first teacher was run out of town by a boy who used stones as weapons of assault. The second teacher met the same agony. But the reign of terror ended when the third teacher had soundly thrashed one boy and also had thrashed the father of another. Still, many students at that Nebraska school considered the teacher "Public Enemy Number One." Today we do not stone our teachers or drive them out of town, but we do expect them to work miracles every single day. We not only call on them to teach the basics, but we also expect them to monitor the playground, police for drugs, reduce teenage pregnancy, and do what our homes, churches, and communities have been unable to accomplish. And when teachers fall short anywhere along the line, we condemn them for not meeting our idealized expectations.

A 1987 Carnegie Foundation survey of 22,000 public school teachers from coast to coast revealed that while teaching is becoming increasingly complex, working conditions in the schools frustrate teachers and reduce the effectiveness of their work. Teachers today are still faced with too many students, too much paperwork, too little time for preparation, and too many mindless interruptions. The survey also found that teachers had few opportunities for professional renewal. Little time is available to meet with colleagues, and few districts provide funds for summer fellowships or funds to support innovative ideas. And the majority of teachers are not involved in selecting teachers and administrators at their schools, nor do they participate in crucial matters such as teacher evaluation, staff development, school budgets, and student promotion and retention policies.

When I was Commissioner of Education, I called together twenty high school students from around the country. We spent the day talking about their schools and about their teachers. At the conclusion of our conversation I said, "Well, before we break today, I'd like to ask how many of you have ever had a teacher who's changed your life?" Every hand went up. And then I asked, "How many of you have ever thanked a teacher?" Not one hand was raised. These high school students had been with dozens of teachers every day for four years, and yet not once—even after an exciting session—did a student stop by the teacher's desk or drop a note to say thank you.

Before we examine the issue of what teachers need to know, we have to understand that we will not attract good teachers into an environment that is demeaning and that lacks empowerment and recognition. Unless we acknowledge that we are talking about a human problem, and not solely a curricular judgment, we will not attract bright young minds into teaching.

The harsh truth is that teaching in this nation is imperiled. There are poor teachers, to be sure, and one bad teacher is more dangerous than one bad surgeon, because a surgeon can only hurt one person at a time. But good teachers outnumber the bad, and I find it disturbing that the current school reform movement is more preoccupied with regulations, testing, and certification requirements than it is with confronting seriously the fundamental and enduring issues: What is it we want our children, in the future, to understand? How can we carefully and authentically assess their work? What do all teachers need to know, and how can we inspire the best and the brightest to enter the profession?

One night several years ago I could not sleep, and instead of counting sheep, I counted all the teachers I had had. I thought of three great teachers in school and college who had changed my life forever. First, I thought of my first-grade teacher, Miss Rice, who, on the first day of school, announced, "Good morning, class. Today we learn to read." It was Miss Rice who taught me that language and learning are inextricably interlocked. And some fifty years later, while writing books on high school and college, I include chapters on the centrality of language, thanks to the influence of an inspired first-grade teacher. I remembered Mr. Wittlinger, my high school history teacher, who one day said to me, "Ernest, you're doing very well in history. Keep this up and you'll get an *A*." It was the first time any teacher had said to me directly, "You're doing very well." My grades slowly crept ahead. I majored in history, and his encouragement changed my life at a time when I was trying to figure out who I was and what I might become. I thought of Joseph Smith, a professor of literature and art. He read Shakespeare aloud to us in class, day after day. Professor Smith relished every line and brought every word to life. He read all those passages with joy, even though he had read *King Lear* and *Macbeth* a hundred times before. What he taught me about the power and magic of language was indelibly impressed, and his influence has lived with me ever since.

What were the characteristics that made these teachers great? First was their effecive use of language. Language is not just another subject; it is the means by which we pursue all other subjects. If I had just one requirement for effective teachers, it would be that they demonstrate not just accurate spelling and grammar but also an understanding that identity is defined and learning achieved through the power of one's language. A teacher who does not know language and cannot instill respect for it in students is inadequate, in my judgment, to meet the challenge of shaping the coming generation.

Writing must be the centerpiece of language development, because it is through clear writing that clear thinking can be taught. Writing in the schools is, in some respects, frozen thought. As our students express themselves in writing, they provide a glimpse into their thinking. Without that capacity, they cannot critique their own thoughts or work toward improvement. Every prospective teacher, then, should be asked to write a coherent essay on a consequential subject. Teachers who are not able to demonstrate that skill successfully must keep trying until they can. So, when we get into this complicated field of what makes a great teacher and how to prepare one, I say the first priority is language. And if teachers are not skilled and successful in the use of symbols, they should not go into the classroom.

The second quality common to my most memorable teachers was being well-informed. They were able to move freely among what we now call the disciplines of knowledge. An essential obligation in the preparation of teachers is not only to guide them toward the mastery of language but also to give them a foundation of knowledge that suggests our interdependence in order to help them prepare students for the complicated world they will inherit.

Teacher education in this country has been endlessly condemned, yet it is the failure of the colleges to define carefully the core of education that has most imperiled the nation's public schools. It is the obligation of the college—not the school of education—to think carefully about the core of common knowledge for all students, not just prospective teachers (Boyer, 1987). How can we expect the school superintendent or principal or teacher to be so enlightened about what children should be learning when many of our colleges seem incapable of defining the meaning of an education? This quest for the commonality of learning is one that colleges and schools together continuously should pursue.

When I was chancellor at the State University of New York, one dreary Monday morning I had a pile of third-class mail on my desk. Instead of turning to the real problems at hand, I peeled off the top item from the stack. It happened to be the student newspaper from Stanford University. They had abolished all core requirements there three years before. But that year, 1971, the faculty had agreed to reintroduce a required course for all students. It was a course in Western civilization, and the student newspaper was mightily offended. A front-page editorial declared that a required course at Stanford was an "illiberal act." The editorial concluded with this blockbuster argument: "How dare they impose a uniform standard on nonuniform people?"

I asked myself how it was that after fourteen or fifteen years of formal education, some of the brightest young people in the nation did not understand that while we are nonuniform, we still have some things in common. Is it conceivable that our brightest young people would grow up and not understand that while we live independently, we are also all dependent on each other?

Several years ago in the Carnegie Foundation essay *Quest for Common Learning* (Boyer and Levine, 1981), we said that the core curriculum should be defined, not just on the basis of the disciplines, but on the basis of the universal experiences shared by all people on Earth. And during a sabbatical at Cambridge, I spent the semester reflecting on what we have in common: we all use symbols; we all are members of groups and institutions; we all have a heritage; we can anticipate the future; we all are engaged in productive work; and we all have values and beliefs that guide our lives. These are universal, whether we are on this continent or the next. A rich commonality goes far beyond a given time or place. Our obligation, then, is not only to become empowered by language but also to start asking about the general knowledge teachers should bring to the classroom to help students look broadly and not narrowly at life.

Third, my best teachers were able to relate their knowledge to the lives of students and to convey it at a level students could understand. Some of this skill can be taught. But frankly, I think working with master teachers in the classroom develops such skills more effectively than do lectures on pedagogy in the schools of education.

As part of a postdoctoral program at the University of Iowa Hospital, I observed young residents in surgery. I stood there and watched as some young surgeon, usually during facial surgery, would come perilously close to a major nerve that, if cut, would leave permanent paralysis. I'll never forget the image of that young doctor with three other master surgeons coaching—"watch it," "yes," "no"—skills developed through the critique of a master teacher. The analogy is not inappropriate to the classroom, where the individual who has been teaching well for years keeps saying, "yes," "OK," "that's good," "watch it." In such a setting, the young teacher should get feedback from students, too. (Here, perhaps, is where the operating room analogy breaks down.) Still, I suggest that the pedagogical growth of teachers develops best through careful guidance and through *coaching,* if I might use that word, by the master teacher.

The fourth characteristic that marked the great teachers I remember was their ability to evaluate the progress of each student. I come back to Mr. Wittlinger. I do not know how he measured student progress, but I do know it involved more than check marks on a paper. Mr. Wittlinger watched my reactions. I loved the course. He saw something bubbling in me. That type of evaluation was not a Scholastic Aptitude Test. It was a teacher pulling together nuances that no paper and pencil test could convey adequately.

I am deeply troubled by the tyranny of testing. We run the risk of reducing students to numbers, measuring not who they are but their capacity to put marks on a paper, which even a chimpanzee can do with some modest training. We urgently need a broader definition of what we are trying to assess. I am intrigued by the work of Howard Gardner (1983) at Harvard, who reminds us that there is more than just verbal intelligence; spatial intelligence, esthetic intelligence, intuitive intelligence, social intelligence, and, if I might be so bold, perhaps ethical intelligence also exist. Are these characteristics less consequential in life than the capacity to recall a word or a number? How is it that we can ignore the potential of children in our measuring instruments? It is frightening to me that millions of children are having their worth denied because of a test score that labeled them a failure.

My wife and I have four children, and every one is wonderfully unique. One child was not fond of school, and teachers concluded that he could not learn. Leaping ahead twenty years, he is now the director of six schools on a Mayan Indian reservation in Belize, building schools, finding teachers, guiding little children, coping with the complicated culture, and forging flooded rivers. My son is achieving year after year what I could not begin to manage. Yet, no tests can measure the combination of social, physical, and intellectual skills that allows him to succeed and to cope in a Mayan jungle. James Agee (1957) wrote that with every child who is born, no matter under what circumstance, the potentiality of the human race is born again. And it seems to me that the great teacher, inspired by the potential of students, conveys that confidence every single day.

This leads me, then, to my final characteristic of great teaching. As I thought of Miss Rice, Mr. Wittlinger, and Professor Smith, I knew their excellence was not just the result of language; it was not just knowledge; it was not just their capacities to relate to me or even their abilities to assess the nuances of potential. It was something else, and this one leaves me a bit bewildered because I do not know how it can be taught. The great teachers I had were believable and authentic human beings. They conveyed an openness and integrity that inspired me to trust them, not for what they knew, but for who they were. They were three-dimensional: willing to laugh, and to cry, and to say, "I don't know." And they became not only good teachers, but also, in a strange way, true and trusted friends.

Most of these characteristics are teachable. I believe we can develop greater skills in the use of language. Colleges can provide a core of common learning that broadens the knowledge base of the teacher. Through master teacher programs, we can help students in the laboratory or in the classroom to develop better pedagogical skills and to relate what they know to the readiness of students. And we can provide prospective teachers guidance on the nuances of testing, as long as we do not have the wearisome interventions of state and federal standards from above.

But, again, I am not yet sure how we can develop that final quality—the integrity and authenticity that will inspire the student to learn. But attracting individuals with these qualities to the classroom is essential if we are to prepare better teachers for the twenty-first century. Clearly, improved working conditions and more opportunities for professional renewal are essential. To talk about recruiting better students into teaching without examining the circumstances that discourage them is simply a diversion. In the end, the quality of American education can be no greater than the dignity we assign to teaching.

References

Agee, J. *A Death in the Family*. New York: McDowell, Obolensky, 1957.

Boyer, E. *High School*. New York: Harper & Row, 1983.

Boyer, E. *College: The Undergraduate Experience in America*. New York: Harper & Row, 1987.

Boyer, E. and Levine, A. *Quest for Common Learning*. Washington, D.C.: Carnegie Foundation for the Advancement of Teaching, 1981.

Gardner, H. *Frames of Mind: The Theory of Multiple Intelligences*. New York: Basic Books, 1983.

Lortie, D. C. *Schoolteacher*. Chicago: University of Chicago Press, 1975.

Part One

Knowledge Essential to the Craft of Teaching

One of the noteworthy components of contemporary discussions of educational reform is the belief that a knowledge base now exists as a foundation for both teacher preparation and teacher assessment. Based in large part on studies that correlate teacher behavior with measures of student achievement, and utilizing systematic observation of teaching in the classroom, this research (Rosenshine and Stevens, 1986) has led to a renaissance of interest in effective teaching. The methodology of this process-product research also has produced concern that it leads to a narrower vision of teaching and teachers (Griffin, 1986). The dependence upon observation, correlation, and standardized measures of achievement has led, in some critics' views (Doyle, 1988; Shulman, 1987), to a focus on indicators of achievement. In contrast, they suggest that a fuller understanding of teaching would lead to a conception of it as an art that involves the teacher's understanding and interpretation of more complex subject matter and that considers the teacher's capacity to relate to individual students and to captivate student attention through the power of expression.

Despite the strong words of caution by some of the leading researchers in the field (Brophy and Good, 1986), effective-teaching research has become the basis of teacher assessment plans that public officials have developed in many states. Thus, general behaviors of teaching identified through research are becoming a prescriptive model for teacher presentation, imposed without sensitivity to subject field, to the physical and psychological characteristics of the students, or to the nature of the educational purposes in the particular classroom.

In this part, we review the knowledge essential to the craft of teaching—while remaining mindful of the progress and the caveats. Authors of the chapters in this section recognize that effective teaching is a product of a complex multivariate equation including knowledge about pedagogy, knowledge about subject matter, and knowledge about the student. Perhaps most important is the recognition that knowledge alone is insufficient. For the teacher, like the surgeon or the trial lawyer or the minister, also must possess professional skills.

In his introduction, Ernest Boyer suggested three components of outstanding teachers: their powers of expression and abilities to relate to students, their abilities to assess the nuances of student potential, and their skills in coaching. These simple points capture some essential truths about the knowledge and skills relevant to effective teaching.

For example, Leinhardt and Smith (1985), in a frequently cited study of mathematics teaching, suggest that effective teachers exhibit both content knowledge and action-system knowledge. Action-system knowledge includes the skills for planning and presenting lessons clearly, for making decisions during the conduct of classes, and for responding to the individual differences and difficulties of students. An important component of this action system is the individual teacher's personal skill or art of presentation and classroom management—what Shulman (1987) has usefully described as "the power of voice and manner." A second important component is the close interrelationship between content knowledge and action knowledge; conceptual knowledge of content, skill of organization and presentation, and thoughtful assessment of students' understanding are woven together in an intricate web. This complexity raises at least three questions we need to ask of the current research on classroom instruction.

First, we need to know more about the interaction of a teacher's knowledge of subject matter and a teacher's techniques of pedagogy—what Shulman (1986) calls "pedagogical content knowledge." What is the knowledge by which teachers in a particular field communicate or structure learning so that students can understand and make sense of key ideas? And what are the ways teachers determine whether students comprehend what is taught?

Second, within this very active process of teaching, what kinds of knowledge and skill lead to conceptual learning and understanding instead of leading to simple memorization or recognition? Much of the research on effective teaching has been conducted at the elementary school level. But to accomplish the goals of teaching and learning desired at the middle school and secondary school level, we will need to focus more on content knowledge and on the skills of organization, discussion, and questioning—skills that characterize higher-order teaching and learning.

Third, what role do teacher beliefs and expectations play in this process of teaching and learning? Sizer (1984) suggests that students and teachers often negotiate informal contracts whereby the teacher demands little of the students and the students in return behave in class. This suggests that in addition to knowledge and skills, teachers' attitudes toward their work and toward their students may be important.

As Boyer observes, within this action system of teaching, the capacity of the teacher to assess the level of knowledge and motivation of the student is obviously crucial. Shulman (1987) makes a consistent case that in addition to content knowledge and pedagogical knowledge, teachers also need an understanding of human development. One danger is that the action-system approach will lead to teachers' learning only generic concepts of human development, much as the effective teaching research led initially to too great an emphasis on generic presentation skills. Rather than learning about the general stages of development that teenagers undergo, a future English teacher's exploration of the relationships between intellectual and cognitive development and the capacity of students to engage with certain subject matter may be more critical. At what age, for example, does character motivation in fiction become important to students? Further, what particular skills need to be developed in conjunction with this understanding of human development in order to assess the stage of the learner and the student's level of understanding?

In the introduction, Boyer's observations on the coaching behavior of his outstanding teachers emphasize the importance not only of essential knowledge but also of essential skills. In this part, both Good and Sigel suggest the importance of skill development, particularly discussion and questioning skills critical to diagnosing student understanding. The concern with skill development in teacher education has encouraged extensive emphasis on the clinical component of teacher education as a means for improving the quality of teacher education (Griffin, 1986). Although students routinely report their student teacher placements to be the most attractive portion of their teacher education programs (Galambos, 1986), some evidence suggests that the internship experience is linked to decline in positive attitudes toward teaching and to deterioration of skills (Evertson, Hawley, and Zlotnik, 1985). Furthermore, as Good suggests, the emphasis on students' field placements as a means of learning about institutional context or about the culture of teaching may be misplaced, given the high probability that many teacher education graduates will begin their teaching in courses, contexts, and locations substantially different from those in which they trained. This view suggests that Berliner's (1986) emphasis on developing individual teachers' skills in inquiry and decision making relevant to active teaching may be a more productive perspective for professional education. The best means for developing these essential skills and the appropriate role of field experiences in teacher training are, therefore, as Evertson and colleagues emphasize, critical questions for teacher training. Finally, since the development of skills inevitably involves coaching, modeling, and active mentorship, what role in this process should master teachers play?

In sum, extensive evidence indicates that teaching is best understood as an active practice in which the teacher constantly makes decisions. The knowledge essential to this practice includes pedagogical content knowledge and human development. The essential skills include expertise in presentation, particularly student questioning and assessment, and the management of classroom settings. These conclusions suggest that the use of content-relevant cases and simulations based upon what Griffin (1986) has called "craft knowledge in use" offers the best hope for developing the level of required teacher thinking and understanding.

References

Berliner, D. "In Pursuit of the Expert Pedagogue." *Educational Researcher,* 1986, *15,* 5-13.

Brophy, J. E., and Good, T. L. "Teacher Behavior and Student Achievement." In M. C. Wittrock (ed.), *Handbook of Research on Teaching.* (3rd ed.) New York: Macmillan, 1986.

Doyle, W. "Curriculum in Teacher Education." Paper presented at the annual meeting of the American Educational Research Association, New Orleans, Apr. 1988.

Evertson, C., Hawley, W., and Zlotnik, M. "Making a Difference in Educational Quality Through Teacher Education." *Journal of Teacher Education,* 1985, *36,* 2-12.

Galambos, E. "Common Directions Toward Improvement." In E. Galambos (ed.), *Improving Teacher Education.* New Directions for Teaching and Learning, no. 27. San Francisco: Jossey-Bass, 1986.

Griffin, G. A. "Clinical Teacher Education." In J. Hoffman and S. Edwards (eds.), *Reality and Reform in Teacher Education.* New York: Random House, 1986.

Leinhardt, G., and Smith, D. "Expertise in Mathematics Instruction: Subject Matter Knowledge." *Journal of Educational Psychology,* 1985, *77,* 247-271.

Rosenshine, B., and Stevens, R. S. "Teaching Functions." In

M. C. Wittrock (ed.), *Handbook of Research on Teaching.* (3rd ed.) New York: Macmillan, 1986.

Shulman, L. S. "Those Who Understand: Knowledge Growth in Teaching." *Educational Researcher,* 1986, *15* (2), 4–14.

Shulman, L. S. "Knowledge and Teaching: Foundations of the New Reform." *Harvard Educational Review,* 1987, *57,* 1–22.

Sizer, T. R. *Horace's Compromise.* Boston: Houghton Mifflin, 1984.

1

Building the Knowledge Base of Teaching

Thomas L. Good

This chapter discusses research on teaching for arts and science faculty and for other professional educators who are not specialists in the area of instructional research. Some critics of colleges of education contend that there is no professional knowledge base on which to design teacher education programs. A basic goal of this chapter is to address and to refute that misconception. I also want to establish that conducting basic research in school settings is a valuable but exceedingly difficult task.

In the past twenty years, improved research and research methodology have increased dramatically our knowledge of teaching. This progress has been achieved despite inadequate funding. Notable progress also has been achieved in the understanding of learning, motivation, and management in complex social settings as well as in the understanding of human development with associated implications for instruction. Research linking teacher behavior to student achievement has thus made enormous strides. What was once a very limited collection of results of various studies that did not combine to form easily interpretable patterns has become an increasingly integrated knowledge base that includes a sizable collection of replicated correlational findings, many of which have been validated experimentally.

However, our understanding of classroom teaching and learning has barely scratched the surface, despite the progress of the past twenty years. This is not because of lack of effort or expertise on the part of educational researchers, many of whom are trained in psychology, sociology, anthropology, and other social science disciplines. In large part, the lack of progress can be attributed to the lack of resources (for example, release time for research, funds to secure equipment, and hiring of coders). However, an equally important obstacle to progress is the complexity of classroom settings, involving countless interacting and changing variables that make understanding instructional effectiveness a difficult task. The study of teaching is a challenging field of inquiry that demands capable scholars.

I must necessarily neglect many important issues related to the teaching profession, including the recruitment of capable teacher education students; the retention of capable teachers in the profession; career ladder and master teacher plans and other efforts to increase the professionalization of teaching; plans for improving the salaries of teachers; strategies for making the conditions of teaching more meaningful and more satisfying; and research and development involving arts and science faculty, education faculty, and local school personnel.

In this chapter, I discuss a few general but important themes of classroom instructional research, including motivation, management, teacher expectations, active teaching, student misconception research, the teaching of learning strategies, and expert-novice comparisons. Another issue that I discuss is the use of research to study and to modify teacher education programs. We have a paucity of data that describe what occurs in teacher education programs, and we need better conceptualizations of these programs and their effects.

Influences on Teaching

As Kennedy (1986) notes, teacher education programs are not independent variables that can be manipulated in any simple way. They are formed by state governments, student bodies, and demands of client school districts. Similarly, what students learn about teaching while participating in these programs depends on what they already have learned elsewhere, on their ability to learn, on their beliefs about teaching, on their dispositions toward teaching, on their inclinations to learn, and on their concurrent learning experiences. We cannot control all of these influences; indeed, we cannot even measure all of them. Kennedy argues that fundamental concerns have been raised regarding what one can expect teachers to learn about teaching during a few semesters of college—relative to what they have learned about teaching throughout their lifetimes and what they will learn about teaching on the job. Yet, almost nothing is known about what prospective teachers already know when they enter teacher education programs or about how that knowledge changes. Figure 1 illustrates what little time formal teacher education has to affect preservice teachers' beliefs about teaching and to provide knowledge relevant to teaching. Prospective teachers have had an average of fifteen years of schooling before they take a formal course in teacher education. After leaving teacher education programs, students are exposed to immediate pressures (for example, a district's evaluation system) and to continuing internal (career ladder) and external constraints (state laws, the media). These forces interact in complex ways with a given teacher's training, ability, and philosophy so that it is hard to conceptualize linkages between teacher education and classroom practice.

Various experiences combine to influence actual teaching behavior. For example, mathematics educators may find that their call for more emphasis on problem solving, estimation, and measurement in elementary school instruction may be neutralized by a school district's implementation of a new mathematics testing program that emphasizes computation and basic concepts. The testing program may be implemented because of the philosophy of school district administrators, but it may be fueled because of external pressures (newspaper articles, influential citizens). However, independent of the

Figure 1. Potential Determinants of Teaching Performance.

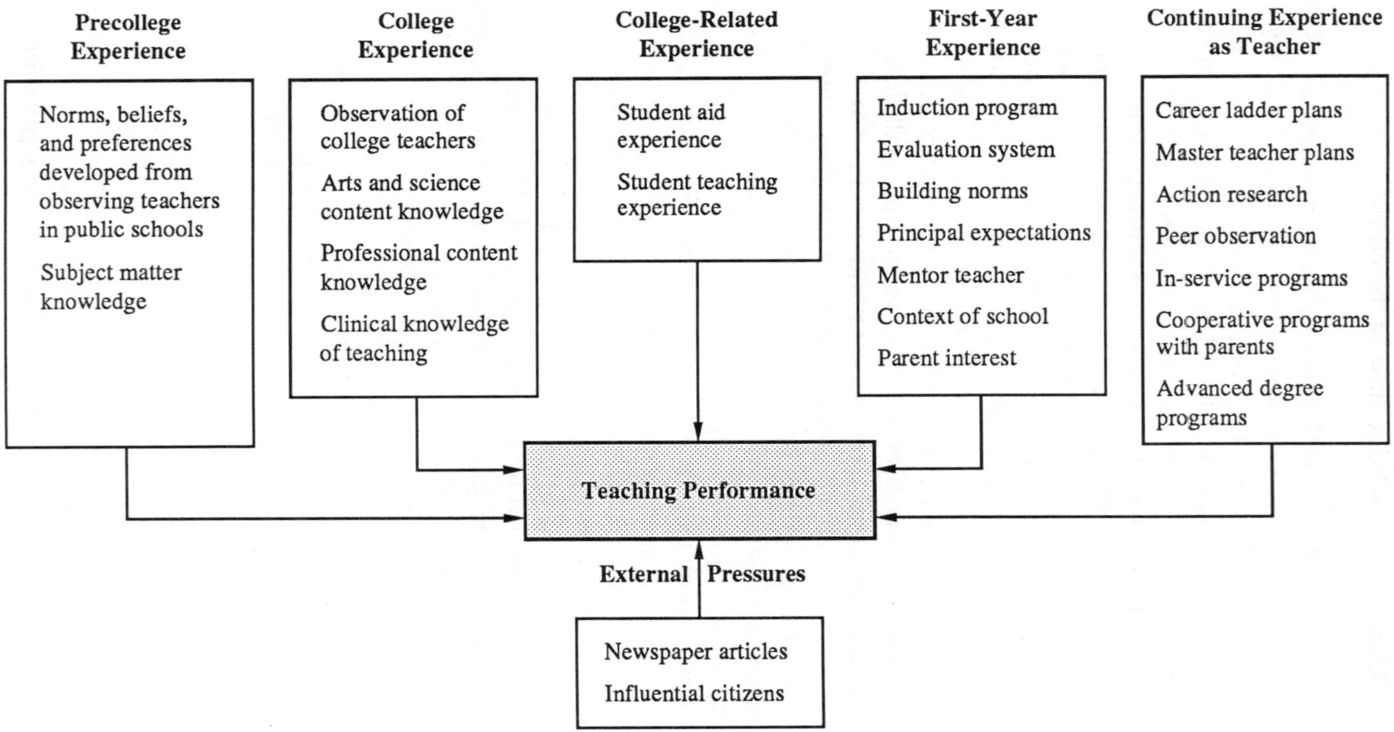

antecedent conditions that led to the development of the testing program, its presence will affect how much instruction is offered in various mathematical topics.

At times, the resistance to change may lie in the teacher education program. For example, a school district offers new and challenging opportunities to a teacher by employing a continuous-progress curriculum with emphasis on critical thinking or by investing in new laboratories or computer equipment, but the teacher's training has not prepared the teacher to fulfill new roles or to use technology appropriately.

Also, it should be clear that the instruction prospective teachers receive from arts and science faculty influences not only their content knowledge but also their knowledge of teaching. How a high school chemistry teacher conducts laboratory activities may be affected (for better or worse) by the teacher's experience in various college laboratory courses more than by teacher education courses.

Some teachers may be well prepared to fulfill one role but find themselves asked to teach in areas for which they have little or no preparation. Similarly, beginning teachers are often assigned to teach the most difficult classes. Such beginning experiences may force new teachers to develop survival skills rather than to experiment, to evaluate, and to grow professionally. Clearly, the present state of affairs in too many teacher education programs and district induction programs makes preparation for a specific professional role extremely problematic.

To reiterate, in this chapter I deal primarily with only one aspect of the teacher education program—knowledge of teaching and its effects on students. I do not discuss other types of professional knowledge (for example, research on student development, motivation, and learning and its implications for teaching; testing and its appropriate use for making educational decisions; state laws that restrict educational programs; and so on). In this chapter, I restrict the discussion to research on classroom teaching. Other issues, such as research on student teaching, the induction experience, and the influence of previous teachers (for example, chemistry teachers in the high school, college chemistry professors, and so on), are beyond the scope of this chapter, although it should be clear that these forces are also important determinants of teacher behavior.

Past Reform Movements

It seems important to comment on reform movements in education—and on the role of research in these movements—since we will find ourselves on the brink of major reform in teacher education if recommendations in recent, impressive reports by the National Commission for Excellence in Teacher Education (1985), the Holmes Group (1986), and the Carnegie Task Force on Teaching as a Profession (1986) are implemented.

There have been many unsuccessful reforms in American education in the past. Standards and criteria that guide reform efforts are rarely based on research. The public often demands immediate change and typically is unwilling to invest the resources necessary to bring about the understanding that can produce meaningful change. For example, at the turn of the century, there was great enthusiasm in this country for whole-class instruction. Then we went to large-group instruction, to individualized instruction, to small-group instruction, and to humanistic instruction. In recent years there has been a great deal of enthusiasm for whole-class instruction again. In eighty years we have gone full circle. This is not a cynical point that change is not possible or that all change is superficial. Rather, the point is that the organizational structure has never predicted instructional effectiveness, although this is where many of our reform efforts have been centered. The issue is not individualized instruction or small-group instruction but rather the quality of thought and effort that occur within these structures (Good and Biddle, 1988). Different organizational strategies can work; the key is quality of implementation. Too often in reform movements those things that are working and those things that are important are swept out along with those that are dysfunctional. Clearly, in some limited sense the system has worked because the characteristics of the problem have changed; however, my argument is that we almost guarantee new problems by overreacting to problems rather than selectively changing and bringing about qualitative reforms. The same thing can happen with reform in teacher education programs and with reform of any other discipline. Single variables do not define problems, and intervention programs that deal with a single factor are not likely to be very successful, especially when change efforts are not based on knowledge from research.

Artley (1981) illustrates the self-defeating nature of using simple approaches to complex problems. He reviews the major individualization techniques used in reading instruction during the 1900s and notes that despite the many desirable features of these methods, the effectiveness of each is seriously limited. Specifically, he claims that any program helps the reading problems of some students but creates (or at least fails to respond to) difficulties for other students. Simply put, in their zeal to provide solutions, educators often overrespond to a problem, so that certain issues are solved in an immediate sense but new problems are created by the systematic application of a solution.

Another problem with reform efforts is our repetition of the same mistakes. For example, the National Commission for Excellence in Education's *A Nation at Risk* (1983) focuses on cosmetic and rather superficial quantitative solutions that ignore educational quality. Nonetheless, in my opinion, it is the most successful educational political document in this century. It has generated a great deal of excitement and has started citizens talking seriously about educational problems. (For an extended discussion of media coverage and the impact of the report, see Tomlinson, 1986.)

However, as a substantive educational document, the report leaves much to be desired. Its recommendations are relatively simpleminded and superficial. The commission recommends a longer school day. One wonders why, if educators are doing such a poor job with the time they have, simply giving them more time would help with the problem. Why do students who are reluctant learners at two o'clock suddenly become intrinsically motivated learners at four o'clock with the advent of the extended school day? The report also recommends a longer school year. With all due respect to the commission members, teaching in June in a room that does not have air conditioning is unlikely to result in improved schooling. The point here is that simple advocacy—more time, more content, a different organizational structure—historically has dominated reforms in American education. *A Nation at Risk* takes this single-variable approach that involves simple linear thinking. (If twenty minutes of homework is good, four hours should be great!)

In contrast, curriculum reforms that address both quality and quantity might be appropriate. For example, in the area of mathematics, finding more time for instruction in problem solving or estimation and in the appropriate use of computers to solve or to represent mathematical problems might be a helpful start. Similarly, extending the school year would allow some teachers and administrators time to participate in curriculum development and coordination and to be paid extra salary for their services. These teachers and administrators could develop new curriculum units (with enhanced academic content) and could improve communication about expectations for students' learning experiences across consecutive grades.

Defining Good Instruction: A Need for Research

Any adequate improvement plan depends partly on the ability to define the problem clearly and accurately. Simply put, the problem is not that students do not spend enough time studying or that students do not learn enough content. What students study and who teaches it are also issues of concern. In this section, I suggest that a thoughtful response to improving student performance must also deal with the quality of instruction and that we need continuing basic research in order to describe more adequately what constitutes quality teaching in various contexts.

Given growing evidence that student performance does not match desirable levels of competence (that is, national assessment of student writing ability, mathematics skill, and science performance), the nation's response has been to increase the quantity of education but not necesarily the quality of education. School districts that offered only three units of mathematics in 1983 now may provide five or six units of mathematics, but unfortunately, there may not be a teacher qualified to teach the calculus course, the advanced French class, or the writing class. Clearly, more content presented by a teacher who is deficient in the subject area or more homework assignments that do not allow for successful practice or critical thinking will not improve student performance (Clune, White, and Patterson, 1989).

Any thoughtful examination of the problem would reveal that inadequate teacher content knowledge is a major issue in some cases and, hence, is part of the problem with inadequate student performance. As Anderson and Smith (1987) note, because of lax standards and an inadequate supply of science teachers, science is being taught by teachers without majors in the sciences. For example, nearly half of those teaching chemistry in Michigan during 1982–83 had not majored in chemistry. Nearly two-thirds of those teaching physics did not have physics majors. Nationally, more than three-fourths of the states reported shortages of general science, chemistry, and physics teachers during the 1981–82 school year. Of teachers newly hired to teach high school mathematics or science in 1981–82, half were unqualified and were teaching with emergency certificates. Clearly, many teachers do not have thorough knowledge of the content they are teaching. To help solve this problem, it is critical that school districts stop the practice of providing teachers with emergency certificates to teach subjects in which they do not have adequate training.

Teachers' lack of content knowledge will likely restrict students' learning, especially when advanced course work is involved (Evertson, Hawley, and Zlotnik, 1985). Indeed, some research suggests that teachers' content knowledge is directly related to classroom instruction and to student performance (Evertson, Weade, Green, and Crawford, 1985). Still, it is important to recognize that research generally has not shown a strong relationship between teacher content knowledge and student performance. For example, Druva and Anderson (1983) conducted a metanalysis of sixty-five studies relating teachers' subject-matter knowledge to the teaching of science and found only moderate relationships between teacher knowledge and student performance.

I believe that more subject matter knowledge, more appropriate course work in the arts and sciences, will help to improve teacher preparation and ultimately classroom performance. A strong core of arts and science courses is a key, basic foundation of any excellent teacher education program. However, teachers must have other knowledge and skills if they are to be successful. Content knowledge alone is not sufficient to guarantee successful teaching. As will be argued in the section that follows, knowledge of teaching methods is also a critical determinant of successful teaching.

Teaching and Learning Science

Research indicates that only a small minority of students learn anything meaningful in science courses. The students who are good in science understand, while all the rest memorize. Consider the following physics problem that students are often asked to solve. When a coin is tossed into the air and it is still moving upward through the air (students refer to a particular point on a diagram), what forces are operating on the coin? The problem involves a very simple application of Newton's laws of motion, which are taught in almost all high school and college physics courses. According to Newton, a coin tossed upward in the air is subject to only two forces—a downward force due to gravity, the major force, and a small additional force due to air resistance. These forces eventually slow the coin to a stop, and it begins to fall back to earth. However, most students also draw or describe an upward force on the coin—a force in the direction of motion. In one study of college engineering majors, most of whom already had taken high school physics, the percentage of students answering the question correctly rose from 12 percent before the beginning of instruction to 28 percent after one semester of physics to only 39 percent correct after two semesters. Despite having had two college semesters of physics, students still could not apply Newton's law to solve an elementary problem.

These students' deficiencies are not due simply to teachers with inadequate content knowledge. The basic problem of conceptual change is an instructional problem. Students cannot add new knowledge to what they already know unless they understand why what they believed to be true is an inadequate conceptualization. Instead, they must abandon habits of thought they have used successfully for many years in favor of new, more complex, and often counterintuitive ways of thinking. There is considerable evidence that good instruction not only exposes students to new information but also helps them to restructure their previous conceptions so they can use new information. Presenting information to students without giving them the opportunity to apply that information and to understand it is usually dysfunctional. Teaching is more than merely transmitting knowledge. Unfortunately, many teachers do not know how to translate knowledge into images that students can understand and internalize (see Carpenter and others, 1988; Duffy and Roehler, 1989).

Managing students and presenting information in a complex social setting demand knowledge of students and how they learn in a social situation as well as knowledge of subject matter. Leinhardt and Smith (1984) distinguish between action-system knowledge and subject matter knowledge. Subject matter knowledge includes the specific information teachers need to present content. Action-system knowledge refers to skills for planning lessons, for making decisions about lesson pace, for explaining material clearly, and for responding to individual differences in student learning. Teachers who possess both action-system knowledge and subject matter knowledge will be more effective than teachers who are deficient in one of these areas.

Teachers' Role

Before discussing selected areas of instructional research, it is important briefly to examine the role of teaching and the complex social conditions that surround the act of teaching in public schools. After conceptualizing the role of the teacher, I will discuss research that helps to clarify how aspects of teaching can be studied and improved.

When teaching is done well, it is a difficult, intellectually challenging task. Although college professors spend more time preparing for their profession, the act of teaching in public schools in some respects is more demanding than college teaching. Public school teachers (especially elementary school teachers) perform tasks that college teachers commonly do not: (1) teach several subjects (science, math, and reading); (2) maintain constant contact with students; (3) negotiate and coordinate individual learning plans for special students; and (4) deal with supervisors, parents, and the public. In addition, teachers in public schools necessarily instruct a higher percentage of reluctant learners who are not in their classrooms by choice.

Given complex, changing social conditions, questions such as what is good teaching or who is an effective teacher can stimulate a variety of responses. However, teacher education programs must inevitably ask these questions. The following brief statement summarizes a description of a good teacher provided by Gary Griffin (1986). A composite of the good teacher is a knowledgeable, well-organized, and consistent classroom leader who interacts with students, colleagues, and community members purposefully and effectively. The individual sees teaching as more than meeting with students and works with peers to identify and act on problems in classrooms and schools. Teachers must also help students raise their own questions and develop self-regulation skills and habits of scholarship that enable students to function as independent and creative learners.

Teaching is difficult in part because it calls for quick decisions under difficult circumstances. Teachers often must make decisions with incomplete information. For example, is the student simply confused on a small point, or has the student failed to read the chapter under discussion (Doyle, 1986)?

Considering this view of the good teacher, and the complexity of classroom teaching, preparing effective teachers is no simple task. Teachers need rich understanding of the subject matter they teach, including an ability to present knowledge so students can understand it. Teachers also need information about student development, motivation, and personality as well as knowledge about intelligence and about how students learn. Teachers must understand the complexity of social environments as well as the organizational and management principles necessary to maintain well-controlled classrooms. They must be able to evaluate students and to identify student learning problems. Teachers need to understand the psychology of teaching methods (selecting, organizing, motivating, presenting information, and making instructional decisions). In order to be effective, teachers need not only to master important subject matter but also to develop the ability to integrate concepts and to utilize teaching strategies that are responsive to the learning needs of particular groups of students (Shulman, 1986).

Reasons for Optimism: An Expanding Knowledge Base

In the past two decades, we have learned a great deal about instruction in American schools. During this period, sophisticated observational research has yielded more knowledge about schooling than was obtained in the previous eighty-five years. There is now an extensive quantitative and qualitative data base for understanding classroom problems and for making decisions about instructional issues. It is not possible here to review all the important advances in our knowledge of classroom learning, because this literature is extensive and complex. However, I will briefly discuss some of the major findings in several areas of this literature and their implications for classroom instruction; those interested in a comprehensive review of the literature should seek other sources (for example, Brophy and Good, 1986; Shulman, 1986; Wittrock, 1986). In particular, the book *Looking in Classrooms* (Good and Brophy, 1987) includes a practical discussion of some of the instructional implications of recent research. In all of these areas, research has yielded concepts and findings that can be used to inform practice, but research has also raised new questions that generate continuing lines of inquiry.

Motivation

Recent research on motivation has changed the way in which motivation is conceptualized. This research has emphasized classroom social factors that impinge on student motivation—effects that do not operate in laboratory experiments. For instance, Stipek (1986) notes that in recent years, two major changes have occurred in traditional assumptions about motivating students to obtain optimal benefits from schooling. First, evidence suggests that frequent use of reward and punishment can actually have the opposite of the intended effect of increasing certain achievement-related behaviors, especially in the long run. Second, recent studies indicate that reinforcement per se does not influence children's behaviors in an achievement setting. Rather, children's cognitions, beliefs, and values determine their behaviors. Students' interpretations of situations, not the objective facts, determine their behaviors. This conceptualization of motivation places the teacher in a quite different role in terms of enhancing student interest in assigned work.

In addition, much of this research is based on the expectancy X value theory of motivation, which suggests that the effort a person is willing to invest in a task is determined by the degree to which the person expects to succeed at the task through reasonable effort and by the degree to which the person values participation in the task itself or access to the reward that successful completion of the task will bring. As Brophy (1983, 1987) notes, people do not invest effort in tasks that they do not value, nor do they try hard to complete tasks that they value if they are convinced that their effort cannot yield success. He argues that teachers should socialize their students to value academic tasks and the knowledge and skills that students develop rather than to confine their motivational attempts to extrinsic incentive systems. His work emphasizes motivating students to learn and getting them to take academic tasks seriously and to develop pride in scholarship.

Grades and other extrinsic incentive systems are inadequate in motivating students to learn how to learn academic content and skills. Students' concentrated effort, careful information processing, and other learning activities must be emphasized. Considering the value of encouraging independent thought, helping students to value the process of academic learning seems an important task—a task that we are beginning to learn about.

It seems especially important not only to think about student behavior as motivation but to begin to explore more systematically the conditions under which students are "motivated" to think. Recent research and conceptualization (for example, Wittrock, 1986) have focused on how students process information from teachers, textbooks, or classroom activities. However, there is virtually no information about which assignments and teacher behaviors are more likely to engage student thinking. What constitutes a good seat work activity or a good end-of-the-chapter question? Does the quality of seat work tasks vary with students' ability and their perceptions of a task, or can some general characteristics be articulated?

Although there is little evidence on the topic, it is popular to assume that when students "do" they are more likely to think. For example, one would not argue that workers on an automobile assembly line engage in much systematic job-related thinking, because they are manipulating concrete activities. Similarly, activities that involve students in applied work may not stimulate their thinking, particularly if students engage in such activities frequently. For example, many students will "tune out" if they frequently work in groups. When teachers lecture for long periods, many students' attention may begin to wander, although certain kinds of teacher talk may stimulate active thinking. Research needs to describe various types of classroom presentations and activities and to consider whether these stimulate student thinking and covert reaction.

Several theories could serve as a basis for this research. For example, Rohrkemper (forthcoming) argues that inner speech guides thought and action as students attempt to deal with learning situations. She notes that two distinct types of inner speech have been identified and represent the potential integration of the affective and the intellectual. Self-involved inner speech reflects control over the self through enhancing motivational and affective statements, whereas task-involved inner speech involves control over a task through problem solving and attempts to modify the task to make it more understandable or more "doable." Thus, in combination, self-involved and task-involved inner speech may allow students to function in adaptive ways by enabling them either to change a task or to modify their self-perceptions and/or effort.

Students bring complex histories to school learning tasks. They differ not only in the ways in which they have achieved mastery over particular concepts or the cognitive skills they possess but also in the degree to which they can use self-involved inner speech in relevant and adaptive ways. Hence, basic research exploring how different classroom tasks stimulate various combinations of student thinking and activity could be extremely important in identifying classroom strategies that engage students in intellectual activities.

Considering that the norms and beliefs of certain minority and socioeconomic groups tend to conflict with the values of a middle-class school setting, subsequent work needs to focus on developing successful strategies for helping low-income and minority students to value learning. It also seems important to extend motivation research to American high schools and colleges. Most work to date has been conducted in elementary, middle, and junior high schools.

The important work of the 1990s will be to validate strategies that help students to develop necessary dispositions for wanting to understand rather than to memorize academic content. Growing evidence indicates that students can perform assigned school work at a satisfactory level even though students do not understand the material (see, for example, Ball and McDiarmid, forthcoming). It is time to begin research to explore how to help students develop the motivation for understanding and for integrating significant bodies of content.

Classroom Organization

Educators often have advocated humanistic outcomes of schooling (socially acceptable behavior, ability to cooperate); however, the effects of related reforms such as individualized programs and open classrooms have been problematic.

There has been a paucity of research on classroom organization. Until extensive programmatic research has been conducted, it is difficult to assess how a program or strategy may work in various contexts. In designing programs for classrooms, it is important to understand why programs work, which features are critical, and which features appear to be less important, nonessential, irrelevant. Slavin (1989) suggests that for any kind of instruction to be effective, four conditions must be satisfied: (1) instruction must be high in quality, (2) instruction must be appropriate to student ability, (3) students must be motivated to work on tasks, and (4) students must have adequate time to learn. Unfortunately, with limited evidence, educators have been prone to make sweeping, simplistic conclusions about which program variables are important. And researchers, with limited funding and almost no backing or rewards for longitudinal work, have been unable to comment intelligently on these sweeping generalizations.

In some areas, enough evidence has accumulated to suggest variables that are important to consider when attempting to implement a particular type of classroom structure. For example, in the past decade, researchers have focused on trying to understand more fully the potential of small-group instruction to promote learning. That is, there have been attempts to explore ways to deal with small groups of students in classrooms rather than instructing thirty students at the same time. Cooperation among group members combined with competition among groups (student-team learning) has proved useful for motivating students to work together—tutoring and giving feedback to one another. These cooperative methods have been used effectively in science and social studies—subjects for which there is some evidence that controlled conflict and debate have helped students understand content and relate it to their own lives.

Some research evidence is accumulating to allow informed decisions about structuring small-group learning. For example, Slavin (1989) notes that a combination of group rewards (based on group members' individual learning) and peer interaction on learning tasks is necessary to produce the learning gains characteristic of effective cooperative learning methods. He has designed experiments comparing classes that used various combinations of the three program components: (1) individualized curriculum materials and assignments, (2) incentive structures that utilize group rewards based on the outcome of competition against other groups, and (3) cooperative task structures that require students to provide tutoring, checking, and other forms of assistance to teammates to prepare them for the competitions. His results demonstrate that achievement gains are due to the incentive structures built into a program rather than to its curriculum materials, assignments, or cooperative task structures.

Still, factors thought to be essential to cooperative learning need additional study. For instance, researchers should compare groups working under group contingencies with those asked to work together to see if peer interaction is affected by reward structures. Also, the students' perspectives on the reward and task structures that compose cooperative learning have been only crudely assessed. It may be that aspects of cooperative learning other than cooperation make it easier for students to interact and to achieve (frequent assessment, clear objectives, and so on). Following the research of Stipek (1986) and others who have explored intrinsic motivation concepts, subsequent work needs to explore what will happen in the long run to cooperative behavior maintained under conditions of external incentives.

Further, it is clear that the curriculum in too many schools is simply focused on covering academic content. If academic progress is to be made in this area, more attention must be placed on the development of classroom curriculum units that allow students to investigate actively (collect data, look for trends) important subject matter concepts. Too often, as is argued in the recent report *Everybody Counts: A Report to the Nation on the Future of Mathematics Education* (National Research Council, 1989), curriculum topics assigned to students are more likely to be appropriate for education students in the industrial age—not for preparing students in the information age. It seems reasonable to begin to provide more opportunities for students to acquire social skills and social communicative abilities; however, when students work with peers, they should be working on meaningful academic content.

Instructional Research and Active Teaching

According to Brophy (1986a, 1986b, and 1986c), recent research suggests that good teachers not only know their subject matter but also understand student development and basic principles of good pedagogy. Unfortunately, many persons do not realize the importance of these factors and persist in suggesting that knowledge of content is the only important prerequisite to instructional effectiveness, particularly in math and science. Not only is this belief incorrect but it also leads to the kind of didactic instruction that produces understanding only in the highest achievers and that leaves the rest of the class memorizing facts, unable to integrate principles they do not understand. Furthermore, this is just as true of instruction at the college level as it is at the elementary and secondary levels. Effective teacher education must prepare teachers to instruct certain types of students in particular content using explanations, examples, questioning strategies, and follow-up practice in application activities to induce integrated understanding and conceptual change.

My own research on mathematics instruction, especially at the elementary school level, provides convincing evidence that teachers do make a difference in student learning and that in-service teachers can be educated in such a way that student performance is increased (Good, Grouws, and Ebmeier, 1983; Good and Grouws, 1987). This system of instruction can be broadly characterized as active teaching. It is instructive to note that in our experimental work, active teaching was an important difference between teachers who obtained higher-than-expected achievement gains and those who obtained lower-than-expected gains. Active teachers presented concepts, explained the meaning of those concepts, provided appropriate practice activities, and monitored those activities. Teachers' looking for ways to determine whether students understood their presentations was particularly important. They assumed partial responsibility for student learning and appeared to be ready to reteach when necessary.

A number of ideas have been developed through careful research on instructional design and on concept teaching (see, for example, Case and Bereiter, 1984). As one example of this growing research, Gropper (1983) describes the nature and difficulty of the responses learners must make and how those factors influence the amount that can be learned at one time, the degree of cueing that is necessary, and the mode of stimulus and response required. Gropper's ideas provide useful guidelines for (1) conceptualizing the task demands built into lessons and assignments, (2) analyzing why students may find certain tasks easier or harder than other logically equivalent tasks that cover the same content, and (3) identifying ways to redesign curricula or to simplify tasks for reteaching when initial attempts have proved to be unsuccessful. Other investigators (for example, Engelmann and Carnine, 1982; Tennyson and Cocchriarella, 1986) also have developed techniques that appear to offer promising hypotheses about how to teach concepts in ways that maximize students' acquisition.

Much work is also being conducted on the effect of organization and presentation of content on learning. Many of these studies have focused on making expository texts easier for readers to comprehend (for example, Armbruster and Anderson, 1984). Other research has concentrated on expository verbal presentations such as teachers' lectures (Brophy and Good, 1986; Good and Brophy, 1989). These studies have identified features of expository presentations that are conducive to better student comprehension: overviews and advance organizers, structuring of the content into logical sequences with clear marking of transitions between sequences and between subparts within sequences, linear redundancy that makes possible the processing of information as an organized body of knowledge rather than as a seemingly random list, highlighting of main ideas and of text structures useful for organizing the content (cause and effect, rules followed by examples, compare and contrast structures, and so on), and reviews or summaries at the end.

In addition to documenting linkages between active instruction and achievement gains, recent research also has yielded information about how teachers should conduct active instruction (Brophy and Good, 1986). Topics include structuring and sequencing of content, clarity and enthusiasm of presentation, difficulty and cognitive levels of questions, choice of students to call on, allocation of response opportunities, and management of seat work.

In addition, Brophy and Good (1986) also argue that despite the noteworthy progress in educational research in the past several years, it has not gone as far as it could have in developing a knowledge base to inform teacher education and teaching practice. Although much knowledge has been gained concerning general aspects of classroom organization and management and about the relatively general, content-free, traditional, whole-class, instruction-recitation-seat-work method, educational researchers barely have scratched the surface of issues surrounding instruction.

Although it is unwieldy to discuss all the individual variables that fall under the broad category of active teaching, it is instructive to review one variable to illustrate the type of research available and to demonstrate that research can yield guidelines adjusted to fit particular situations. Rowe (1974) reported data that at the time seemed remarkable, even hard to believe: after asking questions, teachers tended to wait less than one second before calling on a student to answer. Furthermore, even after calling on a particular student, teachers waited for only about one second for the student to give an answer before supplying it or calling on someone else to respond. These findings do not make sense, because they suggest that teachers were undercutting the value of their questions by failing to give them time to have the desired effect on student thinking.

Rowe followed up these observations by training teachers to extend their wait times from less than one second to between three and five seconds. Surprisingly, most of the teachers found this difficult to do, and some never succeeded. However, in the classrooms where the teachers did extend their wait times to between three and five seconds, important, desirable changes in student behavior were observed (for example, increase in the average length of student responses, increase in the frequency of student-initiated questions, and so on).

Subsequent research (reviewed in Tobin, 1983a, 1983b) has replicated and extended these findings. In particular, this research verifies that increasing wait time leads to longer and higher-quality student responses to teacher questions and to participation by a greater percentage of students in the class.

Subsequent research also has verified Rowe's findings that many teachers experienced difficulty in attempting to extend their wait times. De Ture (1979) found that after training, no teacher attained an average wait time longer than 1.8 seconds. Thus, it seems likely that the pressures on many teachers to maintain lesson pacing and student attention undermine their ability to maintain high-quality dialogue and interactions with students. Some teachers may be reluctant to extend their wait times because they fear, with justification in some cases, that they may lose student attention or even lose control of the class. This is one of many areas in which good classroom management and good instruction appear to be mutually dependent and supportive.

Continuing work in the area suggests that the causal linkages between question level and wait time seem to work in both directions. In addition to noting effects on students, some of the investigators who trained teachers to increase wait times noted interactional changes in which the teachers asked fewer questions per time unit than before but more questions at higher cognitive levels (Fagan, Hassler, and Szabo, 1981; Rice, 1977).

Subsequent research also has shown an interaction with pace and wait time variables as activities and objectives change. Accordingly, although most studies in which teachers were trained to slow the pace and to extend wait time have produced positive outcomes, these studies have tended to be done in intermediate- and upper-grade levels and in contexts of teaching abstract or difficult material. Anshutz (1973) reported no science achievement differences between short and long wait time for students in grades three and four. Riley (1980) found interaction effects on science achievement in grades one through five: a decrease in achievement occurred when wait time was extended from medium to long for low-level questions, whereas an increase in achievement was noted when wait time was extended for high- and mixed-cognitive-level questions.

However, I again want to stress that I have discussed but one of many variables associated with active teaching. In actual classrooms, teachers have to deal with several variables (like wait time) simultaneously if they are to be successful. Further, we know that teaching success is not achieved through the artful mastery of a few variables but rather that instructional excellence involves the coordination of many aspects of instructional process in curriculum (Brophy, 1988b; Fraser, 1989).

One of the weaknesses of the process-outcome research is its concentration on quantity rather than on quality of instruction—it does not attend sufficiently to curriculum issues. Even so, the process-product paradigm has illustrated that teachers make an important difference in how much and how well students learn, as the example of the complexities and dilemmas of wait time demonstrates. Accordingly, future work needs to focus on the quality and appropriateness of various teaching sequences for various concepts at various levels of difficulty and complexity.

Research on pedagogical knowledge is in its initial stages. However, a review by Carter (forthcoming) suggests that research in such specific subject areas as mathematics, social studies, English, and history strikingly illustrates that differences in teachers' disciplinary knowledge, backgrounds, experiences, and orientations have a pronounced effect on how they organize and present instruction. Such research can yield important implications for both preservice and in-service education.

Subsequent research needs to focus on the dynamic interplay between teachers' subject matter knowledge and pedagogical content knowledge. This is especially the case because of increasing evidence that teachers' knowledge and beliefs can be related to students' performance (Peterson, Fennema, Carpenter, and Loef, 1989). Subject matter knowledge involves teachers' understanding of a particular subject (for example, biology), whereas pedagogical content knowledge indicates teachers' abilities to use effectively (from the knowledge they possess about a subject) those ideas that are important to teach to students at a particular grade level. This pedagogical content knowledge especially includes the ability to communicate or to structure learning activities so that students can understand and interrelate key ideas. It seems likely that some teachers are relatively ineffective because their subject matter knowledge is low. However, it is becoming increasingly clear that some teachers who possess advanced subject matter knowledge are unable to use that knowledge in an effective fashion, that is, to transform subject matter knowledge into pedagogical content knowledge. More research evidence is needed about those skills that allow teachers effectively to transform subject matter knowledge into instructional knowledge.

Classroom Management

Historically, classroom management research has focused on teachers' reactions to student misbehavior. The idea was that teachers needed to develop strategies that would enable them to deal with misbehavior but not disrupt students who were engaged in appropriate work. However, this research failed to differentiate between the behavior of teachers who handled classroom discipline problems successfully and those who did not. The focus of research on rewards, punishments, and privileges has yielded insights that can guide teachers in dealing with individual students, but these principles have proved problematic in managing classes of students (Doyle, 1986).

In the early 1970s, researchers broke from the study of the effects of rewards and punishments in laboratory settings and began to move into actual classrooms, videotaping teachers and studying behaviors associated with more and less effective classroom management. In this approach to research, teachers who consistently had high rates of student engagement and little disruptive behavior were carefully compared to teachers who had more classroom management problems.

Perhaps the most influential study was by Kounin (1970), a pioneer in the shift from the study of reactive behavior to a consideration of active teacher behaviors. Careful analysis of videotapes of actual classroom events indicated that teachers' managerial success lay in their ability to prevent problems by eliciting student cooperation and involvement in seat work.

Kounin's observational work led to the identification of several variables that differentiated effective and ineffective classroom managers. His concepts such as "withitness," smoothness, overlapping, momentum, alerting, accountability, and variety led to several experimental studies that attempted to determine whether these behaviors could be taught to other teachers and if those behaviors would lead to better-managed classrooms.

Evertson and Anderson (1979) conducted another important naturalistic study of classroom management. They found that effective managers spent more time at the beginning of the year helping students to behave appropriately. These teachers had carefully thought out general standards for classroom conduct and procedures for students to get assistance, to line up, to use laboratory equipment, and to make up work when they were absent. And they communicated this information to the students. Evertson and Anderson report that better managers were also more careful monitors of student behavior and that they dealt with misbehavior more quickly than did less effective managers. More effective managers alerted students to the behavior they expected and held students accountable. To the extent that students internalized these rules, they could monitor their own behavior more continuously.

Based on the results of such naturalistic research, several successful field experiments on management have now been conducted. For example, Evertson, Emmer, Sanford, and Clements (1983) trained elementary school teachers in effective management behaviors based on naturalistic research. This training resulted in classrooms with significantly fewer inappropriate student behaviors, lower proportions of students off task, and greater proportions of students engaged in appropriate tasks. Clearly, information from research on classroom management has practical value for classroom teachers.

Good management skills provide a necessary but not sufficient structure for student learning. A good management system is requisite for instruction, because it announces clear intentions and makes possible the monitoring of teacher and student behavior to see whether progress is being made toward shared goals. It tells teachers and students who are intrinsically motivated by school tasks how to proceed and to do well in the classroom. It helps students without these orientations to learn self-control and to engage in academic tasks.

Brophy (1979) advocates the study of instructional issues that are independent of classroom management. In addition, future researchers must determine why some management strategies work and must test specific theoretical arguments. Similar attention should be paid to why and how teachers observed to be effective develop their managerial strategies. In particular, researchers should examine how teachers' classroom management styles influence student initiative and self-control. Students need structure and purposeful direction, but they must also have opportunities to learn to determine their own objectives and to develop strategies for evaluating progress toward self-chosen goals. Such abilities become increasingly important as students get older.

Corno and Rohrkemper (1985) stress self-regulated learning (SRL), a form of student cognitive processing at its most complex and integrative level. They argue that students engaged in self-regulated learning take more active mental approaches to academic tasks. They think and actively attempt to use internal resources to solve problems rather than relying on teachers or other students to accomplish tasks for them. Hence, there is a need to explore more carefully how teachers' management strategies and student cooperative learning in small-group formats encourage or discourage students' capacities for self-regulation.

Although existing management research yields important, practical knowledge, we need more research to understand further how management strategies influence learning in various classroom contexts. The boundaries between instruction and management blur upon examination. The managerial or instructional issues that are important to teachers will vary, depending upon the subject matter and whether teachers pursue process or product goals. Classroom management traditionally has been viewed as a product variable (for example, maintaining student attention). Research yields important facts and concepts concerning management, but one must remember that other ways of viewing this variable have not been explored. Most management research has focused on the socialization of the student to accept teacher norms and school norms. Future work needs to explore how to further assist students to manage their own learning. Further, there is growing evidence that the way teachers conceptualize their management role and the way they view themselves as teachers and classroom managers have important implications for the way they actually "manage" classrooms. As Carter (forthcoming) argues, experienced and effective teachers understand the problem of classroom order differently than do inexperienced teachers. It may therefore be important to direct subsequent research to the issues of how teachers view management and how they manage.

Students' Misconceptions

The college physics coin-toss problem in which students did not learn simple principles represented in laws articulated by Newton is an example of misconception research. In another study, Eaton, Anderson, and Smith (1984) examined the teaching (and learning) of a unit on light in fifth-grade science classes. This unit repeatedly emphasized that some light reflects off objects to our eyes and that it is this reflected light we process when we see. The scientific conception of vision is quite different from the commonsense conception that most people develop, namely, that we see objects because the sun brightens them. On a pretest, only about 5 percent of the students were able to define vision correctly. However, even after students had spent several weeks on the light unit, which covered light reflection and vision several times in quite varied contexts, only 24 percent of them were able to define the process of vision correctly, and the majority still entertained the commonsense but incorrect view of vision.

Awareness of such student misconceptions should lead to improved instruction and to improved student performance. For example, when Eaton, Anderson, and Smith (1984) made major adjustments in the way the fifth-grade light unit was taught (including new materials), student performance on a posttest improved from 24 percent to 79 percent. In some cases, the researchers also found they had to deal with teachers' misconceptions of content; however, the more pervasive difficulty was in how teachers conceptualized appropriate instructional strategies (how teachers attempted to convey what they knew to students).

Research has identified a variety of common student misconceptions in both mathematics (Davis, 1984) and science (Champagne, Klopfer, and Anderson, 1980; diSessa, 1982). Matz (1980) includes the following errors in a list of thirty-three algebra errors that high school and college students commonly make:

1. Evaluating 4x, when x = 6, as 46 or 46x
2. Evaluating xy, when x = –3 and y = –5, as –8
3. Computing 2x divided by 2x to be 0
4. Claiming that one cannot multiply by x because the value of x is unknown

Evidence indicates that misconceptions are common, even among college professors (Lockhead, 1980; Rosnick and Clement, 1980). Furthermore, these inaccuracies are often highly resistant to change. Investigators found that mathematics misconceptions were difficult to correct even with tutoring and that errors often reappeared even after learners seemingly had mastered the correct concepts.

Such research on student misconceptions suggests that teaching often involves bringing about conceptual change in addition to the presentation of knowledge. It also implies that certain forms of teaching, opportunities to learn, and types of materials can prevent misconceptions from forming in the first place, thus making teaching more effective, with less time spent on reteaching and review. Subsequent research on misconceptions not only needs to identify other forms but should also develop strategies for preventing students from developing at least some misconceptions and for dealing with the most common of these.

At this point, the field possesses some sophisticated models that explicate possible ways in which patterns of student misunderstanding interfere with the learning of new material (see, for example, Perkins and Simmons, 1988). Now it is time to begin to use these models in classroom research and to assess their potential for improving student learning during classroom instruction.

Teaching Learning Strategies

There is growing recognition among researchers that good teaching includes teaching students how to learn, how to remember, and how to control their own learning (Good and Brophy, 1986; Norman, 1980; Weinstein and Mayer, 1986).

For example, Norman notes that it is odd that we expect students to learn, yet seldom teach them about learning. Most recent attention to the teaching of learning strategies has involved helping students to learn more about how they learn and to control that process more directly. As Weinstein and Mayer (1986) argue, the concept of lifelong learning becomes increasingly vital as students complete their educations and enter a work force that changes rapidly. Students also need to develop effective ways to deal with the increasing knowledge base that society produces as well as to understand their own thinking processes. Organizing knowledge in a meaningful, integrated way becomes a more important task as information continues to explode in this society. Knowing the facts is no longer the key skill; knowing what information one needs, where to obtain it, and how to use that information is profoundly more important.

Study Strategies. Not only must teachers provide adequate time for students to learn how to use their textbooks, but students also must receive instruction on effective study strategies. Two of the most commonly taught study competencies are SQ3R (survey, question, read, recite, and review) and PQRST (preview, question, read, self-recite, and test). Each of these approaches to effective studying provides a model for students to follow in organizing what they read. Once students learn to use such procedures, studying becomes much more than just a disorganized attempt to use textbooks.

Mathemagenic Effects. Mathemagenic effects refer to effects of active information processing by learners. Mathemagenic activities are activities for learners, to prepare and significantly enhance their intentional learning of meaningful material (for example, getting ready to concentrate, approaching the material with the intention of integrating it with material previously presented, answering adjunct questions, or taking notes). When students read material actively, they are much more likely to remember and to understand than when they passively read sentences without thinking about the implications of what they read.

Future Research. I have discussed several strategies that students need to learn in order to facilitate their own learning. Needed now are clearer understandings of when students should learn specific strategies (for example, should second-graders develop note-taking skills as well as listening skills?) and how these strategies can best be taught.

It is also the case that future research on helping students to learn will have to focus upon higher-order thinking skills as well as on routine outcomes of instruction. It will be important for future research to pay attention to students' abilities to use information, to collect data, to pose interesting questions, and to use subject matter knowledge to answer their own self-generated questions. Hence, if the research is to advance, new and sophisticated outcome measures will have to be developed.

Teacher Expectations

A few years ago, an experiment conducted by Rosenthal and Jacobson (1968) proved to be one of the most exciting and controversial reports to appear in the history of educational research. These investigators presented data suggesting that teachers' experimentally induced expectations for student performance were related to actual levels of student performance. Students whom teachers expected to do better, even though there was no real basis for this expectation, did do better.

One of the weaknesses of the original Rosenthal and Jacobson study was that interactions between teachers and students were not observed; therefore, there was no basis on which to determine whether teachers differentially treated students based on the teachers' expectations. Fortunately, in the last fifteen years, many studies have examined the relationship between teachers' beliefs about individual students' achievements and teachers' interactions with students.

In subsequent work (for example, Brophy and Good, 1974; Cooper and Good, 1983; Good, 1981), it has become clear that individual teachers react differently to differences among students. It has been estimated on the basis of many studies that perhaps one-third of teachers behave in ways that sustain the poor performance of low achievers. For instance, some teachers criticize low achievers more frequently than they criticize high achievers for incorrect responses, and they praise low achievers less per correct answer than they do high achievers. In contrast, other teachers praise marginal or incorrect responses given by low achievers. These findings appear to reflect two different types of teachers. Teachers who criticize low achievers for incorrect responses seem to be intolerant of these pupils. Teachers who reward marginal (or even wrong) answers are excessively sympathetic and unnecessarily protective of low achievers. Both types of teacher behavior illustrate to students that effort and classroom performance are not related (Good and Brophy, 1977), and both discourage student thinking.

Passivity Model. Over time, differences in the ways teachers treat low achievers (for example, in the third grade a student is praised or finds teacher acceptance for virtually any verbalization, but in the fourth grade the student is seldom praised and is criticized frequently) may reduce the efforts of low-achieving students and may contribute to a passive learning style. Other teacher behaviors may compound this problem. Low-achieving students who are called on very frequently one year (the teacher believes they need to participate if they are to learn) but who find that they are called on infrequently the following year (the teacher does not want to embarrass them) may find it confusing to adjust to different role definitions. Ironically, those students who have the least capacity to adapt may be asked to make the most adjustments as they move from classroom to classroom. The greater variation in different teachers' interactions with low achievers (in contrast to the more similar patterns of behavior that high-achieving students experience from different teachers) may occur because teachers agree less about how to respond to students who do not learn readily.

Even within a given year, low achievers are asked to adjust to more varied expectations. This may be true in part because many low achievers have several teachers (in addition to the regular teacher, they may have a remedial mathematics, reading, or speech teacher). The chance for different expectations is thus enhanced. During a given year, certain teachers may also be more likely to vary the instructional styles they use to teach low achievers. For example, they may give up on an instructional technique prematurely (for instance, when the phonics approach initially fails, the teacher tries another instructional method). I believe that many low-achieving students' interactions with different teachers are sufficiently varied so as to pose problems for these students ("What am I expected to do?"). In time, this varied teacher behavior reduces student initiative (for example, students become reluctant to raise their hands or to approach the teacher, or they make fewer attempts to think about the meaning of an assignment or a particular subject).

When teachers provide fewer chances for low achievers to participate in public discussion, or wait less time for them to respond when they are called on (even though these students may need more time to think and to form an answer), or criticize low achievers more per incorrect answer and praise them less per correct answer, the implications are similar. It seems that a good strategy for students who face such conditions would be not to volunteer or not to respond when called on. Students are discouraged from taking risks and chances under such an instructional system (Good, 1981). To the extent that students are motivated to reduce risks and ambiguity—and many argue that students are strongly motivated to do so (Doyle, 1983)—students would likely become more passive in order to reduce the risks of critical teacher feedback.

Research on teacher expectations has yielded information and various models of how teachers communicate low expectations to students in classroom situations. That knowledge is useful only if used as a framework for thinking about classrooms rather than as a general definition of how teachers should behave in a classroom. Good and Weinstein (1986b) argue that because of the complexity with which expectations may operate in classrooms, teachers must be decision makers and must apply concepts and research findings to their own classrooms. Expectations are expressed in various ways (choice of curriculum topics, rationale given to students for a curriculum topic, performance feedback). It is not possible to identify a combination of behaviors that can lead to the communication of appropriate expectations. It is also difficult to provide advice to teachers about the utility of particular teacher behaviors (call on, criticism, praise) because students' interpretations of the behaviors depend not only on the behavior but also on the context in which it occurs (what is challenging to a sixth grader may be threatening to a first grader). The quality and style of the behavior, as well as students' interpretations of teacher behavior, are also important aspects that determine the effects of particular behaviors on students. As a case in point, Brophy (1981) notes that praise may erode or enhance motivation, and Mittman (1985) reports that under some conditions, students may interpret teacher criticism favorably (teacher cares—expects good work).

In making decisions, teachers have to apply the concepts to their own classrooms. A review of the literature provides ample evidence that some teachers call on low-achieving students less often than they call on students they believe to be more capable. It makes little sense, however, to encourage all teachers to call on low-achieving students more frequently simply because some teachers call on low-achieving students too infrequently.

Similarly, it does little good to call on low-achieving students more frequently if these students are generally asked only to answer simple factual questions or if they are asked questions they cannot answer. Likewise, it is unproductive to increase the amount of time a teacher waits for a low-achieving student to respond if the increase is independent of a consideration of particular context. If the teacher asks a factual question, simply waiting and providing clues may be an unproductive use of classroom time (the student either knows the answer or doesn't). However, in a situation involving judgment or analysis, more time to think and more teacher clues may facilitate a student response.

Other researchers have expressed concerns that low expectations for classes and even for entire schools have become endemic in American secondary education. Sedlak, Wheeler, Pullin, and Cusick (1986) note that low expectations appear in too many American high schools in the form of a bargain between teachers and students that results in a deemphasis on academic learning. In this bargain, students agree to behave if their teachers do not demand much academic work. Thus, classroom order and pleasantness are achieved at the cost of minimal content acquisition. Sedlak, Wheeler, Pullin, and Cusick argue that there is a vital need to endorse a vision of education that leads to a genuine empowerment of students. In essence, students need instruction and access to concepts and activities that help them develop intellectual insights they can use to make better decisions rather than a steady diet of activities that are designed to keep students busy and under control but that do not require students to reason. Other types of low expectations may be found in a permissive and indiscriminate range of courses that allows high school students to avoid taking substantive courses (Powell, Farrar, and Cohen, 1985).

Why do some teachers noticeably differentiate their behavior toward high- or low-achieving students, while others show only minimal differences in their behavior? Following the work of Dweck and Elliott (1983), Marshall and Weinstein (1984) contend that teachers' beliefs about the nature of intelligence may influence their classroom behaviors. Some teachers view intelligence as a fixed and relatively stable entity. Other teachers view intelligence as incremental, as a repertoire of skills and knowledge that can be increased.

Teachers who hold an entity view of intelligence are more likely to place students in a hierarchy according to performance expectations and to treat these students differently on the basis of expectations. According to Marshall and Weinstein, teachers of low achievers may use performance information to make detrimental social comparisons. However, the statements and curriculum assignments of teachers who hold an incremental view of intelligence communicate the belief that each student has the ability to improve regardless of current status, that individual differences in rates and modes of learning are normal, and that students can learn from those who already have acquired certain skills.

Future Research. Most of the research on teacher expectations has focused on teacher communication of expectations. Future research should examine student awareness of teacher expectations as well as student vulnerability to expectation communication. Rosenthal (1985) notes that much of the research on interpersonal expectancies suggests that mediation of these expectations depends to some degree on nonverbal communication. There are apparently major differences among experimenters, teachers, and other people in clarity of communication through nonverbal channels. Hence, it is important to study student sensitivity to expectations, and especially to nonverbal expectation communication, more carefully.

The usual product measures that researchers use (student performance, IQ, and achievement tests) appear to be too narrow to reveal much about the relationship between expectations and classroom performance. Meyer (1985) suggests that aptitude and achievement outcomes are likely to underestimate the beneficial effects of early school experiences as well as the effects of teacher expectations. Subsequent research needs to include various social adjustment measures (ability to work cooperatively with others, to assume responsibility, and so on) as well as cognitive outcomes.

Future research should also focus upon expectations that teachers and students hold about subject matter. It seems clear that expectations regarding subject matter influence how teachers attempt to present subject matter and how students attempt to master it. For example, how do teachers conceptualize mathematics? Does it imply speed and right answers or the search for patterns and understanding? Much more research needs to examine subject matter expectations and their relationship to classroom learning.

Effective Schools

In the past several years, educational researchers have produced a significant body of literature on schools as social institutions (for comprehensive reviews, see Good and Brophy, 1986; Purkey and Smith, 1983). Despite the controversial findings of Coleman and others (1966), who argued in the late 1960s that schooling did not significantly affect student achievement and that achievement could be predicted on the basis of individual student characteristics (such as aptitude and home background), recent research that employs sophisticated methods to examine school processes illustrates that schools do make a difference in student outcomes (Good and Weinstein, 1986a). Variation in achievement among schools serving similar populations is often substantial and has significant implications for social policy. There is a growing awareness that school environments can support or detract from the quality of teaching. Available evidence strongly suggests that schools with comparable resources (including student talent) can and do have very different climates that can be related to student achievement. Simply put, the environments in some schools support learning, and norms for scholastic achievement in these schools are much clearer and higher than in comparable schools serving similar populations (see Good and Brophy, 1986, for a discussion of factors that differentiate schools with high student performance).

Along these lines, work by Rosenholtz (1989) provides clear evidence that the normative culture varies in more and less effective schools. She notes that teachers in some schools conceptualize teaching as routine, whereas staffs in other schools view it as nonroutine. In schools in which teachers view teaching as routine, teachers tend to work alone, using only their own observations and habits as a basis for reflection and growth. In schools in which teachers see teaching as nonroutine, teachers attempt to gain and share technical knowledge about instruction. More research is needed to better understand how teachers' dispositions and beliefs about collegial relationships affect their sharing of knowledge and their enrichment of the curriculum.

Research on schools as social institutions has conceptual and methodological limitations, such as its atheoretical nature and the instability of outcomes. However, it is clear that schools as social institutions differ in their ability to affect student performance on outcomes such as standardized achievement tests. We now need research that addresses the theoretical and methodological problems and that begins to specify what school variables affect important student outcomes other than achievement (ability to engage in self-evaluation and independent thought, and so on).

Although reports such as *A Nation at Risk, Becoming a Nation of Readers, A Nation Prepared, A Call for Change in Teacher Education,* and *Tomorrow's Teachers* have spurred interest in schooling, we must now develop new models, expand old models of effective schools, and use models that are built on and tested by new types of research. Increased funding will be necessary to conduct this research because it is labor-intensive and because it requires a pool of talented observers to collect reliable and useful data. It is important that this research be conducted by a wider range of social scientists in order to complement the efforts of the relatively small number of scholars who currently explore school environments (Good and Weinstein, 1986a). If public education is to be understood and improved, it must be studied using diverse theoretical frameworks. To increase cooperation between colleges of arts and science and colleges of education in studying local school districts, it is important to include political scientists, anthropologists, sociologists, psychologists, mathematicians, and other talented academicians in the study of schooling.

Integrative Curriculum Work

It is beyond the scope of this chapter to discuss the many important advances that have occurred in the teaching of particular subject matter (for comprehensive reviews of teaching subject areas—mathematics, writing, and so on—see chapters in Wittrock, 1986). However, it is useful to mention briefly that present-day curricula stress the importance of integrating various subject matter and making teaching more demanding (that is, requiring more careful planning and more preparation). The focus on teaching writing in content-area courses is a good example of this new trend.

As Nelms (1987) indicates, there is an increasing need to use writing as an aid to reading and learning in the content areas in elementary schools (for example, Beyer and Gilstrap, 1982; Thaiss, 1986; Welton, 1983). Other studies demonstrate the need to integrate the language arts—reading and writing, composing and comprehending, speaking and writing, and reasoning—in order to facilitate learning in the content areas (for example, Jensen, 1984; Petersen, 1986). According to Nelms, useful specific suggestions for developing elementary school social studies units that include reading, writing, and speaking are available in the literature. He argues that imaginative, relevant writing assignments can be constructed on almost any conceivable topic. Nelms argues that too often the use of writing in content areas is relatively superficial. He cites the example of students who simply regurgitate information that is available in an encyclopedia or in an atlas and then add pictures or photos in order to produce a thick report. Such assignments merely require students to report facts that others have collected. Genuine learning, however, requires students to use language to respond to what they see and hear and to integrate new reading into other knowledge they possess about a topic. Thus, it is important that students have opportunities to express their ideas in conversation and in writing and to do so across curricula, not just in language arts. This is especially important in social studies, because social responsibility requires citizens who are responsible for their own learning and thinking. According to Nelms, the regular practice of actively responding through writing exercises is good preparation for such responsibility. However, to reiterate, the important issue is the quality of writing assignments, not the use of writing per se. Nelms summarizes several different types of writing that can be used to promote active learning in various content areas: writing to inventory knowledge, writing to initiate learning, writing to consolidate learning, writing to personalize learning, and writing to clarify thinking.

Nelms notes that the new reform movement in education emphasizes traditional academic content (for example, history and sociology), but he contends the important issue is that content not be taught as a closed system and that the teaching method involve a learning of process, not just learning how to learn, in some vague sense. Thus, as we attempt to adapt schooling to the coming information age, we must not denigrate the value of facts and content, but we must teach subject matter in a way that encourages thinking and application rather than rote memorization.

New curricula integrate the language arts to facilitate instruction and learning in the content areas. Researchers need to assess the effects of these curricula and the idea, for example, that every teacher should be a teacher of writing. Careful observational studies must examine the trade-offs that occur when integrative subject matter units are taught and when teachers try to achieve multiple objectives. Needed are better conceptualizations and statements about how such units can be used to encourage student initiative, thinking, and application. These materials have interesting possibilities but need to be tested and improved through careful classroom research.

Expert Versus Novice Teachers

Berliner (1986) acknowledges the value of previous process-product research (that is, the research briefly described earlier in the "Instructional Research and Active Teaching" section of this chapter) and argues that it is important to extend our knowledge of what effective instructors do in the classroom to include an understanding of why effective teachers behave as they do. He also points out the need to examine teachers' instructional decisions, the rules or criteria teachers use to make classroom decisions, and how teachers vary instruction to meet the needs of different students. According to Berliner, educators need to develop a system of research that allows information to be codified and formalized, such as the systems in, for example, medicine, chess, or physics (see, for example, Chi, Glaser, and Farr, 1988; Duda and Shortliffe, 1983).

Berliner (1986) notes that information about experts and novices in other fields also applies to teaching. His research identified several characteristics of novice and expert teachers. For example, novices held literal views of objects and events, whereas experts made inferences about those objects and events. That is, experts applied their domain-specific knowledge to make sense of the classrooms they viewed. When novices were shown slides of classrooms, they simply described the superficial characteristics of classrooms. The expert teachers that Berliner and others have studied had the following characteristics in common with experts in other fields: they were able to categorize problems to be solved at some higher cognitive level; they used higher-order systems of categorization to analyze problems; they were extraordinarily fast and accurate at recognizing events that were taking place in the classroom; they were sensitive to the task demands and the social structure of the job situation; and they were opportunistic planners, who were able to change quickly when things were not moving at a productive pace.

Leinhardt (1986) reports on a comparison of a small group of expert teachers and novices (student teachers). Expert teachers were selected from among teachers whose students' scores were in the top 15 percent in the district for at least three years in a five-year period. Teachers were observed over a three-and-one-half month period that included classroom observations, interviews, and videotapes of up to twenty-five hours of math classes. One of the key differences between expert teachers and novice teachers was that experts were able to provide interviewers with a more explicit, detailed plan of their intended actions in a lesson. Expert teachers were also more likely to make explicit references to students' actions in their descriptions and to mention planning for a key decision point (or several) within the lesson—a point at which the teachers would determine whether to present new material or to repeat concepts in a different way to ensure student understanding. Leinhardt argues that the mention of a student action suggests that teachers maintain ongoing plans for both the teacher's and the students' actions and for goal sequences. This appears to be a difficult but necessary part of being an effective teacher. Expert teachers' agenda descriptions were far richer and more detailed than those of novice teachers. It is interesting that experts always started their planning statements by telling what they had done the day before. In contrast, none of the novices did so. Experts thus saw lessons as connected. Leinhardt notes that novices may very well have had more elaborate plans than the ones they first described, but the plans were not accessible in the moments just prior to teaching or while teaching.

Another interesting difference between experts and novices was that expert teachers' explanations of content contained components that students already knew (88 percent of the cases); however, none of the novices' explanations included common phenomena that students knew. Experts gave better explanations than did novices, and their explanations contained more critical features and fewer errors. When errors did occur in expert teachers' explanations, they were not as serious.

Leinhardt notes that novice teachers' lessons were characterized by fragmented structures and long transitions between lesson segments, by frequent confusion caused by missent signals, and by an ambiguous system of goals that often appeared to be abandoned rather than achieved. Interviews with novices indicated that they knew the subject matter but did not use that knowledge while teaching. The lessons of novice teachers did not fit well together within or across topics. Leinhardt found that novices were aware of these problems to some extent. However, novices lacked the analytical skills to understand where failures occurred or when goals that were implicit in certain actions were not achieved.

Researchers have studied other differences between expert and novice teachers. For example, Housner and Griffey (1985) found that one out of five instructional strategy decisions experienced teachers made had to do with adaptation of instruction in case planned lessons did not work out. In comparison, only one out of ten strategies of less experienced teachers dealt with how to adapt lessons. It seems that experienced teachers do a better job of anticipating learners' difficulties and have a variety of ways to offer instruction and well-worked-out rules for when to vary instruction.

Huberman (1985) attempted to determine when experienced teachers mastered the problems that perplexed first-year teachers. Included here were issues of discipline, effectiveness with the class, effectiveness with slow and quick learners, sustaining the interest of poorly motivated students, having a variety of materials that students like to work with and that were appropriate as well, and establishing satisfactory sets of rules and systems of communication in the classroom. It is interesting that Huberman found that the majority of teachers solved only five of the original eighteen problems of first-year teachers in fewer than three years. It may take several years for teachers to solve problems such as classroom management and organization. Without appropriate intervention, many problems of teaching practice do not lend themselves to quick solutions.

Although the study of expert teachers is important, there are probably limits to our ability to specify the components of expertise that nonexperts need (Doyle, 1986). Chess players and grand champions may think and approach the game differently, so that different strategies, especially in the short run, are probably necessary for nonexpert chess players. Similarly, in the area of teaching, it may be that there are times when young teachers have to teach in ways different from more experienced teachers, and it may be that a focus on expert teachers in certain contexts could be misleading if we are not careful about the way in which those results are applied. For example, work by Borko and Niles (1987) suggests that young teachers may have to plan more than do experienced teachers if they are to be successful. Hence, research on expert teachers needs to be balanced with continuing work on teachers of varying ability who teach in diverse situations.

Teacher Education

I have stated that our knowledge of teaching and of other school processes has improved substantially in the last decade, in large measure because of better observational research. However, we know little about teacher education programs and about the values and norms articulated therein—partly because teachers are faced with countless decisions that, although practical in nature, represent difficult analytical challenges.

For a variety of reasons, few researchers have studied teacher education programs. (See Lanier and Little, 1986, for a discussion of how limited resources, low status among university programs, and institutional politics have hindered the development of systematic knowledge about teacher education programs.) Although demographic and survey data exist, there is virtually no information on what occurs in teacher education programs. There is every reason to believe that teacher education programs vary widely, from the dismal and disappointing to the exciting and important. Unfortunately, we cannot propose even tentative answers to rudimentary questions such as whether the knowledge from research on teaching is being taught in teacher education programs and, if so, whether such knowledge is being presented as the solution to educational problems (an approach that I believe is self-defeating) or as findings and concepts that teachers must apply flexibly to particular contexts (for example, Biddle and Anderson, 1986). Educational problems have multiple causes and thus do not lend themselves to simple, generalized solutions.

Research on Teacher Education

Mary Kennedy (1986) and her colleagues at the Teacher Education Center at Michigan State University argue that it is important to document the purposes and quality of teacher education programs, largely because serious accusations have been launched against these programs for their lack of attention to the teaching of academic subject matter and for their generally low academic quality. Yet, these accusations appear to be made not only in the absence of evidence but even in the absence of any ideas about what is meant by the terms *academic subject matter* and *academic quality.* It is time to ground these debates in research. We need to know the extent to which teacher education courses are academically demanding and the extent to which they improve students' capacities for independent thought.

As Kennedy notes, researchers should examine the effects of various teacher education programs on teachers' knowledge, skills, and dispositions. Until now, there has been more argument than research about these issues, and many of the issues have not yet been conceptualized in a way that would allow careful investigation. Furthermore, teacher education is only one of many influences on teachers, and we should examine its role relative to that of other influences, such as formal induction programs, state-mandated testing, and so on (see Figure 1).

Other basic and interesting questions also need to be answered: How stable are teachers' conceptions of academic learning? Where and how do teachers acquire their understandings of pedagogy (Ball and McDiarmid, forthcoming)? When and how do teachers develop views on critical issues such as what to expect from low- and high-achieving students and how to pursue excellence and equity goals at the same time?

One program of research at the Teacher Education Center compares different types of teacher education programs with one another, and it compares teacher education with liberal arts programs. In liberal arts–teacher education comparisons, four types of information appear useful to collect: (1) how the mathematics skills and writing skills of teacher education students and other students differ when they begin college; (2) how students' conceptions of writing and mathematics change as they move through college and, where applicable, into teaching positions; (3) to what extent teacher education students and other students improve their abilities to use writing and mathematics instrumentally as they move through college; and (4) whether teacher education students and other students improve their abilities to teach writing or mathematics as they move through college and into teaching positions. (Do they increase the number of ways they can present a mathematical concept? Do they improve their abilities to critique students' writing assignments and their abilities to enable students to revise their writing?)

There is a need for careful conceptualization of teacher education if empirical research is to be helpful. As Kennedy and her colleagues argue, many of the components of preservice teacher education have not been carefully conceptualized. For example, student teaching is often thought to be an important part of the teacher education experience (although some claim that the effects of teacher education programs are minimal once students enter the conservative environment of schools). However, researchers have not fully conceptualized student teaching, despite the research in this area. Many important questions remain unanswered. For example, is student teaching the time for prospective teachers to put it all together to demonstrate that they can teach? Is it an occasion for novices to test different approaches and ideas and to begin seeing how to learn from their own practice? Although these questions are not mutually exclusive, they represent different views of student teaching.

Also, we need more research on teacher movement from college into the teaching profession. It is important to avoid making implicit assumptions about the relationship between what teachers encounter in preservice programs and what they subsequently do in classrooms (are they supervisors or mentors?).

Howey and Zimpher (1986) suggest that it is difficult to conceive of reform of teacher preparation, either baccalaureate or postgraduate, that does not also attend to the general studies curriculum. They note that there are dramatic differences in what students can study in arts and sciences or in general studies curricula. Thus, researchers should examine what disciplines, what types of courses, and what sequences of courses would best serve as the foundation for a person- and service-oriented profession such as teaching. Are all courses taught in arts and science equally appropriate, and if not, what are the criteria for making distinctions in career planning and program planning? If reform in teacher education is to occur, it will be necessary to reexamine the entire college curriculum of prospective teachers. Howey and Zimpher note that better utilization of our current research base and, most important, the expansion of this research as rapidly and as widely as possible are of critical concern. Because teacher education suffers from institutional isolation, they call for a national consortium similar to the Holmes Group to examine the state of teacher education. Teacher educators also need to encourage local educators and arts and science faculty to join in this effort.

Summary

I have argued that research on teaching yields important concepts and findings that can be valuable to classroom teachers. However, these findings are valuable not because they yield rules for teaching but rather because they help teachers to assess the likely consequences of alternative strategies and thus to make more informed decisions. Recent research clearly indicates that seemingly simple actions, such as calling on a student, actually involve complex decisions. Fortunately, there is a growing literature that is beginning to assess directly how teachers make decisions and use pedagogical content knowledge to make complex classroom decisions (Carter, forthcoming).

There is growing recognition that teachers need more than subject matter knowledge if they are to be effective in the classroom. As the report of the National Commission for Excellence in Teacher Education (1985) notes, teaching and learning are difficult and subtle endeavors, and successful teachers need extensive professional training and knowledge to complement subject matter knowledge.

However, it is also the case that successful teaching involves more than effective communication (Brophy, 1988a, 1988b; Good and Mulryan, forthcoming). It also entails the application of principles of cognitive development, understanding of human motivation, knowledge of subject matter, as well as pedagogical skills necessary to help students to understand the curriculum. Although recent research is valuable, it yields only limited knowledge about the full range of knowledge, dispositions, and skills that teachers need if they are to be successful in the classroom across several student outcomes. Continued research on instructional process is of considerable importance.

Well-developed teaching skills are absolutely necessary for successful teaching. The observational literature reminds us repeatedly that teachers are incredibly busy; they interact with many students, attend to numerous factors simultaneously (remediation, enrichment, management, supervision, and instruction), and make decisions under adverse conditions (see Good and Brophy, 1987).

Although questions about classroom practice are easy to ask, they are exceedingly difficult to study. Information a teacher presents may mean quite different things to various students in a class. Unfortunately, the difficulty of doing classroom research is often minimized because the research is practical. Berliner (1986) notes that when a physicist studies a problem and announces that the problem involves Newton's second law, he or she is considered an expert. When an experienced teacher classifies a child's learning problems into three categories that lead to certain actions, it is often considered to be an example of something less. The complexity of teaching is minimized, however, when we confuse the validity of the inferences being made with their practical characteristics.

Berliner argues—and I agree—that making decisions in unstructured contexts such as classrooms is a much more complex task than is solving problems in well-structured domains such as mathematics or chess. Teaching occurs in a complex social setting in which student attention and effort are always problematic to some extent.

I contend that the problems of practice represent difficult analytical challenges that merit research and model development that will enable us to distinguish the many variables that affect teaching. We have much more detailed knowledge of teaching in many areas now than we had a few years ago. In addition, we also better understand how school structure and culture (climate, incentives) affect teaching and learning. Still, new models and concepts of teaching must be developed. These new models have to be built with the recognition that there is currently a growing teacher shortage, at the same time that the proportion of college graduates preparing for careers in teaching is at an all-time low (Hawley, 1986).

If universities wish to improve public schools, they can best do so by encouraging teacher educators, arts and science faculty, and local school personnel to combine resources in studying problem areas of mutual concern. It is imperative that teaching become a profession if schools are to attract and to retain capable teachers. I believe that at the heart of any profession are status, financial rewards, and knowledge not possessed by the average citizen. Institutions of higher education cannot directly affect salary increases that teachers need, nor can they bestow status. However, they can facilitate the development of a coherent knowledge base, which is the core of any profession.

Zeichner (1986) notes that one of the distinguishing characteristics of teacher education today is its low investment in systematic research, development, and evaluation. He argues that relatively few schools and colleges of education are significantly involved in research related to any aspect of schooling, and a minute proportion of this scholarship focuses on teacher education. It is imperative that this situation change.

References

Anderson, C., and Smith, E. "Teaching Science." In V. Richardson-Koehler (ed.), *Educators' Handbook: A Research Perspective.* New York: Longman, 1987.

Anshutz, R. "An Investigation of Wait-Time and Questioning Techniques as an Instructional Variable for Science Methods Students Microteaching Elementary School Children." Unpublished doctoral dissertation, Department of Education, University of Kansas, 1973.

Armbruster, B., and Anderson, T. "Structures of Explanations in History Textbooks or So What If Governor Stanford Missed the Spike and Hit the Rail?" *Journal of Curriculum Studies,* 1984, *16,* 181–194.

Artley, S. "Individual Differences and Reading Instruction." *Elementary School Journal,* 1981, *82,* 143–151.

Ball, D., and McDiarmid, G. "The Subject Matter Preparation of Teachers." In W. R. Houston (ed.), *Handbook of Research on Teacher Education.* New York: Macmillan, forthcoming.

Berliner, D. "In Pursuit of the Expert Pedagogue." *Educational Researcher,* 1986, *15,* 5–13.

Beyer, B. K., and Gilstrap, R. *Writing in Elementary School Social Studies.* Boulder, Colo.: Social Science Education Consortium, 1982. (ED 213 631)

Biddle, B., and Anderson, D. "Theory, Methods, Knowledge and Research on Teaching." In M. Wittrock (ed.), *Handbook of Research on Teaching.* (3rd ed.) New York: Macmillan, 1986.

Borko, H., and Niles, J. "Descriptions of Teaching Planning: Ideas for Teachers and Researchers." In V. Richardson-Koehler (ed.), *Educators' Handbook: A Research Perspective.* New York: Longman, 1987.

Brophy, J. "Teacher Behavior and Its Effects." *Journal of Educational Psychology,* 1979, *71,* 733–750.

Brophy, J. "Teacher Praise: A Functional Analysis." *Review of Educational Research,* 1981, *51,* 5–32.

Brophy, J. "Conceptualizing Student Motivation." *Educational Psychologist,* 1983, *18,* 200–215.

Brophy, J. "Improving Teacher Quality in Science and Mathematics Education: What Can Research Tell Us?" Paper presented at the annual meeting of the American Educational Research Association, San Francisco, Apr. 1986a.

Brophy, J. "Mathematics Education: A Presentation to the Special Interest Group in Mathematics Education." Paper presented at the annual meeting of the American Educational Research Association, San Francisco, Apr. 1986b.

Brophy, J. "Teaching and Learning Mathematics: Where Research Should Be Going." Paper presented to the special interest group on Research in Mathematics Education at the annual meeting of the American Educational Research Association, San Francisco, Apr. 1986c.

Brophy, J. "Socializing Students' Motivation to Learn." In M. L. Maehr and D. A. Kleiver (eds.), *Recent Advances in Motivation and Achievement.* Vol. 5. Greenwich, Conn.: JAI Press, 1987.

Brophy, J. "Research on Teacher Effects: Uses and Abuses." *Elementary School Journal,* 1988a, *89,* 3–22.

Brophy, J. "Teaching for Meaningful Understanding and Self-Regulated Learning." In J. Brophy (ed.), *Advances in*

Research on Teaching. Vol. 1. Greenwich, Conn.: JAI Press, 1988b.

Brophy, J., and Good, T. *Looking in Classrooms.* New York: Harper & Row, 1974.

Brophy, J., and Good, T. "Teacher Behavior and Student Achievement." In M. Wittrock (ed.), *Handbook of Research on Teaching.* (3rd ed.) New York: Macmillan, 1986.

Carnegie Task Force on Teaching as a Profession. *A Nation Prepared: Teachers for the 21st Century.* New York: Carnegie Forum, 1986.

Carpenter, T., and others. "Using Knowledge of Children's Mathematical Thinking in Classroom Teaching: An Experimental Study." Paper presented at the annual meeting of the American Educational Research Association, New Orleans, Apr. 1988.

Carter, K. "Teachers' Knowledge and Learning to Teach." In R. Houston (ed.), *Handbook of Research on Teacher Education.* New York: Macmillan, forthcoming.

Case, R., and Bereiter, C. "From Behaviourism to Cognitive Behaviourism to Cognitive Development: Steps in the Evolution of Instructional Design." *Instructional Science,* 1984, *13,* 141–158.

Champagne, A., Klopfer, L., and Anderson, J. "Factors Influencing the Learning of Classical Mechanics." *American Journal of Physics,* 1980, *48,* 1074–1079.

Chi, M.T.H., Glaser, R., and Farr, M. J. *The Nature of Expertise.* Hillsdale, N.J.: Erlbaum, 1988.

Clune, W., White, P., and Patterson, J. *The Implementation and Effects of High School Graduation Requirements: First Steps Toward Curricular Reform.* New Brunswick, N.J.: Center for Policy Research in Education, 1989.

Coleman, J., and others. *Equality of Educational Opportunity.* Washington, D.C.: U.S. Government Printing Office, 1966.

Cooper, H., and Good, T. *Pygmalion Grows Up: Studies in the Expectation Communication Process.* New York: Longman, 1983.

Corno, L., and Rohrkemper, M. "Self-Regulated Learning."

In R. Ames and C. Ames (eds.), *Research on Motivation in Education.* Vol. 2. Orlando, Fla.: Academic Press, 1985.

Davis, R. *Learning Mathematics: A Cognitive Science Approach to Mathematics Education.* London: Croom Helm, 1984.

De Ture, L. "Relative Effects of Modeling on the Acquisition of Wait-Time by Preservice Elementary Teachers and Concomitant Changes in Dialogue Patterns." *Journal of Research in Science Teaching,* 1979, *16,* 553–562.

diSessa, A. "Unlearning Aristotelian Physics: A Study of Knowledge-Based Learning." *Cognitive Science,* 1982, *6,* 37–75.

Doyle, W. "Academic Work." *Review of Educational Research,* 1983, *53,* 159–199.

Doyle, W. "Academic Work." In T. Tomlinson and H. Walberg (eds.), *Academic Work and Educational Excellence.* Berkeley, Calif.: McCutchan, 1986.

Druva, C., and Anderson, R. "Science Teacher Characteristics by Teacher Behavior and by Student Outcome: A Meta-Analysis of Research." *Journal of Research in Science Teaching,* 1983, *20* (5), 467–479.

Duda, R., and Shortliffe, E. "Expert Systems Research." *Science,* 1983, *220,* 261–268.

Duffy, G., and Roehler, L. "Tension Between Information Giving and Mediation: Perspectives on Instructional Explanations." In J. Brophy (ed.), *Advances in Research on Teaching.* Vol. 1. Greenwich, Conn.: JAI Press, 1989.

Dweck, C., and Elliott, E. "Achievement Motivation." In P. Mussen and E. Hetherington (eds.), *Handbook of Child Psychology IV: Socialization, Personality, and Social Development.* New York: Wiley, 1983.

Eaton, J., Anderson, C., and Smith, E. "Students' Misconceptions Interfere with Science Learning: Case Studies of Fifth-Grade Students." *Elementary School Journal,* 1984, *84,* 365–379.

Engelmann, S., and Carnine, D. *Theory of Instruction: Principles and Application.* New York: Irvington, 1982.

Evertson, C., and Anderson, L. "Beginning School." *Educational Horizons,* 1979, *57,* 164–168.

Evertson, C., Emmer, E., Sanford, J., and Clements, B. "Improving Classroom Management: An Experiment in Elementary School Classrooms." *Elementary School Journal,* 1983, *84,* 173–188.

Evertson, C., Hawley, W., and Zlotnik, M. "Making a Difference in Educational Quality Through Teacher Education." *Journal of Teacher Education,* 1985, *36,* 2–12.

Evertson, C., Weade, R., Green, J., and Crawford, J. *Effective Classroom Management and Instruction.* Washington, D. C.: National Institute of Education, 1985.

Fagan, E., Hassler, D., and Szabo, M. "Evaluation of Questioning Strategies in Language Arts Instruction." *Research in Teaching of English,* 1981, *15,* 267–273.

Fraser, B. "Instructional Effectiveness: Processes on the Micro-Level." Paper presented at the International Congress for School Effectiveness, Rotterdam, The Netherlands, Jan. 1989.

Good, T. "Listening to Students Talk About Classrooms." Paper presented at the annual meeting of the American Educational Research Association, Los Angeles, 1981.

Good, T., and Biddle, B. "Research and the Improvement of Mathematics Instruction: The Need for Observational Resources." In D. Grouws and T. Cooney (eds.), *Perspectives on Research on Effective Mathematics Teaching.* Reston, Va.: National Council of Mathematics Teachers and Lawrence Erlbaum Associates, 1988.

Good, T., and Brophy, J. *Educational Psychology: A Realistic Approach.* (1st ed.) New York: Holt, Rinehart & Winston, 1977.

Good, T., and Brophy, J. *Educational Psychology: A Realistic Approach.* (3rd ed.) New York: Longman, 1986.

Good, T., and Brophy, J. *Looking in Classrooms.* (4th ed.) New York: Harper & Row, 1987.

Good, T., and Brophy, J. "Teaching the Lesson." In R. Slavin (ed.), *School and Classroom Organization.* Hillsdale, N.J.: Erlbaum, 1989.

Good, T., and Grouws, D. "Developing Inservice Training Programs for Increasing Understanding of Mathematical Ideas." *Phi Delta Kappan,* 1987, *68* (10), 778-783.

Good, T., Grouws, D., and Ebmeier, H. *Active Mathematics Teaching.* New York: Longman, 1983.

Good, T., and Mulryan, C. "Teacher Ratings: A Call for Teacher Control and Self-Evaluation." In J. Millman and L. Darling-Hammond (eds.), *Handbook of Teacher Evaluation.* (2nd ed.) Beverly Hills, Calif.: Sage, forthcoming.

Good, T., and Weinstein, R. "Schools Make a Difference: Evidence, Criticisms, and New Directions." *American Psychologist,* 1986a, *41* (10), 1090-1097.

Good, T., and Weinstein, R. "Teacher Expectations: A Framework for Exploring Classrooms." In K. Zumwalt (ed.), *Improving Teaching: 1986 ASCD Yearbook.* Alexandria, Va.: Association for Supervision and Curriculum Development, 1986b.

Griffin, G. "Clinical Teacher Education." In J. Hoffman and S. Edwards (eds.), *Reality and Reform in Clinical Teacher Education.* New York: Random House, 1986.

Gropper, G. "A Behavioral Approach to Instructional Prescription." In C. Reigeluth (ed.), *Instructional-Design Theories and Models: An Overview of Their Current Status.* Hillsdale, N.J.: Erlbaum, 1983.

Hawley, W. "Toward a Comprehensive Strategy for Addressing the Teacher Shortage." *Phi Delta Kappan,* 1986, *67* (10), 712-718.

Holmes Group. *Tomorrow's Teachers: A Report of the Holmes Group.* East Lansing: Michigan State University, 1986.

Housner, L., and Griffey, D. "Teacher Cognition: Differences in Planning and Interactive Decision-Making Between Experienced and Inexperienced Teachers." *Research Quarterly for Exercise and Sport,* 1985, *56,* 45-53.

Howey, K., and Zimpher, N. "The Current Debate on Teacher Preparation." *Journal of Teacher Education,* 1986, *33,* 41-49.

Huberman, M. "What Knowledge Is of Most Worth to Teachers? A Knowledge-Use Perspective." *Teaching and Teacher Education,* 1985, *1,* 251-262.

Jensen, J. (ed.). *Composing and Comprehending.* Urbana, Ill.: National Council of Teachers of English, 1984.

Kennedy, M. *Proposal for Continuation of the National Center for Research on Teacher Education.* East Lansing: Michigan State University, 1986.

Kounin, J. *Discipline and Group Management in Classrooms.* New York: Holt, Rinehart & Winston, 1970.

Lanier, J., and Little, J. "Research on Teacher Education." In M. Wittrock (ed.), *Handbook of Research on Teaching.* (3rd ed.) New York: Macmillan, 1986.

Leinhardt, G. "Expertise in Mathematics Teaching." *Educational Leadership,* 1986, *43* (7), 28-33.

Leinhardt, G., and Smith, D. "Expertise in Mathematics Instruction: Subject Matter Knowledge." *Journal of Educational Psychology,* 1985, *77,* 247-271.

Lockhead, J. "Faculty Interpretations of Simple Algebraic Statements: The Professor's Side of the Equation." *Journal of Mathematical Behavior,* 1980, *3,* 29-37.

Marshall, H., and Weinstein, R. "Classrooms Where Students Perceive High and Low Amounts of Differential Teacher Treatment." Paper presented at the annual meeting of the American Educational Research Association, New Orleans, 1984.

Matz, M. "Towards a Computational Model of Algebraic Competence." *Journal of Mathematical Behavior,* 1980, *3,* 93-166.

Meyer, W. "Summary, Integration, and Perspective." In J. Dusek (ed.), *Teacher Expectancies.* Hillsdale, N.J.: Erlbaum, 1985.

Mittman, A. "Teachers' Differential Behavior Toward Higher- and Lower-Achieving Students and Its Relationship with Selected Teacher Characteristics." *Journal of Educational Psychology,* 1985, *35,* 149-161.

National Commission for Excellence in Education. *A Nation at Risk.* Washington, D.C.: National Institute of Education, 1983.

National Commission for Excellence in Teacher Education. *A Call for Change in Teacher Education.* Washington, D.C.:

American Association of Colleges for Teacher Education, 1985.

National Research Council. *Everybody Counts: A Report to the Nation on the Future of Mathematics Education.* Washington, D.C.: National Academy Press, 1989.

Nelms, B. F. "Response and Responsibility: Reading, Writing, and Social Studies." *Elementary School Journal,* 1987, *87* (5), 571–589.

Norman, D. "Cognitive Engineering and Education." In D. Tuma and F. Reif (eds.), *Problem Solving in Education.* Hillsdale, N.J.: Erlbaum, 1980.

Perkins, D., and Simmons, R. "Patterns of Misunderstanding: An Integrative Model for Science, Math, and Programming." *Review of Educational Research,* 1988, *58,* 303–326.

Petersen, B. (ed.). *Convergences: Transactions in Reading and Writing.* Urbana, Ill.: National Council of Teachers of English, 1986.

Peterson, P., Fennema, E., Carpenter, E., and Loef, M. "Teachers' Pedagogical Content Beliefs in Mathematics." *Cognition and Instruction,* 1989, *6,* 1–40.

Powell, A., Farrar, E., and Cohen, B. *The Shopping Mall High School: Winners and Losers in the Educational Marketplace.* Boston: Houghton Mifflin, 1985.

Purkey, S., and Smith, M. "Effective Schools: A Review." *Elementary School Journal,* 1983, *83,* 427–452.

Rice, D. "The Effect of Question-Asking Instruction on Preservice Elementary Science Teachers." *Journal of Research in Science Teaching,* 1977, *14,* 353–359.

Riley, J. "The Effects of Teachers' Wait-Time and Cognitive Questioning Level on Pupils' Science Achievement." Paper presented at the annual meeting of the National Association for Research in Science Teaching, Boston, 1980.

Rohrkemper, M. "Self-Regulated Learning and Academic Achievement: A Vygotskian View." In D. Schunk and B. Zimmerman (eds.), *Self-Regulated Learning and Academic Achievement: Theory, Research, and Practice.* New York: Springer-Verlag, forthcoming.

Rosenholtz, S. *Teachers Workplace.* New York: Longman, 1989.

Rosenthal, R. "From Unconscious Experimenter Bias to Teacher Expectancy Effects." In J. Dusek (ed.), *Teacher Expectancies.* Hillsdale, N.J.: Erlbaum, 1985.

Rosenthal, R., and Jacobson, L. *Pygmalion in the Classroom: Teacher Expectation and Pupils' Intellectual Development.* New York: Holt, Rinehart & Winston, 1968.

Rosnick, P., and Clement, J. "Learning Without Understanding: The Effect of Tutoring Strategies on Algebra Misconceptions." *Journal of Mathematical Behavior,* 1980, *3,* 3–27.

Rowe, M. "Wait-Time and Rewards as Instructional Variables, Their Influence on Language, Logic, and Fate Control: Part I: Wait-Time." *Journal of Research and Science Teaching,* 1974, *11,* 81–94.

Sedlak, M., Wheeler, C., Pullin, D., and Cusick, P. *Selling Students Short: Classroom Bargains and Academic Reform in the American High School.* New York: Teachers College Press, 1986.

Shulman, L. "Paradigms and Research Programs in the Study of Teaching: A Contemporary Perspective." In M. Wittrock (ed.), *Handbook of Research on Teaching.* (3rd ed.) New York: Macmillan, 1986.

Slavin, R. "Cooperative Learning and Student Achievement." In R. Slavin (ed.), *School and Classroom Organization.* Hillsdale, N.J.: Erlbaum, 1989.

Stipek, D. "Children's Motivation to Learn." In T. Tomlinson and H. Walberg (eds.), *Academic Works and Educational Excellence.* Berkeley, Calif.: McCutchan, 1986.

Tennyson, R., and Cocchriarella, M. "An Empirically Based Instructional Design Theory for Teaching Concepts." *Review of Educational Research,* 1986, *56,* 40–71.

Thaiss, C. *Language Across the Curriculum in the Elementary Grades.* Urbana, Ill.: National Council of Teachers of English, 1986.

Tobin, K. "The Influence of Wait-Time on Classroom Learning." *European Journal of Science Education,* 1983a, *5* (1), 35–48.

Tobin, K. "Management of Time in Classrooms." In B. Fraser (ed.), *Classroom Management.* Bentley: Western Australian Institute of Technology, 1983b.

Tomlinson, T. "A Nation at Risk: Background for a Working Paper." In T. Tomlinson and H. Walberg (eds.), *Academic Work and Educational Excellence.* Berkeley, Calif.: McCutchan, 1986.

Weinstein, C., and Mayer, R. "The Teaching of Learning Strategies." In M. Wittrock (ed.), *Handbook of Research on Teaching.* (3rd ed.) New York: Macmillan, 1986.

Welton, D. "Social Studies and the Elementary Teacher." *Social Education,* 1983, *47* (7), 523-540.

Wittrock, M. "Students' Thought Processes." In M. Wittrock (ed.), *Handbook of Research on Teaching.* (3rd ed.) New York: Macmillan, 1986.

Zeichner, K. "Social and Ethical Dimensions of Reform in Teacher Education." In J. Hoffman and S. Edwards (eds.), *Reality and Reform in Clinical Teacher Education.* New York: Random House, 1986.

2

What Teachers Need to Know About Human Development

Irving E. Sigel

Teacher education today is a critical problem, especially for public education, because there has been an erosion of confidence in the public school system. This erosion of confidence can in part be attributed to the public's lack of confidence in the nation's teachers. What is basically lacking in teacher preparation, and contributes to much educational failure, is a sound and profound grounding in human development as a critical underpinning of the educational enterprise.

Various reform efforts have been proposed, and are being proposed, ranging from raising the standards of admission for educational programs to revising the way teachers are to be educated. The Holmes Group (1986) report, for example, is one of the more radical suggestions offered to the schools of education, contending that a more intensive educational experience in the liberal arts and subject matter areas will enhance the quality of this country's teachers. Admirable as this effort is, I contend that it misses the mark, because the suggested reforms tend to place the emphasis on the content of the program rather than on the quality of education and instruction the teachers receive in their college or university. Unless there is a considered overall theory in teachers' preservice education, particularly regarding integrating their understanding of human development with other pedagogical requirements, educational progress will be impeded. I base this assertion on the understanding that human development principles define and describe the cognitive and social-emotional characteristics of prime constituents in the educational enterprise—the children. Everyone else in the system, from board of education members to school superintendents, has only one justification for their efforts—to provide a sound education for children. Human development principles derived from the behavioral and social sciences furnish the state-of-the-art knowledge regarding how children develop cognitively, socially, and emotionally in the context of a vertically structured school system.

The role of the educator is to provide appropriate experiences in an appropriate context to ensure that students are involved in an educational environment that strives to optimize their development. For this to happen, teachers must be prepared to become aware of and to keep abreast of the knowledge of human development, since their charges are developing human beings. Teachers generally are not adequately trained in the utilization of human development principles. In fact, the educational enterprise tends to minimize the importance of our knowledge of human development as it goes about the business of educating children.

School as Socializing Agent

The school is a prime socializing agency, preparing students to take their place in society by teaching (1) basic communication skills—reading, writing, speaking, (2) good study and work habits, (3) appropriate social values, (4) thinking and problem-solving skills, and (5) subject matter in the basic disciplines. These are but some of the goals of education. What a heavy burden we place on our teachers! And what are the support systems and the rewards we provide our teachers? Not much.

Criticisms of this nature of our society are not new. Teachers are not adequately trained to meet the demands placed upon them; teachers are not prepared to carry out the necessary performances required to accomplish society's expectations. Coupling inadequate preparation with a relatively poorly financed social support system, is there any wonder why public education is an endangered institution? Unless teachers are trained in ways proximal to their everyday functions, all reforms are doomed to failure.

Given this context, what contribution can a developmental perspective make to teaching youngsters from kindergarten through twelfth grade? First, a developmental perspective is not just acknowledging that children at one age are different from children at another age. To say that four-year-olds have different needs and talents than five-year-olds is not a very meaningful statement. Development is not just getting bigger and smarter; it is getting qualitatively different. It is more than the accumulation of size, shape, and experience.

Development is a process of ongoing qualitative change, of transformations proceeding in a progressive, orderly manner. Development proceeds with various systems, biological and psychological. These systemic changes are interdependent. There is a synergistic quality to the transformation, so that while the child does not change in one system, the system changes. For example, the elementary school child has acquired new ways of thinking and reasoning as well as increased physical control of eyes and hands—in essence, visual integration. This combination of competencies enables the child to learn how to read and to write, to handle equipment, and so on.

For the educator, the developing intellectual structure is probably most salient, since intellectual growth is a goal of education. However, we must not forget that the developing child forms a total system. Even if education focuses on the intellectual side of life, educators must not forget that intellectual functioning can be affected by emotional states such as stress, anxiety, and depression. Although there is an interaction between the two systems, the prime responsibility for education is to use the student's intellect in the service of acquiring and utilizing knowledge.

Education Is Developmental Effort

At every level, preschool through college, the educational effort must be rooted in human development. Students are developing organisms, developing in basic physical, psychological, and social ways. Teachers must understand this change process. They must have a perspective that orients them to identify the markers that signify change. Knowledge of human development enables teachers to organize their teaching materials, teaching strategies, and classroom environments with such a development context. I am convinced that teachers (in fact, educators in general), textbook writers, and creators of instructional materials and assessment materials are generally exposed, but not sensitized, to a developmental perspective. Consequently, they do not have the framework to approach their mission with that kind of perspective.

The intellectual (cognitive) development domain of developmental psychology has produced the greatest advances in knowledge and understanding of cognitive growth. The seminal work of Piaget (1950) as well as a host of investigators he influenced has demonstrated that cognitive development is a complex process proceeding by invariant sequential stages from infancy to adulthood. Each stage of growth enables the child to master particular classes of material. The sequence is invariant and sequential, which means that stages follow in a fixed, sequential order (Case, 1985; Ginsberg and Opper, 1969; Piaget, 1950; Sigel and Cocking, 1977).

Since development proceeds in an orderly fashion, curriculum and instructional strategies should be calibrated accordingly. Piaget's approach can be used as an organizational basis for developing curriculum and instructional strategies.

Piagetian Perspective

Piaget argues that the four stages of invariant order in cognitive growth are sensorimotor, preoperational, concrete operational, and formal operational stages. Each stage includes certain cognitive operations that are ways of thinking and reasoning. During the months of infancy, children tend to have primitive understandings of means-end relationships, of cause and effect, and of the ability to plan and to anticipate. An overview of the earliest, or sensorimotor, period appears in the original text of Piaget ([1936] 1952) and in Gallagher and Reid (1981). I will focus on the subsequent periods of cognitive growth beginning with age two.

The second period, preoperational, covers ages two through six. This period of life can be broken down into two subphases: preoperational and intuitive. In the preoperational phase, the child begins to understand symbols (that is, a word or a picture can represent an object or an event) and to categorize on the basis of single, but not multiple, characteristics of objects and events. Also during this period, the child seems to believe that his or her point of view is shared by everyone. The child at this level is essentially characterized as perceptually dominant, since organization, classification, and concepts are largely determined by the potency of the physical attributes of objects and events. A key characteristic of a child's thinking at this period is that it is centered on or dominated by particular characteristics of instances individually experienced. There is a considerable body of research covering this period of the child's life. Although this phase of cognitive development is not highly relevant to teachers in the public schools, it is part of an ongoing life process, and it involves prototypes of thinking and reasoning operations.

The second subphase of development is referred to as intuitive: the years from preschool (usually age four) to the beginning of elementary school (age five or six years). Three fundamental operations now make their appearance: (1) the ability to think in terms of logical classes, (2) the ability to identify relationships, and (3) the ability to handle number concepts.

These competencies are still influenced by the child's limited perspective, but the observant teacher will begin to notice that children can be encouraged to shift from one approach to another. For example, the child at this level may begin by categorizing a group of geometric forms by color and then shift to form. By the end of this period, the child can combine color and form into what is called a *conjunctive classification.* For example, a child has a group of geometric forms varying in shape (triangles, squares, circles) and in color (red, green, yellow). When asked to classify these, the four-year-old may use either color or form, for example, red shapes or all the squares, whereas the seven-year-old might use two attributes, for example, big or red squares. At this stage, the child still cannot combine the two attributes and group the items as a single class—big red squares. The reason I focus on classification skills is because they are basic to many types of school curricula. For example, in social studies, communities, events, and social groupings are described in terms of classes.

The stage most germane to education is the period called *concrete operations* (ages six to eleven). Gradually, during this period, children become increasingly able to shift from direct action on objects or numbers to dealing with them abstractly. There is still a need for direct engagements with objects, however, and it is easy to misjudge the child's competence. Children at the concrete operations stage still need hands-on experience with objects. In learning mathematics, expressing concepts by using different sized blocks (such as Cuisinarre rods) in the earlier stages is easier than using abstract numbers. With the passage of time, the child is able to use imagination and to think in abstract symbolic terms. New competencies also become possible. The child's classification skills reflect a more complex understanding. In this period, the child can group an array of objects hierarchically. Dogs can be members of the class mammals, which in turn can be in the class vertebra. This is a classification system in which each subclass is merged into a higher class. The child can also move down from a higher-order class to a lower one, as in breaking the class mammals down into classes such as cows, sheep, and dogs. The mental operation involved in this activity is called *reversibility.* Children can also order instances asymmetrically, as exemplified in counting. This operation is referred to as *seriation.*

Another logical operation increasingly available to the child is *transitivity.* This is the logical process of defining relations. For example, if A is heavier than B and B is heavier than C, then A is heavier than C.

Critical to all these achievements is the fundamental logical understanding that Piaget refers to as *conservation.* Conservation means that certain properties of objects remain invariant in spite of change in form or appearance. For example, in a familiar experiment, a child is presented with two balls of clay. The child attests to the equality of the two balls in size and weight; then one of the balls is flattened. The child is asked if the two pieces of clay—the ball and the flattened piece—are the same. If the child acknowledges equivalence, then the conservation concept has emerged, an understanding that quantity remains invariant in spite of change in shape.

Understanding of equivalence is a critical cognitive achievement that underlies logical thinking. One can readily imagine a variety of contexts in which this principle operates. Think of the riddle so often asked by children, "Which weighs more, a pound of feathers or a pound of lead?" To solve this problem, an individual must realize that the unit of measure is equivalent in spite of the difference in materials.

Understanding the cognitive changes in this period of the elementary school grades should provide teachers and textbook writers with a framework by which to develop instructional strategies and lesson plans.

The formal operational period (age eleven and on) is the final stage of intellectual development that Piaget and his co-worker, Inhelder, describe (Inhelder and Piaget, 1958). During this period, the student takes the final steps to true abstract thinking, demonstrating that the logic of an argument provides necessary guidance. Not only is the student in this period able to present a logical argument but he or she is also able to take the perspective of another. The primary achievement during this period is the ability to formulate hypotheses in a formal sense, to make logical inferences, and to evaluate the logic of hypotheses. With the development of the capacity for creating and employing hypotheses comes the capacity for deductive and inductive reasoning.

These intellectual competencies, as well as those that have developed earlier (for example, reversibility and hierarchical classification), enable the student to handle complex mathematical functions, such as proportions, to plan scientific investigations and to engage in combinatorial thinking.

Validity of Stage Theories

There is some controversy regarding the stage theories of cognitive growth (Sigel, 1981), but psychologists generally agree on three points: (1) While there may be controversy as to the specifics of the sequence proposed by Piaget, and while the presence of some mental operations at a particular stage may be questioned, there is general agreement that cognitive development does proceed in a progressive manner, with each set of achievements dependent on past experience. It is unlikely that children could solve complex classification problems unless they had acquired an understanding of conservation. One major contribution of Piaget and his colleagues is therefore the emphasis on development as a process of qualitative change. (2) The cognitive operations that Piaget describes are definable mental actions that have validity in their own right. Psychologists who are students of cognitive functioning will agree that mental operations such as classification (both simple and hierarchical), seriation (ordering), and symbolic comprehension are identifiable. An educator familiar with these various operations can use them for instructional and curricular analysis. (3) Although we in the United States know Piaget best for his descriptions of the development of intellect, his theory has much more to offer—especially in describing how children come to interpret their social world relative to moral development and in describing the significance of peer relations.

My presentation of the theory, while offered as an exemplar of a point of view, does not preclude educators seeking alternative conceptualizations of development. Other theorists are beginning to provide perspectives that have merit and that are used in research (Vygotsky, 1978; Werner, [1957] 1978; Wertsch, 1985). However, no one to date has integrated these ideas into a single comprehensive whole.

The task for college and university instructors preparing teachers for all grade levels is to abstract general principles of cognitive growth and to help the student teachers appreciate how such knowledge would enhance the quality of instruction.

Does this emphasis on cognitive development contradict the notion that children develop as total organisms? Is it not the case that the child's emotional state influences his or her cognitive functioning? There is no denying that cognitive functioning is dependent on a lot of emotional conditions. Fear of failure; lack of interest in the subject matter; and attitudes toward teachers, peers, and self are among the types of emotional factors that influence children's use of their intellectual skills.

The very interdependence of cognitive functioning and emotional affect justifies the need to articulate the nature of the child's developing intellect. When teachers make academic demands on children, and when these demands are inadequately tuned into children's cognitive developmental levels, the children are immediately positioned for failure. The consequences can be devastating for a child's concept of self as a learner. However, when the teacher understands the child's competence level, chances are the child will not get bored or develop a false sense of competence. Striking the right balance is critical and occurs when teachers have developed for themselves a conceptual model that enables them to devise appropriate instructional strategies and concomitant diagnostic skills appropriate to the child's developmental level.

Instructional Strategies and Developmental Principles

I have alluded to the notion that if teachers were trained to work with a well-developed developmental conceptual framework, they would have a rational base for devising instructional strategies. My own research with experienced teachers has shown that they seem to have no well-articulated rationale for their classroom strategies. Most instructional strategies seem to derive from unsophisticated understanding of development. Teachers presume pictures to be simple depictions of events, so pictures are used in primers as aids. But pictures are not simple messages. Children learn to "read" pictures, and, in fact, pictures can interfere with learning to read (Sigel, 1978). Most instructional strategies follow the adult's notion of moving from the simple to the complex. Simple language and audiovisual aids are examples of presumed simplicity.

One instructional approach receiving continued attention is the entire questioning process (Sigel and Kelley, 1988). It seems obvious that questioning would be an integral part of teaching. Through the use of questions, a teacher can know what the child knows and how the child reasons. Most research, however, has shown that teachers' questioning is primarily in a test format, asking closed questions primarily to test knowledge. Overall, teachers infrequently ask provocative questions. Why? Teachers are not adequately trained to do that. More important, teachers generally are not exposed to a conceptual base from which they could derive the principles for determining the appropriate way to construct or to employ questions (Sigel and Kelley, 1988). Is it surprising that student teachers are not properly prepared to use questioning strategies? After all, they most likely have been exposed to didactic methods.

Skill in the use of questioning techniques requires (1) awareness of the developmental level of the student, (2) appreciation of the need for clear and precise formulation of the question, (3) attention to the student's response, (4) awareness of the need to wait (at least five seconds) between the question and the student's answer, and (5) follow-through using the student's response as a base.

Not only are teachers inadequately trained to use questioning strategies, they are equally unprepared to carry out profitable discussions with their students. Discussion strategies, as well as every other instructional mode, must be calibrated to a student's developmental level. Unless this is done, it is unlikely that the students or the teachers will find any strategy actively worthwhile.

Although the focus on the relationship between cognitive development and teaching strategies is necessary, it is insufficient. Social and emotional factors are of profound importance in children's learning, broadly speaking. Children's learning is a product of these complex factors, each of which contributes differentially. For example, children from deprived backgrounds are probably more subject to learning difficulties, due in large measure to their social history. For more privileged children, cognitive factors may be of greater moment.

The task for teachers is learning how to balance these factors in the context of a classroom environment organized to facilitate learning. Social background variables come into focus in the classroom. How all of this is played out depends in large measure on the classroom environment. Some recent research in this area has proved to be relevant, showing that "Children's autonomy in the learning process may, in fact, have important consequences for learning outcomes, particularly with regard to quality of learning" (Grolnick and Ryan, 1986).

To this point, I have dealt with instructional issues in human development. What about the curriculum? What does our human development knowledge have to say about curriculum? Curriculum is the heart of the educational endeavor, for it is content the student is expected to master. Teaching stages are the instrumental means that serve to enable the student to master the content.

Available knowledge is currently classified by subject matter—math, history, economics, physics, chemistry, and so on. We use various classification systems, but most are not systematically organized on developmental principles as conceptualized in this statement. Rather, they appear to be based on traditional concepts of the domain or organized on implicit epistemological criteria. However, those scholars who organize knowledge domains along such criteria do not attend to the learners. Piaget, however, has studied the ontogenesis of knowledge of space, time, geometry, mathematics, and logic by examining children's understandings of these knowledge domains over time. His discoveries indicate that there is an "invariant order of acquisition from birth onward" (Flavell, 1963).

Children have perspectives regarding each of these basic knowledge areas, and, with age, the understandings shift. Preschool children's sense of calendrical or clock time is different from that of adolescents. Since young children's time concepts are gross and tied closely to the ongoing present, understanding the relationship between the eighteenth century and the twentieth century is beyond their comprehension. Concepts of two hundred years ago are meaningless.

The implications of a Piagetian perspective for teaching social studies is clear: gauge the time frame to be used against the child's cognitive level. The major point here for educators to realize is that acquisition of knowledge must be tied to the process of developing cognition—not to the epistemological sense of the structure of the particular discipline. To use an adult model of the structure of knowledge alone is to reject comprehension of the student.

One strategy we can use in the context of employing a cognitive developmental model is to do task analyses to examine specifically what the task demands are in problems presented to a child. The first step in analysis of a task is to ask what cognitive processes are involved in the problem. What does the child have to do to solve the problem? Take a seemingly simple task. The child is asked an arithmetic problem: Johnny has five apples and Mary gives him six apples. How many apples does Johnny have? What does the student have to do to solve the problem? First, of course, the concept of number must be present. The child has to know the meaning of number concepts, has to translate the idea of giving an equivalent to addition, and above all, has to have the addition schema in mind.

Task analysis can be done for virtually every problem a

teacher gives to a student. The basic requirement is that the teacher have knowledge of cognitive processes and how they evolve. Working from this knowledge base, the teacher will be in a position to analyze the cognitive demands inherent in the tasks the child has to master and, of course, to analyze the content of what is to be taught. A good example of this issue is the developing of classification skills. The evidence is clear that children's abilities to organize and to classify material change over time from simple groupings of items along a single dimension to logical classifications, as exemplified in taxonomies of insects or animals. The basic process may be evident early, but over time, the quality of the process changes.

Task analysis is a practical and viable approach to the ordering of curriculum sequences. Training student teachers in task analysis can provide them with two important teaching tools: first, a basis from which to understand what the child has to master in order to deal with the task and, second, a basis for deciding on the instructional strategies appropriate to teach the task. In the event the child has trouble with the problem, the teacher, by using task analysis, can identify the source of the child's error or difficulty. Preparing teachers to develop ways to analyze tasks should facilitate teaching and learning.

Every curriculum task involves some kind of cognitive process, even though it may not be a problem-solving task. For example, memorizing certain facts such as dates, names, or events involves mnemonic strategies. The skills in memorization and retention of material learned, even by rote, follow developmental principles—principles that limit young children in the amount they can retain. But teachers can teach strategies to facilitate retention. Awareness of how children acquire knowledge and the amount of material they can retain, as well as an awareness of the principles involved in ensuring relatively long-term retention and the strategies for enhancing memorization, can be derived from an understanding of how memory and learning develop.

Acquisition of technical skills, such as reading, doing calculations, and mastering a computer, depends on the child's developmental level. Clearly, a fundamental understanding of developmental processes is a critical prerequisite for adequate instruction. The ideas and the framework are there, and texts, research reports, and a body of research literature provide the basis for teachers to build a developmental conceptual framework.

Developmental Approach to Training Teachers

The courses required of student teachers include educational psychology and child development, as well as courses in teaching the special child, the gifted child, or the retarded child. These courses are required, so how can I claim that teachers do not have a developmental perspective? I make that claim because these developmental courses are not presented as integral to the preparation of teachers. The courses are taught in isolation from a student teacher's practicum, often by individuals from different departments. For example, the instructor in an educational psychology course is not even in the classroom with the student teacher to see how he or she applies the principles acquired in the course. Does the teacher of developmental psychology know how the curriculum is structured? Where does the student learn how to apply the principles learned in a developmental psychology course to curriculum analysis? The integration of human development principles in teacher training is usually left to the student. This is irresponsible behavior on the part of teacher training faculty, because students have neither the background nor the sophistication to do this on their own.

In a school district in which I have worked, the fifth-grade teachers were having a terrible time with a mathematics text. After they learned how to analyze the text according to developmental principles in terms of a child's acquisition of mathematics, they discovered that the text chapters were in the wrong sequence. Once they switched the sequence of the chapters, the problems were solved. Neither the textbook writers nor the publisher were aware of the problem. The fault was laid at the door of the teachers. How could the teachers have known the problem unless they were trained to examine the developmental sequence of the tasks involved in the text?

Who are the models for the student teachers? Are they their professors? Are they the critic teachers? Are they the teachers these student teachers had when they were students in elementary school and high school? From this array of individuals, student teachers identify their models. There might be one particularly exciting teacher or perhaps a composite of several teachers. How the student teacher creates an ideal is unclear, but if the model is generated from experience, the student should articulate the model in the preparation period.

What if the student teacher does not become aware of such an influence (Sigel and Saunders, 1983)? Faculty members must be aware of this situation and must realize that they are part of the modeling complex. If they are interested in their student teachers' learning to engage in discussion and inquiry, they should employ such strategies themselves. For instance, instructional opportunities in seminars, in practicum courses, or even in tutorials might include some time devoted to the model question.

I am pleading for an integration of human developmental principles with curriculum and instruction. No matter what the subject matter is or what the grade level is, we still need to focus on the student as a learner and as a developing individual. The developmental level of the student is a major determinant influencing the quality and quantity of knowledge, the competencies, and the skills that the student will acquire during the school years. If our intent is to prepare teachers to prepare students for the future, where skills in problem solving and thinking are vital, it is incumbent on the educational establishment to realize they are working with developing student teachers and developing children whose developmental progress must be ensured as a criterion for gauging the educational effort.

Conclusions

Current developmental psychology and the broader field of human development have been able to identify the course of intellectual and social development of children. The knowledge acquired in these fields, while not complete, is of sufficient power to form the basis for developing and organizing curricula, for deriving appropriate instructional methods, for providing teachers with criteria for developing their lessons, and for diagnosing children with learning difficulties.

However, this body of knowledge is not now being integrated into teacher preparation. Rather, it is fragmented and isolated from the context in which it should be used. Consequently, such knowledge does not play a significant role in teacher preparation. Teacher behavior in classrooms is often not developmentally appropriate. The consequence of this is that teachers are losing their effectiveness in reaching many of their students.

There are ways of integrating human developmental principles for teacher preparation. To do so would require reorganization of teacher education programs by breaking down some of the barriers that exist between departments and even within colleges of education. Until such reforms are instituted, there is little likelihood that we can adequately create dramatic and constructive changes in the way the educational enterprise is carried out.

References

Case, R. *Intellectual Development: Birth to Adulthood.* Orlando, Fla.: Academic Press, 1985.

Flavell, J. *The Developmental Psychology of Jean Piaget.* New York: D. Van Nostrand, 1963.

Gallagher, J. M., and Reid, D. K. *The Learning Theory of Piaget and Inhelder.* Monterey, Calif.: Brooks/Cole, 1981.

Ginsberg, H., and Opper, S. *Piaget's Theory of Intellectual*

Development: An Introduction. (1st ed.) Englewood Cliffs, N.J.: Prentice-Hall, 1969.

Grolnick, W. S., and Ryan, R. M. "Autonomy in Children's Learning: An Experimental and Individual Difference Investigation." *Journal of Personality and Social Psychology,* 1986, *50* (3), 550–558.

Holmes Group. *Tomorrow's Teachers: A Report of the Holmes Group.* East Lansing: Michigan State University, 1986.

Inhelder, B., and Piaget, J. *The Growth of Logical Thinking from Childhood to Adolescence.* New York: Basic Books, 1958.

Piaget, J. *The Psychology of Intelligence.* Boston: Routledge & Kegan Paul, 1950.

Piaget, J. *The Origins of Intelligence in Children.* New York: International Universities Press, 1952. (Originally published 1936.)

Sigel, I. E. "The Development of Pictorial Comprehension." In B. S. Randhawa and W. E. Coffman (eds.), *Visual Learning, Thinking, and Communication.* Orlando, Fla.: Academic Press, 1978.

Sigel, I. E. "Child Development Research in Learning and Cognition in the 1980s: Continuities and Discontinuities from the 1970s." *Merrill-Palmer Quarterly,* 1981, *27,* 347–371.

Sigel, I. E., and Cocking, R. R. *Cognitive Development from Childhood to Adolescence: A Constructivist Perspective.* New York: Holt, Rinehart & Winston, 1977.

Sigel, I. E., and Kelley, T. D. "A Cognitive Developmental Approach to Questioning." In J. T. Dillon (ed.), *Questioning and Discussion: A Multidisciplinary Study.* Norwood, N.J.: Ablex, 1988.

Sigel, I. E., and Saunders, R. A. "On Becoming a Thinker: An Educational Preschool Program." *Early Child Development and Care,* 1983, *12,* 39–65.

Vygotsky, L. S. *"Mind in Society: The Development of Higher Psychological Processes."* Cambridge, Mass.: Harvard University Press, 1978.

Werner, H. "The Concept of Development from a Comparative and Organismic Point of View." In S. S. Barten and M. B. Franklin (eds.), *Developmental Processes: Heinz Werner's Selected Writings.* Vol. 1. New York: International Universities Press, 1978. (Originally published 1957.)

Wertsch, J. V. (ed.). *Culture, Communication, and Cognition: Vygotskian Perspectives.* New York: Cambridge University Press, 1985.

3

Bridging Knowledge and Action Through Clinical Experiences

Carolyn M. Evertson

Clinical experiences are those components of professional teacher education programs that place preservice teachers into the classroom in some capacity. They are traditionally of two general types: early field experiences, such as those involved with the practica accompanying methods courses or other courses on pedagogy, and student teaching or practice teaching, which comes at the end of the sequence of professional course work leading toward certification.

Recent concerns about improving the quality of teaching have resulted in increases in the time students spend in schools and classrooms. Kluender (1984) and Egbert (1985) examined the catalogues of approximately forty institutions that prepare teachers and found that clinical experiences made up just under 10 percent of the total program hours in both elementary and secondary programs for which students receive separate credit. Egbert also noted that in addition, 34 percent of human development and psychology courses, 41 percent of reading methods courses, 38 percent of social studies methods courses, and 45 percent of foundations and introductory courses required a field experience or practicum of some kind, thus raising the percentage even higher. In the fifteen-year span between Johnson's (1968) and Heald's (1983) surveys, the field experiences component of professional education grew from around 280 clock hours to almost 420 hours.

More recently, studies of teacher preparation curricula have shown that of 142 responding teacher preparation institutions in fifteen states in the South and Southeast, 64 percent reported increased field requirements, and only 2 percent reported a decrease. Forty-nine percent of these institutions listed increases in the amount of time teacher candidates spend in field experiences as one of the three most important changes made in the way they educate teachers (Hawley, Austin, and Goldman, 1988).

The increase in emphasis on field experiences, often in response to political pressures from practitioner organizations and legislatures, signals a growing conviction that if students are to learn to teach they must spend a significant amount of time in classrooms and schools and that this must start earlier in their training. Many reforms, both statewide and nationwide, have resulted in state certification requirements that increase the clinical component, particularly early field experiences. However, the value of these experiences, in terms of their contribution to learning to teach effectively, is often less certain than most proponents would believe (Evertson, Hawley, and Zlotnik, 1985). The contribution of field experiences to a preservice teacher's learning how to teach must be gauged by the quality of those experiences themselves. Dewey (1938) made the distinction between educative and miseducative experiences. He argued that the belief that all genuine education comes about through experience does not mean that all experiences are genuinely educative. Any experience is miseducative that has the effect of arresting or distorting the growth from further experiences. The central question becomes whether field experiences lead preservice teachers to become students of education, open to reflecting about their experiences, able to be active constructors of effective learning environments, and able to solve the complex problems of daily classroom life.

Case Analysis of a Field Experience

Too often, early field experience programs proceed according to an oversimplification of the apprenticeship model, whereby preservice teachers simply model the strategies and techniques of their cooperating teachers and assist them. This approach, if narrowly interpreted, can lead to miseducative experiences because of the lack of opportunity for new teachers to reflect upon and to analyze the purposes of their involvement and to use these analyses to direct further growth. The following is an all too familiar example.

The preservice teacher is assigned to a primary classroom as part of the practicum component of a reading methods course in the preparation program. Part of the classroom assignment is to listen to members of a low-ability group reading a story from a basal reader. The preservice teacher is not familiar with the reading series or specific curriculum goals, has not been involved in planning the activity, does not know the skill levels of the individual students, does not know what the learning objectives are for the story to be read, has not prepared discussion questions, and does not know how performance will or can be evaluated. While the regular classroom teacher may have knowledge and understanding of the purposes of the reading lesson, often he or she does not communicate this to the preservice teacher.

In a sense, practicum experiences of this sort misrepresent the concept of a true apprenticeship, because the actual experiences for the cooperating teacher and for the preservice teacher are substantially different. The experienced teacher may be familiar with the curriculum, may have taught the material before, and may be able to lead an effective story discussion without detailed preparation. This is not so for the novice teacher (see Erdman, 1983).

Feiman-Nemser and Buchmann (1985) pinpoint examples of three common pitfalls that result from trusting firsthand experience in learning to teach. The first is the familiarity pitfall. They argue that unquestioned familiarity is a pitfall because it arrests thought and may mislead it. This problem stems from the human tendency to trust what is most memorable in personal experience. Students approach the early field experience with preconceptions about what classrooms are like and what teachers do, based upon their own years as pupils in classrooms. Their perspectives remain unchanged from the time they themselves were students. This kind of framework for viewing, with its accompanying standard for judging, may only represent a sort of self-evident and taken-for-granted perspective that actually overlooks the essential commonplaces.

The second, the so-called two-worlds pitfall, reflects the typical experience in courses similar to those in educational psychology and others, wherein students are placed in classrooms to observe and to use the classrooms as one would use a laboratory. One example involves the student who has been given a project in which he or she spends one afternoon a week in a second-grade classroom observing one or two target students. Because the observation is for only half a day, the pupils' names, the classroom routines, the purposes for the lessons, the curriculum decisions, the teacher's intentions, and the culture of the community are all unfamiliar. For most of the observation time, the teacher education student is supposed to focus on three pupils whom the teacher has identified as being worthy of observation in some ways. The task for the university student is really to concentrate on mastering the ways of observing (that is, perfecting the use of observation as a tool) and thus to get a good grade in the course on the campus. These conflicting purposes become pitfalls because the performance standard required for an acceptable grade is indigenous to a university culture and not necessarily to the culture of schools and teaching.

To bridge these two cultures, the student also needs to reflect upon the role of observation in the inquiry process and in the enhancement of teaching skills. The very structure of the assignment shows that the two kinds of learning are distinctly different.

Applegate (1986) reports that students may even ignore or devalue the university course requirements to practice specific skills in their field assignments because the cooperating teacher redefines, devalues, or does not understand the assignment. The student may resolve these conflicts by suspending the assignment and concluding that just being out in the schools and doing something is the important thing.

Third, the cross-purposes pitfall centers on the student

teaching experience. Feiman-Nemser and Buchmann (1985) point out that classroom teachers are legitimately focused on the teaching of their students and that classrooms are generally not designed as laboratories for teaching the preservice teacher how to teach. Because the primary role of the teacher is that of instructing students, the cooperating teacher may find praiseworthy the student teacher's attention to the status quo. After all, this view is functional in maintaining the existing social structure and instructional framework. Yet without instructional intervention, learning from practice teaching and from other such experiences presupposes acting and understanding. If a student teacher cannot identify critical variables, analyze successes, or construct the practical arguments, there is little reason to believe that replication can occur in another setting.

The common theme throughout these problems seems to be the discontinuity between the content and skills to be learned and the feedback and reinforcement for learning. The cultural and social demands of each setting often require the student to decide on appropriate actions that will best allow him or her to meet the needs of the moment.

Effectiveness of Student Teaching

Student teaching is usually identified by new teachers as the most rewarding and useful aspect of their preservice professional programs. Interviews and follow-up studies of beginning teachers repeatedly have shown that new teachers look upon this as their most valuable professional course work (Griffin, 1986; Griffin and others, 1983; Nemser, 1983; Veenman, 1984). These claims, coupled with the current doubts about the present usefulness and rigor of preservice preparatory course work, probably have contributed as much as anything to the proliferation of proposals for increasing the field experience.

However, existing research (Evertson, Hawley, and Zlotnik, 1985) provides little evidence that supervised practical experience in itself, as it is currently encountered, is a very effective way to educate teachers. Reviews of experimental studies in research on teacher education have concluded that by the end of student teaching, students almost universally showed decrements in attitude and teaching behavior, as compared with their starting levels prior to the field experience. In addition, they showed a shift toward conservatism in overall attitudes (Hawley, 1989; Malone, 1985; Peck and Tucker, 1973). Malone (1985, p. 19) concluded that "students receiving a few to a moderate number of field experiences seem to benefit from them. When students are exposed to more than three or four courses involving a significant field experience component, desired outcomes may not be affected and may, in fact, decline."

In an intensive study of student teaching, Griffin and others (1983) found little change in student teachers on numerous classroom teaching psychological and attitudinal variables. However, the authors did detect a trend toward conservatism. They concluded that the experience of student teaching, at least for the group of participants they studied, was not powerful enough to alter what might be deep-seated personal and professional beliefs. In addition, they found that the participants in the student teaching experience, while well-meaning and caring, operated from a perspective that promoted the well-being and comfort of self rather than a perspective based on a set of carefully articulated performance standards. Furthermore, student teachers were exposed almost exclusively to situation-specific teaching strategies, apparently with no conceptualized point of view driving the experiences, rather than to a variety of theoretically sound options for decision making.

In the face of a great deal of evidence showing that practicing teachers rate the student teaching experience as the most valuable of their college preparation, it appears that students may well be learning a kind of organizational literacy—a sociocultural understanding of the norms, roles, and expectations of the organization. Moreover, the experience is personally memorable, immediate, and powerful only in contrast to their campus course work.

Evidence suggests that increasing the clinical experience component, at least in preservice preparation, by requiring more hours in the field is hardly a panacea. While the research demonstrates the need for circumspection regarding the structure and quality of those experiences, such a cautious approach does not mean that these experiences cannot also be valuable and effective. It does mean we must work conscientiously to provide meaningful and powerful experiences in other preparation courses as well.

Recasting the Preservice Teacher Education Program

What might an effective teacher education program look like? Unfortunately, little hard evidence is available to guide us regarding the selection of essential content and the settings of these experiences. However, best guesses suggest the following.

Undergraduate Preparation. Preprofessional education should focus on broadly based studies in the humanities, social sciences, and physical sciences. While differences among college curricula make it difficult to be prescriptive about specific course distribution, this general course work probably should make up at least half of the undergraduate major. However, reformers should recognize that change in teacher education also means restructuring general education. The presumption of most reformers is that teachers should acquire and bring to teaching a broad knowledge derived from their liberal arts education. However, courses in liberal arts and sciences are coming under increasing attack for being poorly taught, and students seldom select their programs of study to include the most rigorous and well-articulated sequence of courses. Instead they may choose the easiest path through the college curriculum (Galambos, Cornett, and Spitler, 1985; DeLoughry, 1989). In addition, college students apparently do not transfer what they learn in one course to what they learn in another unless the linkages are made explicit and unless the tools for making such transfers are well developed. However, in some cases, students report better models of teaching provided by professors in pedagogy. These same students also indicate that they learn how to learn and how to make applications to their liberal arts courses (Neely, 1987; Travers and Sacks, 1989).

Preprofessional education should also include a thorough grounding in the subjects to be taught. Although this suggestion is self-evident for teachers in secondary classrooms, it leaves open the question of an appropriate area of concentration and sequence of course work for students in elementary education and early childhood education—areas that necessitate a thorough grounding in human learning and development.

Professional Course Work. Required education courses should include recent research on teaching and learning. This growing body of knowledge about student learning, effective instructional strategies, and effective schools has yet to make its way into most of our professional courses for teachers.

Courses in general social and behavioral theory should involve the redesign of curricula. In this way, students preparing to be teachers are better able to recognize and to analyze issues in areas such as equality and equity for individuals within the confines of society, as well as issues regarding the consequences of conflict and the importance of race and class status in interpersonal relationships.

Students should be provided with course work in which they are asked to develop problem-solving skills by addressing complex issues using systematic and diverse modes of inquiry. Tasks that teachers must perform are varied, and there are few if any generic teaching strategies that work equally well in all settings and with all students. Therefore, teachers must possess analytical capabilities and be active learners, capable of reflection and flexibility.

Education courses should convey knowledge about schools as organizations because many nonschool sources of learning for students can have serious repercussions for their learning and development. Linking schools to parents, to the community, and to other social agencies will become increasingly important as the nature of the family changes and as the community responds to the new roles and attitudes of its participants.

Finally, course requirements should include instruction in educational technology. The full potential of educational technology will likely be realized only if teachers are aware of and competent in the use of these powerful teaching and learning tools. Few teacher education curricula include the use of computers. However, if teachers find that their goals can be furthered through computer-based learning, they are more likely to become users of such technologies.

Clinical Experiences and the College Setting

The clinical experiences that might be included in most of the recommended course work discussed above can be quite diverse, perhaps even occurring in on-campus laboratory settings. Berliner (1985) argues that pedagogy needs to change, to become a laboratory-based field of study. Through these experiences, one comes to reflect upon one's own work, to analyze the work of others, and to be innovative and divergent without fear of negatively affecting students. He further states that as the knowledge base grows larger in the area of preservice teacher education, and because of the competing agenda for the time and the contexts in which this learning can occur, extensive practice opportunities must be provided in on-campus settings.

Laboratory experiences should be an important part of teaching methods courses. For example, students can learn the techniques of classroom observation and ways of structuring those observations to highlight specific teaching tasks, student and teacher interactions, verbal and nonverbal communication patterns, and the development of content and instructional routines. Furthermore, students can come to understand these not as isolated behaviors, but as part of the ongoing evolution of class processes that affect teaching tasks. Students learn observational skills and reflect on what they can and cannot learn from observing teaching and learning processes. This reflection can take place within a framework developed from what we have learned about effective teaching practices. Observation cast in this way is a teaching tool that allows the preservice teacher to focus specifically on the tasks of teaching and on the evolution of classroom events over time. In this way, students can construct the knowledge base for their own practice using and incorporating the research.

Students can also analyze case studies and descriptive accounts drawn from real classrooms and from research on teachers' classroom management practices and methods of instruction. Cases such as these have the advantage of slowing the action and allowing students to see the sequence of events at a more instructive pace, providing the focus for discussion of and reflection on teaching and learning processes.

Demonstration videotapes and videodiscs often make classroom events and teaching practices look so smooth and effortless that it may be difficult to identify the critical actions. But group discussions can center on vignettes of problem situations for which students can derive systematic and alternative methods of solution.

Approaches to classroom management techniques and ways of intervening with student misbehavior, a perennial concern for beginning teachers, can be acted out through role-playing, with students in groups practicing with such strategies as resolving interpersonal conflicts with students, holding a class meeting to develop rules and procedures, or helping students control their own behavior through cognitive monitoring. Preservice teachers can work in groups to develop scenarios that demonstrate the use of specific approaches with the rest of the class involved as participants in the process. While becoming tangibly familiar with these techniques is unquestionably useful, an even more important benefit is the knowledge of how these techniques can be used and when they are and are not appropriate (Wolfgang and Glickman, 1986).

Course content can be regularly evaluated through follow-up of students during their solo teaching. Careful and regular supervision aids in understanding how to articulate the sequence of courses, how to evaluate course content for usefulness in supporting the preservice teacher, and how to assess what should be added, excluded, or kept but restructured.

Microteaching can take many forms, but it essentially involves preservice teachers' organizing and delivering short lessons. These brief lessons often demonstrate specific competencies, such as planning, interactive teaching, questioning techniques, teaching a procedure to students, and evaluating the lesson. Microteaching is a useful tool when used in combination with other laboratory experiences. It can provide immediate feedback, practice, and assistance in self-analysis of specific teaching skills (Borg, 1972; Copeland, 1975).

Computer software and videodisc technology has been designed to simulate problem situations for which students choose alternative solution strategies (Bransford, Hasselbring, and Sherwood, 1986; Skeel, 1989). Increasingly complex problems are presented through these simulations that require students to make quick decisions, to attend to two or more simultaneous events, and to react accurately but rapidly. However, teacher education programs are only beginning to explore technology as a tool to support the process of learning to teach.

Induction to Teaching Through Professional Development Schools

The current pattern of moving from college directly to the isolation and complexity of classroom teaching leaves many first-year teachers frustrated and disillusioned. One solution to this problem is the development of a new stage in the teacher education process—a year-long internship in a school that is especially organized to induct teachers.

Models for year-long internships are being developed through many school-university partnerships. These experimental models vary a great deal; however, many of them attempt to address the need to provide centers for training both preservice teachers and teachers. An example of one such model involving university and school faculty might include a selected group of (1) year-long interns involved with other preservice teachers who have completed teacher preparation and bachelor degree programs except for student teaching, (2) semester-long student teachers in the process of completing their professional course work, or (3) experienced teachers who have applied for training as staff developers of specific techniques. The initial stage might involve trainees working under mentor teachers especially selected for their teaching expertise and for their skills as teacher educators. The intent is for the professional development school to function much as a teaching hospital that trains interning physicians—with the realization that teacher education is a joint responsibility. A management team with representatives from each institution can function to coordinate and to share the joint responsibility for field experiences, at least in the student teaching and induction phases, with the schools.

Role of the Teacher Educator

We must also ask who assumes the role of teacher educator in the clinical setting. Lanier (1986) points to the difficulty in locating a cadre of people who willingly state that their primary area of concentration is teacher education. She says, quoting from Borrowman (1965), that the situation in institutions preparing 90 percent of the teachers in the United States is that the majority of faculty members have an interest in teacher education that is at best tangential to their most active concern, their substantive area. It is not the public schools' primary purpose to train teachers. But if we urge the schools to take on this role, we cannot assume that it can happen as a responsibility added to what schools already do. Those who participate will need support and the skills to become mentors and teacher leaders; filling this need may be problematic at best within the present school structure.

Classroom teachers who are to serve as role models and coaches often have no training in facilitating adult learning. Cooperating teachers may lack the time and even the motivation to play a major role in the education of the preservice teacher. Explanations for this include the absence of economic or career incentives for the extra effort, the absence of release time from teaching duties, and the absence of support from principals or from fellow teachers for supervisory activities that might take them away from their primary responsibilities in the classroom (Hawley, 1989).

As we begin to examine more closely the quality of clinical experiences, we can readily see that faculty who participate in the preparation of teachers will have to become involved for more substantial amounts of time and in roles very different from those to which they are accustomed. Cazden (1976) has documented the difficulties in bridging the gap between the theoretical and academic world of the university and that of the classroom teacher. In a paper she wrote after taking sabbatical leave from her Harvard teaching position to become a first-grade teacher in San Diego, she describes her own subjective impediments that were added to the objective conditions she found in the normal classroom. The first was her rustiness as a teacher of children. She felt that a repertoire of ideas was not readily available to her. Second, whereas in the university every day is different and the schedule is somewhat flexible, in a public school there are six or seven hours every day with the same twenty-five students, with visual and auditory stimulation that cannot be tuned out. Finally, her goals intruded on her often conflicting ideas of what kind of teacher she wanted to become after years of studying teaching and studying child language.

In order for clinical experiences to fulfill the promise they hold for preservice teachers, so that this training can become a meaningful part of their education, it is clear that we must address these and other issues central to teacher preparation. At their best, clinical experiences bridge the world of knowledge and the world of action.

References

Applegate, J. H. "Undergraduate Students' Perceptions of Field Experiences: Toward a Framework for Study." In J. D. Raths and L. G. Katz (eds.), *Advances in Teacher Education.* Vol. 2. Norwood, N.J.: Ablex, 1986.

Berliner, D. C. "Laboratory Settings and the Study of Teacher Education." *Journal of Teacher Education,* 1985, *36* (6), 2-8.

Borg, W. "The Minicourse as a Vehicle for Changing Teacher Behavior: A Three-Year Follow-Up." *Journal of Educational Psychology,* 1972, *63,* 572-579.

Borrowman, M. "Liberal Education and the Professional Education of Teachers." In M. L. Borrowman (ed.), *Teacher Education in America: A Documentary History.* New York: Teachers College Press, 1965.

Bransford, J. D., Hasselbring, T. S., and Sherwood, R. D. *Computers, Videodiscs, and the Teaching of Thinking.* Learning Technology Center, Technical Report 86.1.1. Nashville, Tenn.: Vanderbilt University, 1986.

Cazden, C. "How Knowledge About Language Helps the Classroom Teacher—Or Does It?: A Personal Account." Cambridge, Mass.: Harvard University, 1976. (Mimeographed.)

Copeland, W. D. "The Relationship Between Microteaching and Student Teacher Classroom Performance." *Journal of Educational Research,* 1975, *68,* 289-293.

DeLoughry, T. J. "Study of Transcripts Finds Little Structure in the Liberal Arts." *Chronicle of Higher Education,* Jan. 18, 1989, pp. A1, A32.

Dewey, J. *Experience and Education.* New York: Macmillan, 1938.

Egbert, R. "The Practice of Preservice Teacher Education." *Journal of Teacher Education,* 1985, *36* (4), 16-22.

Erdman, J. "Assessing the Purposes of Early Field Experience Programs." *Journal of Teacher Education,* 1983, *34* (4), 27-31.

Evertson, C., Hawley, W., and Zlotnik, M. "Making a Difference in Educational Quality Through Teacher Education." *Journal of Teacher Education,* 1985, *36* (3), 2-12.

Feiman-Nemser, S., and Buchmann, M. "Pitfalls of Experience in Teacher Preparation." *Teachers College Record,* Fall 1985, pp. 53–65.

Galambos, E. C., Cornett, L. M., and Spitler, H. D. *An Analysis of Transcripts of Teachers and Arts and Science Graduates.* Atlanta: Southern Regional Education Board, 1985.

Griffin, G. "Issues in Student Teaching: A Review." In J. D. Raths and L. G. Katz (eds.), *Advances in Teacher Education.* Vol. 2. Norwood, N.J.: Ablex, 1986.

Griffin, G., and others. *Clinical Preservice Teacher Education: Final Report of a Descriptive Study.* Austin: Research and Development Center for Teacher Education, University of Texas, 1983.

Hawley, W. D. *New Directions for Teacher Education in the United States.* Paris: Organization for Economic and Cooperative Development, 1989.

Hawley, W. D. "Systematic Analysis, Public Policy Making, and Teacher Education." In W. R. Houston (ed.), *Handbook of Research on Teacher Education.* New York: Macmillan, forthcoming.

Hawley, W. D., Austin, A. E., and Goldman, E. S. *Changing the Education of Teachers.* Atlanta: Southern Regional Education Board, 1988.

Heald, J. E. *Report to the Profession.* Washington, D.C.: American Association of Colleges for Teacher Education, 1983.

Johnson, J. A. *A National Survey of Student Teaching Programs.* Report produced under HEW Grant#OEG-7-068182-2635. DeKalb: Northern Illinois University, 1968.

Kluender, M. "Teacher Education Programs in the 1980s: Some Selected Characteristics." *Journal of Teacher Education,* 1984, *35* (4), 33–35.

Lanier, J. "Research on Teacher Education." In M. C. Wittrock (ed.), *Handbook of Research on Teaching.* (3rd ed.) New York: Macmillan, 1986.

Malone, M. "Preservice Field Experience in Teacher Education: A Quantitative Synthesis." Paper presented at the annual meeting of the American Educational Research Association, Chicago, Apr. 1985.

Neely, A. M. "Using the Research on Teaching Effectiveness: Applications for Teacher Education." Paper presented at the annual meeting of the Association of Teacher Educators, Houston, Tex., Feb. 1987.

Nemser, S. F. "Learning to Teach." In L. Shulman and G. Sykes (eds.), *Handbook of Teaching and Policy.* New York: Longman, 1983.

Peck, R., and Tucker, J. "Research on Teacher Education." In R.M.W. Travers (ed.), *Handbook of Research on Teaching.* (2nd ed.) Skokie, Ill.: Rand McNally, 1973.

Skeel, D. J. "Using Technology to Build Teacher Decision-Making Skills." *Foreign Language Annals,* 1989, *22,* 149–155.

Travers, E. F., and Sacks, S. R. "Joining Teacher Education and the Liberal Arts in the Undergraduate Curriculum." *Phi Delta Kappan,* 1989, *70* (6), 470–474.

Veenman, S. "Perceived Problems of Beginning Teachers." *Review of Educational Research,* 1984, *54* (2), 143–178.

Wolfgang, C. H., and Glickman, C. D. *Solving Discipline Problems: Strategies for Classroom Teachers.* (2nd ed.) Newton, Mass.: Allyn & Bacon, 1986.

Part Two

Knowledge Essential to Teaching in a Discipline

A central component of the effectiveness of middle school and secondary school teachers is what Boyer (Chapter One) termed "their strong foundation in the knowledge taught." In the preceding chapters, the authors emphasized that effective teachers require not only command of their subject matter but also understanding of sufficient complexity to enable them to teach it. This has been termed "pedagogical content knowledge" (Shulman, 1986, p. 8)—the ways of knowing, representing, and formulating a subject that make it comprehensible to others. Traditionally, teacher education students acquired this knowledge through two experiences. First was the disciplinary major or minor in a specialty, such as English literature or mathematics. The second was one or more methods courses in the education program adapted to the particular specialty. The current reform movement in teacher education has criticized heavily the traditional education methods courses (Doyle, 1988), and therefore educators have focused attention on increasing the amount of student course work dedicated to the content specialty. Some evidence, however, indicates that this obvious solution simply defers the question of what core knowledge of content is essential for teaching at the middle school and secondary school levels. Is it the equivalent of a college major in the discipline, or, if not, in what way should it be different? In this part we explore these issues in three representative but critical fields: English literature, mathematics, and science.

The conventional belief has been that more course work in a discipline will produce a better teacher; but research has, until recently, not supported this obvious assumption (Byrne, 1983). One reason for this finding may be the simplistic measure of teacher disciplinary knowledge used in the research (for example, number of courses), or the reliance on standardized student achievement tests, which emphasize basic skills, as the measure of teacher effectiveness. More recent studies that focus directly on the classroom behavior of teachers more knowledgeable in the subject matter suggest that such teachers are better able to detect student preconceptions, to exploit opportunities for fruitful digressions during teaching, to interpret insightful student comments, and to emphasize conceptual understanding. Conversely, teachers with less knowledge may reinforce student misconceptions, may inappropriately criticize correct student responses, may avoid teaching critical material altogether if they do not know it well, and may be unable to appraise critically the adequacy and accuracy of relevant texts (Grossman, Wilson, and Shulman, 1989). And some evidence indicates that when teachers lack knowledge of the appropriate content, they emphasize didactic lecturing to avoid the embarrassment of difficult questions (Grossman, 1989).

Unfortunately, however, the means for increasing appropriate subject matter knowledge is not as obvious as it might appear. Undergraduate general education programs vary substantially in quality and permit students wide latitude in avoiding more demanding course work (Boyer, 1987; Galambos, Cornett, and Spitler, 1985). Even the requirements for a major field like English literature may vary substantially from college to college, and studies of students with extensive preparation to teach fields such as mathematics, physics, and history reveal wide gaps in their subject matter understanding of basic concepts (McDiarmid, Ball, and Anderson, 1989). In defining the appropriate knowledge in the content area, several themes continue to emerge.

One issue is the relevance of the knowledge taught in academic disciplines at the college level to the content covered in middle schools and secondary schools. College English majors focus on literature and interpretation; language arts at the school level emphasizes grammar, composition, and a full range of language-related activities, such as dramatics, speech, and reading. There is a similar gap between the college mathematics curriculum and what is covered in the schools. As Peter Hilton emphasizes, the school mathematics curriculum covers material that is dealt with nowhere else in the modern world!

Nonetheless, the emphasis on linear algebra and differential equations at the college level may not adequately prepare students to teach arithmetic, geometry, and business math as they are offered in the schools. Similarly in science, the specialized majors in chemistry and physics at the college level may offer inadequate preparation for teaching the more integrated courses at the school level, particularly the middle school. Even if we expect schoolteachers to focus on the experimental logic of science in their teaching, there is little reason to expect that they directly experienced scientific investigation as undergraduates, unless they were honors students. Clearly, bridging this gap between the content of college majors and the content of school teaching is a significant problem.

A second issue is the way to approach the content knowledge to be learned. John Dewey (1983, pp. 285–286) once observed: "Every study or subject thus has two aspects: one for the scientist; the other for the teacher as teacher. These two aspects are in no sense opposed or conflicting. But neither are they immediately identical." Recent research (Wilson, Shulman, and Richert, 1987) has suggested at least two dimensions of subject matter knowledge essential for teaching: (1) the subject content—knowledge of the facts, organizing principles, and central concepts—and (2) the subject method of inquiry—what Harold Morowitz (Chapter Six) terms "how we know the things we know." Recent studies, particularly in the field of mathematics, suggest that teachers with greater knowledge of the subject have a deeper, conceptual understanding of the field, and are able to make sense of the subject in a manner not typical of less knowledgeable teachers (Lampert, 1985; Leinhardt and Greeno, 1986; Leinhardt and Smith, 1985). Knowledge of conceptual structure and knowledge of a field's inquiry methods help teachers to comprehend more effectively their students' levels of learning and understanding, and such knowledge is critical to the teachers' pedagogical choices. The substantive knowledge of all fields is large and growing, and teachers need to comprehend the concepts and inquiry methods of a field so they can effectively make selection decisions in content. Further, teachers must be able to plan their own future learning and professional development in the content knowledge. Defining the best means to educate for this type of deep understanding remains a critical issue.

A third issue derives from academic politics—how best to decide what knowledge in a subject field is essential for teaching? Should the decision be made by those in teacher education programs, by those in the discipline (and by which faction within a discipline?), by teachers and policy makers in public education, or by some amalgam of all these groups? The process for defining the essential knowledge is itself unclear.

For the chapters that follow, we have selected three distinguished faculty members from the content fields, each of whom has extensive experience and interest in the preparation of subject matter teachers for the schools. In their respective chapters, Professors Lloyd-Jones, Hilton, and Morowitz explore the issues central to defining the knowledge essential to their respective fields of English, mathematics, and science. One noteworthy aspect of their arguments is that the criteria for defining the knowledge essential to teaching may lead us to the most efficacious definition of knowledge for all students. An academic experience that can evoke excitement and commitment among students for their subjects, that can make students literate in the symbols and language of their specialties, and that can provide a depth of understanding sufficient to guide a lifetime of learning in one's field is a program worthy of the term *the knowledge most worth having*.

References

Boyer, E. L. *College: The Undergraduate Experience in America.* New York: Harper & Row, 1987.

Byrne, C. J. "Teacher Knowledge and Teacher Effectiveness: A Literature Review, Theoretical Analysis and Discussion of Research Strategy." Paper presented at the 14th annual convention of the Northeastern Educational Research Association, Ellenville, N.Y., Oct. 1983.

Dewey, J. "The Child and the Curriculum." In J. A. Boydston (ed.), *John Dewey: The Middle Works, 1899–1924.* Vol. 2. Carbondale: Southern Illinois University Press, 1983.

Doyle, W. "Curriculum in Teacher Education." Paper presented at the annual meeting of the American Educational Research Association, New Orleans, Apr. 1988.

Galambos, E. C., Cornett, L. M., and Spitler, H. D. *An Analysis of Transcripts of Teachers and Arts and Science Graduates.* Atlanta: Southern Regional Education Board, 1985.

Grossman, P. L. *A Tale of Two Teachers: The Role of Subject Matter Orientation in Teaching.* Knowledge Growth in a Profession Publication Series. Stanford, Calif.: Stanford University School of Education, 1989.

Grossman, P. L., Wilson, S. M., and Shulman, L. S. "Teachers of Substance: Subject Matter Knowledge for Teaching." In M. C. Reynolds (ed.), *Knowledge Base for the Beginning Teacher.* Elsmford, N.Y.: Pergamon Press, 1989.

Lampert, M. "Mathematics Learning in Context: The Voyage of the Mimi." *Journal of Mathematical Behavior,* 1985, *4,* 157–167.

Leinhardt, G., and Greeno, J. "The Cognitive Skill of Teaching." *Journal of Educational Psychology,* 1986, *78,* 75–95.

Leinhardt, G., and Smith, D. "Expertise in Mathematics Instruction: Subject Matter Knowledge." *Journal of Educational Psychology,* 1985, *77,* 247–271.

McDiarmid, G. W., Ball, D. L., and Anderson, C. W. "Why Staying One Chapter Ahead Doesn't Really Work: Subject-Specific Pedagogy." In M. C. Reynolds (ed.), *Knowledge Base for the Beginning Teacher.* Elmsford, N.Y.: Pergamon Press, 1989.

Shulman, L. S. "Those Who Understand: Knowledge Growth in Teaching." *Educational Researcher,* 1986, *15* (2), 4–14.

Wilson, S. M., Shulman, L. S., and Richert, A. E. "150 Different Ways of Knowing: Representations of Knowledge in Teaching." In J. Calderhead (ed.), *Exploring Teachers' Thinking.* London: Cassell, 1987.

4

What Teachers Need to Know About English

Richard Lloyd-Jones

In 1986, the National Council of Teachers of English (NCTE) published its revised booklet, *Guidelines for the Preparation of Teachers of English Language Arts* (Wolfe, 1986). It was drawn up over two or three years by the NCTE Standing Committee on Teacher Preparation and Certification, a diverse group that takes up the task of revision every decade or so to represent the collective views of the 55,000 members. The draft statement was circulated among many other NCTE groups, including the commissions on language, literature, composition, reading, media, and curriculum, as well as various standing committees. Overall, it represents the best agreement of several hundred people unusually well-informed on the questions. It could provide the basis for specialty certification.

In this discussion, I will focus on the basic assumptions of those who created the guidelines and of those who subsequently participated in the three-week Conference of the English Coalition in 1987. That conference, sometimes described as the successor to several major reviews of English made in the fifties and sixties, brought together sixty elementary, secondary, and college teachers and scholars to assess the current state of English studies at all levels of teaching. The general views of the coalition conference (Lloyd-Jones and Lunsford, 1989) reinforce the specific materials of the guidelines and imply directions likely to be followed by standing committees of the NCTE or of its constituent group, the Conference on English Education, in proposing modifications in the nineties. The coalition, in addition to these associations, includes the Modern Language Association, the College Language Association, the College English Association, the Association of Departments of English, the Conference on College Composition and Communication, and the Conference of Secondary School English Department Chairs, but the statement of the conference does not necessarily bind any of the groups.

General Objectives of English Studies

Those of us in departments of English teach people to speak and write, listen and read more effectively. In the process, we teach them about language in general and about English in particular, and we introduce them to notable examples of writing and speaking. That sounds simple enough. The problem is that such goals lead one into almost every kind of human experience and knowledge, for language mediates our relationships with other people and with the external world in general. Francis Bacon suggested that all knowledge was his province, and so it is for us—a determined person can justify assigning almost any task to teachers of language arts.

A corollary to this proposition is that most of what people learn about using the language comes from daily experience, not from school. Since the language is so inclusive, individuals acquire different bits of linguistic knowledge, and they acquire those bits in different sequences, so teachers have to deal with groups of students who have markedly dissimilar preparation. To be sure, all disciplines have to average out instruction to suit a varied population. But for teachers of English, the scope of variation is so great that we spend a fair amount of time just guessing at the meaning of some bit of language outside of our own previous experience. As a result, we are occasionally trapped into tolerating a particular teacher's ignorance of the language in the name of open-mindedness about options or, more likely, into chasing with messianic fervor after another teacher's "sure-fire" but simple-minded explanation or rule book.

The primary use of language is to represent the world we perceive, but what we perceive is immediately distorted by the limits of our minds and by the pressures of our needs and wills. No representation is ever pure. Jonathon Swift, in reporting Gulliver's travels in Laputa, ridicules the absurdity of imagining discourse so spare as to consist only of things, the objects themselves carried about in bags; we represent things as words, or as words combined by grammar; and we generally suggest our interpretation and evaluation of what is represented as well. We should not imagine that the words represent all of the reality; the signs in language emphasize the part of our perception that is important to us collectively, as a group, defined by our language. We share a view of the world enforced by our language. One reason some purists are so eager to change the language of other people is in fact to change the people; one reason we study a foreign language is to try to get outside of the limits of our own language; one reason we study alien literature is to discover in it the demonstrated sense of reality of people unlike us.

The practical mastery of language, which is basic to our definition of humanity, is a preoccupation for those who want to turn infants into children. We reassure babies not only with our touch but also with our voices. We are delighted when these bundles of nerves seem to recognize words and try to make their own. We celebrate the first sentence—or even clear evidence of any infantile predication. We do all we can to make sure that in five or six years, children will have mastered the grammar of the home language. The vocabulary may be limited—perhaps parochial even to one household—and the skill in manipulating grammatical structures may be naive, but children come to first grade with a large body of knowledge and skill. Even after school begins, the influence of home language, discourse in the neighborhood, and (eventually) public talk in the media dominate life. After all, the use of language allows one to survive where one lives, and school often seems to deal with a distant future. A child can master all sorts of verbal refinement to remain in good standing with a street gang while claiming to be quite baffled by school instruction in adult hoity-toity usage.

Essence of the English Teacher

For a teacher, the centrality of language to any form of human survival is a potential lever to learning, just as the incredible variety is a challenge to one's sense of control or social unity. Both centrality and variety exert unusual demands on the teacher's competence.

First, the teacher must use the language well in daily discourse. Speaking and even writing are learned primarily by imitation and actual use. Good listening and reading are less easy to observe, but students soon discover which teachers really pay attention and understand language, and the students copy accordingly. It is not enough merely to be a good example, and children need many additional good examples outside of school, but being a model is the first obligation of the teacher.

At the outset, teachers of English must be fascinated by the language. They need not be universal experts. Not all short-story writers have to be able to write technical reports, and not all orators have to conduct negotiations, but everyone should be compulsive about some segment of creation in language and should let it show. It is not enough to be minimally competent or duty bound; teachers of English must find life itself in how words go together. If I had to devise for prospective teachers a training program with but one segment, I would concentrate on enhancing each teacher's performance as a user of language. If you want to translate that as having an English major, fine, although I doubt that the undergraduate major is sufficient for any teacher, except possibly for those who have a well-established passion for language when they elect English.

The problem with enthusiasts is that they sometimes mistake their own special excellence for total excellence.

Their dialect seems to be the only dialect; their readings become the 100 required items for the nation. Often journalists or lawyers or genteel essayists fall into the trap, perhaps because they are ordinarily very good at some kinds of writing, while being innocent of any serious theory of language. People who want to sell five feet of well-bound books, or college entrance examiners, or even secretaries of education take advantage of the American longing for predigested knowledge, of the eagerness for short lists of the "very best." One wishes to avoid having to know too many special cases. The purveyors of a limited canon of useful literary texts deprive us of the joy of discovering flawed brilliance by making us concentrate on their monuments. In the extreme form, they are tyrants of language, and through language, they are tyrants in the society, sometimes just because they do not understand the options, sometimes because they do.

We all need literature that enlarges and gives additional meaning to our world, but our students (and we) gain most when the work that is new to them (or us) primarily moves out from a base of what is already familiar. Not everyone automatically begins with the visions and conventional assumptions of prosperous Caucasian males, so we need some works with other points of departure.

Much of teacher training should be devoted to increasing the options. The first options are those implied by the term *general education.* Even more than most other teachers, the teacher of English needs to be curious, to be delighted by all kinds of knowledge. The language takes us into every discipline, so we at least have to become willing tourists in the domains of our students and friends. Like the elephant's child, we must have "insatiable curiosity." Still, we also have special interests to develop. We start with our particular superior skill in using the language, and then we acquire other skills; we discover the variations in language important to other people. From this great range, we draw the specifics to help our students discover the language they need in their lives. We are the linguistic catalysts for the academy.

Writing

Writing is usually identified as a school skill, sometimes to distinguish it from speaking. To the extent that we are talking about scribal skills, that is probably true. In school, we learn the systems of representing speech in marks on paper. The arts of stenography are important in providing attractive, unimpeded access to the language, so we should not disparage them. Moreover, the invention of writing undoubtedly changed society in many ways. It altered the role of memory; our past is now bound in libraries rather than carried in our heads. Writing makes it easy to remove statements from their contexts; as a result, we emphasize discourse in which immediate social exigencies are suppressed, as in much academic or scientific writing.

Nonetheless, we can be distracted by taking too seriously these scribal skills. Some rather simple-minded people are excellent scribes, and some brilliant folks are badly coordinated or impatient or even hostile and produce sloppy papers. Possibly, word processors or other machines will reduce the problem, and clearly the elementary skills will still have to be learned in school as a craft, but those are not the problems of composition crucial to a teacher or writer. They do not define the real tasks of the high school teacher.

Any writer must first make sense. Sense is not defined alike in a news story, a lyric poem, a business proposal, a Zen parable, and a political stump speech. Each form has its own rules for sense. A teacher needs an encyclopedia of rule books, just as the writer has to acquire enough tact to recognize what kind of rule applies in what situation. But the point is to make sense, at least to oneself, and usually to others as well.

To some school people, making sense means logic. I can remember exercises in formal logic in my freshman handbooks. But even those who like the slogan implying that good writing is good thinking ordinarily do more than chase syllogisms. They add workbook versions of Mill's principles of induction and perhaps present disguised forms of Aristotle's *topoi.* Still more likely are standard patterns of organization and rules for examples and evidence, a few exercises in definition, and a bit of propaganda analysis. Systems of Western thought are numerous, and they work at many different levels of abstraction. For the writer, most of the systems provide means for asking questions, for developing ideas, and for anticipating what a doubtful reader will need to know. The systems provide practical ways for guiding a writer who is stuck, so teachers ought to know several of them in order to devise ways to help stuck students.

Beyond that, as liberally educated people, teachers should also be curious about what the Western mind calls thought and how psychologists and neurologists think we develop thoughts; in a practical sense, both the creator and the interpreter of language need many ways of considering how language allows us to develop and to relate the fragments of our perceptions. Given the brevity of a college education, probably most techniques for making sense have to be learned in practice, as most uses of language are. Although writing should be a part of every course in the curriculum—for writing provides the careful and committed means for examining knowledge of all sorts, and writing, after all, can be examined thoughtfully for revisions—still special courses in writing open up a fuller range of human situations and concentrate on how the language actually shapes experience and understanding. For prospective teachers I prefer a survey course asking students to try many different kinds of writing, but I would settle for any course emphasizing decisions of craft. The theories I would save for the master teachers.

Linguistics

This distinction between mastery of the craft and mastery of theory suggests my attitude toward the formal study of grammar, too, although I emphasize that I am talking of grammar, not usage, and I really am concerned with a far more inclusive understanding of what language is. Grammar is what holds the language together; we learn it tacitly as we acquire our native language. When we study foreign languages, at least as adults, we ordinarily make explicit use of descriptions of grammar in order to learn quickly about how other languages use different strategies for combining ideas. Many systems of description are available, and each represents some different objective of description. Generative grammars of English suggest mental processes, and structural grammars are more useful for stylistic description. One learns systems of description so one can stand back from the language to think about it.

Most school grammars, ordinarily watered down versions of neoclassic adaptations of Latin grammar, probably help one learn Romance languages, offer some grammatical vocabulary, assist in making one pay attention to revision, and baffle the unwary. Prudence suggests that teachers know it because so many elders invested so much painful effort in learning it that they will harass any teacher who cannot talk about it. Maybe, too, a teacher will feel stronger in the fight by knowing that the bishops who shaped traditional descriptions knew Latin and believed Latin superior to English; they also thought that Latin grammar, being derived from Greek grammar, was closer to a pre-Babel grammar and therefore closer to some true grammar. That is partly why they were willing to create rules that ran totally in the face of actual practice. They also had the *Eton College Latin Grammar* to borrow from. Most experimental evidence suggests that knowledge of school grammar does not improve one's writing and that by taking time from the actual practice of writing, it may actually inhibit the student.

For most people, the real issue is not grammar, but usage. We are concerned about what words or structures are chosen in what situations to represent what set of values. The variations establish the social, ethnic, and regional ties of the writer; they represent the history of the language and the people who use it. They drag us into politics and all sorts of social tensions. At a simple level of *who* and *whom* or apostrophes, usage identifies who is fussy. At the level of contractions or personal pronouns, it suggests degrees of intimacy and social conformity. At the level of dialects, it suggests the subcategories of the society. Most of our practical interest in usage deals with the effect of any of myriad forms on particular readers, through a standard list of "classics," in which the student acquires enough knowledge to decorate conversation at a cocktail party. The teachers may be ill equiped to do anything else.

These perversions of objectives of literary learning have given rise, partly, to cries of alarm on matters of education from political leaders such as William Bennett, Lynn Cheney, Allan Bloom, and E. D. Hirsch. They deplore what they perceive as less emphasis on knowledge about works they value. Whether ignorance of standard works is judged to be greater than it was depends on what groups are being compared, on what works are considered standard, and on how the assessment of the knowledge is conducted. But as a rule, concern over specific works or short lists rises from a restrictive social or political bias; it may be sensible and suitable for a particular time and place, but it also may be improperly restrictive in an open society. Teachers of the nineties and beyond have to be responsive to complexly mixed culture.

One problem for them is that the body of knowledge is too large for anyone to cover. Even our new Ph.D.'s have barely begun to sample the body of excellent works in English, much less the important works in translation. One must have a system that allows a student to sample intelligently, to interpret richly, and to develop preferences. The prospective teacher, as a guide, needs a range of literary experience to match that of the society as well as some sense of priority in identifying which writings should come first in the growth of each particular student. Traditional courses present the works chosen essentially to respond to the needs of nineteenth-century America. The choices favor the values of the British royal court, because in earlier periods, those who hung around the government produced most of the literature. Even the republican literature of the eighteenth century and socially conscious literature of the nineteenth grew from the values and daily perceptions of middle- or upper-class English and American men. Their educations usually included some contact with major classical writers—nowadays only in translation—so a few ancient writers enter the canon of works to be studied.

To a point, such agreement on what ought to be read is helpful in establishing a common ground of allusion. People who talk about "cultural literacy" seek such ground, but it is probably not now enough. We may wish for a tightly knit culture of white males bred in the elegant verbiage of the churches of England and Scotland, but we live in a world that has absorbed many other views. American literature itself demands a broader sample. The problem for curriculum makers is to provide prospective teachers a manageable sample in about a year of college work. On the record of college catalogues examined by a committee of the Association of Departments of English, the last twenty years have seen almost no change in college requirements for the major. What actually happens in classrooms is less clear, as Charles Harris, chair of the committee, points out. Styles in criticism have changed, so courses probably have changed more than titles of courses have. A broader range of authors may be taught in standard courses, and elective courses further increase the range.

If coverage in the traditional sense is impossible, the word *sampling* requires definition. We need to show off the problems of reading different genres, produced in different ages and cultures, for people of many needs. We need to supply cultural background to help students become readers capable of interpreting works of writers unlike themselves. But we also need to nurture them with works providing pictures and interpretations of their own special world. We will have to settle on some titles simply because they are available. We will probably take some works specially written for adolescents, so they recognize how literature can be used to shape the materials of their own experience. We will probably take some old standards precisely because they have become part of our language, sometimes like flies in amber. In short, we will shuffle among titles in order to serve the primary goal of making students better able to interpret whatever writing falls into their hands. That implies efforts to help them for brief moments to live outside of our time and culture and to draw into themselves a part of the cultural memory we regularly entomb in libraries. The teacher needs a range of background to identify particular works that can gently enlarge the experience of students in the class.

Additional Studies

I have not tried to deal with the alternative languages of cinema and graphics and mathematics, nor the special dialects of journalism and technical writing, nor the dynamics of language in speech, although at times all of these concerns fall to the teacher of English—and might legitimately do so. In the colleges, various fratricidal wars have placed the subjects in separate departments, but the size of the collegiate academy also dictates subdivision into interest groups, which become socially and intellectually isolated. When our graduate assistants complain of having to teach speech in our freshman course, they are imitating the senior neoclassicists who will not teach Victorian literature. This compartmentalization is a problem for anyone who tries to base certification of teachers on course titles or on hours of work taken in college departments. But it is also an issue in high school programs, so secondary teachers may well be hired because they are competent in areas of English not specifically mentioned here—directing plays, coaching debate, or tutoring nonnative speakers. The language arts teacher in the elementary school is most often responsible for the full range of competence represented by English studies. Doubtless, that is why the elementary teachers at the English coalition conference set the agenda for discussion, for they more than the others grapple the full range of language activities.

I also have passed over the crafts of teaching; most are best learned in apprentice situations. Probably some present apprenticeships are ill supervised, too short, and peripheral to sustained professional experience, but some of the professional restructuring proposed for the schools will help extend the acculturation of new teachers to their tasks. General knowledge of how societies transmit their cultures and specific survival skills, or how individuals learn, should be part of the general education for all graduates, not just background for teachers in colleges of education. Such knowledge is fundamental for any society and its governors, though all teachers might seek additional knowledge in order to interpret their own practices.

Conclusion

The essential question for identifying a teacher of English is whether the person is alive to language. That implies a strong will to discover, to try out another idea or experience. That implies an openness to people of all kinds and to the worlds they express. Whatever specific training is required, whatever tests for admission are designed, the goal should be to identify and encourage people who are eagerly expanding their verbal range. All of us have come a long, wordy way from birth, but the possibilities for travel in language exceed by far the distance we have come. We seek as our teachers those who are compulsive travelers, those who have learned the means of travel and have the itch to wander. They are the Pied Pipers, and we and the children will follow them together.

References

Lloyd-Jones, R., and Lunsford, A. (eds.). *Report of the English Coalition Conference: Democracy Through Language.* Urbana, Ill.: National Council of Teachers of English, 1989.

Wolfe, D. *Guidelines for the Preparation of Teachers of English Language Arts.* Champaign, Ill.: National Council of Teachers of English, 1986.

5

What Teachers Need to Know About Mathematics

Peter J. Hilton

Before embarking on a detailed discussion of the essential content of mathematics courses for teachers and students, it is natural to lay down certain principles that underlie the recommendations. I will enunciate these principles in the form of propositions. However, whereas mathematical propositions must be accompanied by proofs in order to command belief, propositions about the teaching of mathematics are not susceptible to proof. Thus, these propositions will be accompanied by commentaries to promote their reasonableness. In addition, I will specify certain content areas and treatments I view as crucial to the education of prospective secondary teachers.

Principles

Proposition 1: The specific future needs of the prospective secondary teacher should not be reflected in the precollege curriculum of that teacher, or even in the undergraduate curriculum of that teacher.

Commentary: The first half of this proposition is obviously true, being a special case of the universal principle that specific future professional needs should not influence the precollege curriculum of any student. As to the second half of the proposition, I am here referring to content and not to treatment. That a student will later be teaching mathematics at the secondary level should not influence the content of mathematics courses that student studies as an undergraduate; the content should be that of an enlightened, contemporary mathematics major. The argument rests on two related assertions. First, the teacher needs to understand the significance, mathematical and real world, of the mathematics he or she is teaching, and it is in the nature of the dynamics of good mathematical instruction that this understanding comes from studying the sequels to that mathematics; thus for the secondary teacher, from studying undergraduate mathematics, especially the core curriculum. Second, the teacher's mathematical understanding must always go beyond the level at which he or she is teaching, in order that the teacher be confident to present new material, to encourage questions, and to foster experimentation. The only good teacher is one who welcomes divergent trends among the students; convergence, which leads to easy classroom management and a sterile atmosphere, is the refuge of the timid teacher, fearful of finding himself or herself out of his or her depth.

Unfortunately, it is necessary today to violate this principle because of the presence in the traditional school curriculum of anachronistic elements that are encountered nowhere else in contemporary life. The presence of these elements at the elementary level is notorious. At the secondary level, the most conspicuous of these anachronisms is formal geometry, presented as a sort of arcane religion with its symbols, rituals, and holy writ. Future secondary teachers, but nobody else, need to master this obscure theology masquerading as mathematics. A healthy education for future secondary teachers of mathematics naturally presupposes a healthy secondary curriculum, and this we do not yet have.

Proposition 2: The education of future secondary mathematics teachers, at college or university, should depart very little from that of other mathematics majors.

Commentary: The contrary argument is based on the claim that the future teacher should be provided with the opportunity to test the power to explain mathematical ideas to students, to illustrate, apply, and otherwise motivate them. But all undergraduates should have, indeed need, this opportunity. As a general rule, we do not know if we have understood something unless and until we have successfully explained it to somebody else. Moreover, the responses of those to whom we try to teach some material may well enrich and give direction to our own understanding. Parenthetically, I would broaden this general rule to include computers among our students; for we can be in some doubt as to whether a human student has understood, but a computer's grasp of an idea is unmistakable.

Some also maintain that future teachers need a number of courses of a pedagogical nature. It is doubtful that these are crucial in the preservice education of future teachers, whatever their role in the in-service education of teachers. Therefore, there can be no justification for taking time from the study of content in order to free time for courses in pedagogy. Courses in pedagogy should be carefully coordinated with content courses, and no student should be deterred from becoming a teacher or denied provisional certification for want of credit in pedagogical courses.

Proposition 3: The most important attribute of a secondary mathematics teacher is a positive attitude toward mathematics. The essential knowledge of mathematics is concerned with the nature of mathematics itself—its unity and its essence as a discipline.

Commentary: This proposition is valid for the teacher of mathematics at any level and is absolutely crucial when applied to the elementary teacher. For him or her, it would constitute the *Hauptsatz,* or principal proposition. The teacher must understand what mathematics is and what it is not. Mathematics is a system of thought incorporating but transcending a uniquely well-adapted language. It is not a set of skills, though its practice requires and inculcates skill. It is not a set of separate disciplines, but a single unity comprising many interrelated areas of study. Thus, what matters is that a student and the student's teacher learn to think mathematically; any significant part of mathematics can be used to convey to them the necessary understanding and thinking ability. Conversely, no part of mathematics, however seemingly appropriate, can prepare the student really to understand mathematics, and hence to be in a position effectively to teach it, if he or she learns it as a set of isolated skills to be retained by the exercise of undiscriminating memory.

It is sad that this has to be said, but we must recognize that the contrary view seems to prevail very widely in the United States. To quote but one particularly conspicuous example, we find Saxon (1986) bewailing the availability of hand calculators in the elementary classroom, arguing that their use there leads to mathematical illiteracy. Saxon crusades energetically and very successfully for a return to the nineteenth century; we should, he argues, teach by rote and oblige the child to learn by memory. The sale of his textbooks testifies to the plausibility of his message. This deplorable philosophy, not so surprising in one with a strong military background, may well lead to short-term success. It will certainly not lead to the ability to understand and apply mathematical ideas. It may even, at the most optimistic estimate, continue to give the student the illusion of success through the first two college years. Then comes the student's rude awakening that he or she has learned no real mathematics and, hence, can use none. It is almost always too late then to change; and the student, feeling disillusioned and betrayed, will usually become embittered.

Proposition 4: It is vital that the future teacher understand the distinction between education and training.

Commentary: This proposition, broader than its predecessor, is nevertheless closely related to it. A training in skills that are by their very nature ephemeral can only serve the short-term interests of the trainee and can provide him or her only with temporary mastery of some aspect of some profession. An education will benefit the whole person, in all aspects of that person's life. A mathematical education, if successful, leads inevitably to the acquisition of skills (mathematics should be something you do, not merely something you learn); but a training in skills need not involve any genuine mathematical education.

Evidence of the fallacy inherent in the confusion of education with training is provided by the proneness to deplore the loss of skills by today's children. A failure in their education is surely always regrettable; but the loss of a skill may be a sign of progress. In nineteenth-century Britain, many women and children had substantial coal mining skills; should we regret that no woman or child has these skills today? The dishwasher, the washing machine, the automobile—all these gadgets have rendered certain skills obsolete. Let those who advocate continued emphasis on accuracy in executing the dreary algorithms of elementary arithmetic, on the grounds that the battery of one's hand calculator may be dead, at least be sufficiently consistent to keep a horse in readiness in case the car battery is dead. Indeed, the latter procedure is far more rational, since one may stand in urgent need of transportation, whereas a long division is only urgent if the teacher quite artificially declares it to be so.

Further evidence of this widespread confusion is provided by the terms *teacher training* and *driver education.* No group of people needs education more than the teachers, and no group needs training more than the drivers of automobiles. It is regrettable that many parents, in their well-meant concern for the future well-being of their children, contribute to the confusion by looking for an immediate connection between what students learn at school and the way the students will subsequently earn their livings. We can sympathize with the motives of those parents; we should, however, have nothing but scorn and contempt for those self-styled educators who pander to this parental concern and conspire to rob our children of their birthright.

Proposition 5: Tests should be kept to a minimum. Moreover, they should reflect and not influence the curriculum.

Commentary: Currently, tests distort the curriculum at every level. Students are, in general, concerned only with doing well on tests and with getting good grades, and teachers teach for success on the tests. Of course, some testing is necessary so that teacher and, more importantly, student can monitor progress made. But the teacher must also find the means of continuously monitoring student progress, and this requires a sensitivity that cannot be achieved without a thorough mastery of the mathematical material in question.

Especially pernicious is the influence of standardized tests on the actual mathematical curriculum, as distinct from the official curriculum. Such tests, as a general rule, have nothing to do with genuine mathematics and put a most undue emphasis on the acquisition of skill. Multiple choice questions are utterly ridiculous unless, perhaps, one is testing for competence in finite group theory, for which the method of solution by elimination is often appropriate. When we do mathematics to solve real-world problems, the real world does not inform us that the answer is one of five possibilities. Moreover, if we are given a finite list of possible answers, then we have available a method that is likely to be quicker and easier to apply than is the method presumably being tested.

It is no coincidence that the teaching of geometry is in a sorry state in this country, for it does not lend itself to mechanical testing. Indeed, no real mathematics does. We should declare ourselves inexorably opposed to any form of testing that gives credit only for the so-called answer and pays no attention to the reasoning of the student or the explanation of the choice of method.

The tyranny of tests and the hegemony of testers can be broken only by the determination of confident and well-educated teachers at all levels. Future teachers must acquire an awareness of the immensity of this problem during their own education.

Crucial Content

We can outline certain rather precise specifications for the necessary mathematical content of the education of a future secondary mathematics teacher. The reader might have supposed from the previous discussion that such specificity would be out of place; have we not said that mathematics is a unity, that any significant part of mathematics can serve as the vehicle to convey the essential nature of mathematical thought, and that attitude toward mathematics is of supreme importance? But we must make choices, and we do claim that there are features common to all worthwhile mathematics at the undergraduate level that should be brought out. Moreover, it is unreasonable to anticipate a revolutionary change of mathematical content—or, rather, intended mathematical content—at the secondary level. To fix our ideas, we should, however, assume that the secondary curriculum shows an awareness that we are living in the computer age.

I present the crucial content under five heads: applications, algebra, geometry, number systems, and functions and rates of change. Again, these are not separate courses, but essential features of a well-rounded mathematics education.

Applications. The future teacher must understand the role of applications in stimulating mathematical activity and the role of applications in motivating the study of mathematics. Both these roles are subtle, however. It is rarely the case that new mathematics is discovered (or created, according to your philosophical position) in response to a real-world problem. Rather, new significance attaches to an already known piece of mathematics when we study and understand its connection with a real-world situation. Examples abound today of exciting new connections between modern theoretical physics and active areas of mathematics—such as fiber-bundle theory, infinite dimensional Lie algebras, and representation theory. It is remarkable that, whereas the study of partial differential equations may be said to have originated with the attempt to model the nature of flux in the real world, these other areas of mathematics were invented for purely mathematical reasons.

One must be careful in seeking to motivate the study of mathematics through applications. First, the applications must be of genuine interest to the students; it is not enough that they be important. All too often, teachers, with naive optimism, hope that by exhibiting a connection between a dull piece of mathematics and an uninteresting application, they will simultaneously encourage an interest in both. Of course, this does not work. Second, simplifying the mathematical model arising from a real-world problem is usually necessary in order that it be susceptible to treatment with the mathematical tools available to the student. It is crucial that we undertake such "falsification" openly and honestly; it is often better to describe such crude models as illustrations rather than as applications. Third, it is a mistake to insist on motivating every new mathematical item by reference to a problem outside mathematics. In most cases, mathematical progress depends on the autonomous dynamic of mathematics itself, and seeking such outside motivation in all cases would therefore be artificial and misleading. Fourth, the spirit of applied mathematics is to be found also in good pure mathematics; thus, generalization and abstraction take place within mathematics itself, and mathematical progress often consists of revealing previously hidden connections between different parts of mathematics (most typically, at the secondary level, between algebra and geometry).

Algebra. First and foremost, the future teacher has to understand that algebra at the secondary level (that is, until abstract algebra is encountered) is simply arithmetic made mathematical—arithmetic expressed in an appropriate mathematical language. This language leads to systematic procedures for getting answers to mathematical questions, but it is unlikely to lead, of itself, to the formulation of natural, interesting questions. Such questions arise from modeling the real world, very often mediated through geometrical presentation. It is thus a fundamental pedagogical blunder to teach algebra or geometry in isolation. An exclusive diet of the former produces boredom, of the latter, frustration.

The future teacher not only should be able to execute significant algebraic manipulations but also must understand why they are significant. For example, he or she should be familiar with the behavior of quadratic polynomials in one or two indeterminates. Familiarity with a formula for solving a quadratic equation is certainly not enough. The relation to properties of conic sections and quadric surfaces should be part of the curriculum, along with facts about the maxima or minima of quadratic polynomials. Thus are geometry and algebra united.

Geometry. As already stressed, geometry should not be studied as a separate discipline at the secondary level; rather, the geometrical viewpoint should permeate the whole of the mathematical experience. We are not recommending the study of axiomatics, nor a heavy dose of Euclidean geometry as currently administered. The future teacher should be able to think geometrically (in two and three dimensions) and should know how to prove geometrical statements both synthetically and analytically.

Of great importance are the concept of similarity of geometrical figures (the basis of trigonometry) and the analytical geometry of straight lines and circles in the plane. The role of algebra in answering genuinely geometrical questions should, as we say, be clearly understood by the future teacher and sharply distinguished from the current role of coordinate geometry as a thin excuse for doing some dull algebra.

We believe that it is within geometry, and specifically in the passage from polygonal paths to curves, that the link is forged that will eventually enable the student to study both discrete and continuous mathematics and to understand their similarities and differences. Unfortunately, today one goes from the geometry of triangles and more general polygons to the geometry of circles, as if no essentially new mathematical idea had been introduced. Notions like arc length, area enclosed by a smooth closed curve, and tangent to a curve involve sophisticated concepts of continuous mathematics and are not to be derived in an elementary fashion from linear geometry. There is no smooth transition to smooth geometry.

Number Systems. Of outstanding importance to the precalculus student is an understanding of the real number system with its several interrelated structures—that is, its algebraic, topological, differentiable, and order structures. (I have said before that I would happily undertake to teach calculus to any student who really understood the mathematics of the rational number system and who had some geometric intuition.)

The future teacher must understand how, why, and with what consequences the number system is built up, starting with the natural numbers. For example, the nature of the order relation changes substantially as one passes from the natural numbers **N** to the integers **Z** (there is no longer a first element and hence no straightforward induction principle) and then from **Z** to the rational numbers **Q** (there is no longer a "next element"). The inadequacy—more technically, the incompleteness—of **Q** should be understood geometrically, and the set of real numbers **R** should be constructed by means of infinite decimals. This, of course, implies that the future teacher should understand the notion of the limit of a convergent sequence and should be able to provide students with a convincing, intuitive conception of this idea. This is especially necessary in order to understand the arithmetical operations in **R.**

It is very important to demystify the nature of real numbers and, preferably, also complex numbers before the student embarks on calculus. This demystification will surely have a geometrical flavor; yet a crucial element is imparted to the process through the general availability of hand calculators and computers. The teacher must understand that calculator arithmetic is not the same as human arithmetic. Let us consider the field of real numbers **R**; it is a field in the strict sense that the operations of addition and multiplication in **R** satisfy certain axioms. On the other hand, the real numbers are certainly not "real"! Irrational numbers have no real-world significance, and complex numbers (including pure imaginaries) are quite as real as real numbers and substantially less complex if we consider their algebra and function theory. Thus, the real numbers form a beautiful mathematical system, which the computer rejects. However, in rejecting irrational numbers, computer arithmetic is obliged to incorporate many awkward and ugly features into its simplified number system, for the computer admits only a very restricted part of the rational number system. The teacher must understand the principles of approximate arithmetic (Hilton and Pedersen, 1986) and, in particular, of round-off error and the trade-off involved in passing between the world of the mind and the world of the machine.

Functions and Rates of Change. All students at the secondary level require a clear, even if essentially intuitive, notion of rate of change. They must understand that change, or flux, is the natural state of the universe and that the principal role of mathematics in the real world is to model that state of flux, just because the principal role of science is to explain, predict, and ultimately influence that flux.

In the first instance, the idea of variation requires that the notion of function be clearly understood. We do not advocate, at the secondary level, the study of nonnumerical functions; but it is important to have the notion of functions defined on **N**, **Z**, and **Q** (or subsets of these) as well as functions defined on subsets of **R**. For example, a real sequence is a function defined on **N** with values in **R**.

It is also important to the future teacher to be perfectly clear about the distinction between a genuine variable and the x's and y's of elementary algebra, which are, almost always, merely numbers that cannot yet be specified (unknowns) or that do not need to be specified (indeterminates). The distinction must be conveyed to students so that they avoid the stereotyped thinking that always regards an equation as representing something to be solved instead of as describing a locus or a process. (Naturally, inequalities should also be regarded in this multicolored light.)

Finally, it is essential that the secondary teacher be able to present and motivate for students the mathematical notion of rate of change. This idea, of enormous importance in the history of mathematical thought, is certainly rendered no less significant today either by the availability of computer programs for symbol manipulation or by the fact that the computer will often replace a differential equation by a difference equation. Starting with the idea of the differential coefficient, the rate of change of a function at an interior point of its domain, one proceeds to the derivative as itself a function. It would be especially satisfactory if the view of the tangent line to a curve as the best possible linear approximation could also be conveyed to students; the chain rule would then appear in its true light as the statement of the compatibility of linear approximation with composition of functions rather than in the spurious light, familiar to today's students, as a means of differentiating functions one would never have occasion to meet.

I would add parenthetically the suggestion that a good introduction to the idea of rate of change would be by means of a discussion of speed and average speed. Everyday language suggests that in order to understand the term *average speed,* one must understand the noun *speed* and the adjective *average.* In fact, this is quite wrong, since the concept of average speed, over a given time interval, is quite simple, being the quotient when distance traveled is divided by time taken. Obviously, this concept is much easier to comprehend than is either of the notions of average or speed. One may indeed present average speed both as a special case and as an extension of the usual notion of average—and one can then present speed as a limiting case of average speed. One then sees, in a new form, the significance of the statement, for example, that the average age is not an age and the average family is not a family—that one should more correctly speak of the average of the ages and the average of the families, so that both average age and average family are averages.

Conclusion

This then is our minimal prescription for the future secondary teacher. Any well-conceived undergraduate program of mathematical studies should provide this for all its mathematics majors, and no reasonable duties for the secondary mathematics teacher should require anything that, from the conceptual rather than the purely technical point of view, goes substantially beyond what I have prescribed.

References

Hilton, P., and Pedersen, J. "Approximation as an Arithmetic Process." In H. L. Schoen (ed.), *Estimation and Mental Computation.* Reston, Va.: National Council of Teachers of Mathematics, 1986.

Saxon, J. "Classroom Calculators Add to Math Illiteracy." *Wall Street Journal,* May 16, 1986, p. 22.

6

What Teachers Need to Know About Science

Harold J. Morowitz

Teaching consists either of the transmission of information, facts in the broadest sense, or of training in the use of tools necessary to obtain and evaluate information. When students are set to memorizing the names of the world's continents, they are accepting facts, and when they learn to read, they are acquiring a tool or method of unlimited application. Elementary schooling must consist of both aspects. However, even a technique such as reading has its limitations if all the available materials are authoritarian in character and if students never face the question "How do we know the things we know?" That question, including the ability to deal with it, represents the most powerful universally available device for obtaining knowledge and for evaluating the baffling set of inputs that come to everyone in a highly pluralistic media-oriented society. Inquiry-directed learning has played a small educational role in Western culture. Nevertheless, this approach, as a method of acquiring knowledge and evaluating statements, must be a central feature of general education in future progressive societies.

The two great anti-utopias envisioned by authors of this century, *1984* (Orwell, 1949) and *Brave New World* (Huxley, 1946), both represented societies in which it was not possible to ask, "How do we know?" In one case, repression was employed, and in the other, intense distraction was used—but always to prevent use of inquiry as part of the intellectual equipment of the citizens. Both societies were thus deterred from exercising options, and individuals were unable to develop their human potential. This transmission of statements without the opportunity to inquire into their source or validity is brainwashing in its most general sense.

To avoid the appeals to authoritarianism, the teacher must be equipped with a deep understanding of the acquisition and validation of knowledge. What has been regarded as a philosophical fine point must become central to teacher training. The following pages focus on what the educator should ultimately impart to the student. Consideration of this program will define the kinds of knowledge and approaches that will become part of the teacher's conceptual framework.

Historical Setting

The inquiry method of education has its roots in classical Greece and is vividly presented to us in Plato's retelling of the conversations between Socrates and various citizens and young men of Athens. Socrates unrelentingly pursued questions to their roots by repeatedly asking, in many different circumstances, "How do we know? What is truth? What is beauty? What is justice?" All of these concepts came under probing inquiry. The citizens of Athens perceived that Socrates's questions were engaging the young and that the answers might upset the established order. The philosopher was brought to trial, accused, among other things, of misleading his students. As Plato concluded, "Such was the end, Echecrates, of our friend, whom I may truly call the wisest, and justest, and best of all the men I have ever known (Jowett, 1911, p. 447).

The naive question "How do we know?" seems to have lain dormant from the end of the golden age of Athens until the early 1600s when René Descartes resolved to accept nothing as true which he did not clearly recognize to be so. From that time forth, the problems of epistemology, the theory of knowledge, became an intimate part of the philosophical thought of the Western world, and the succeeding investigations of David Hume, Immanuel Kant, and a number of others established the framework within which we approach problems even today. However, this tradition has never been widespread and is, at present, chiefly seen in advanced courses in epistemology, which enroll only a small fraction of college students.

A second approach to ways of knowing has accompanied the growth of science as a major intellectual and practical endeavor of contemporary civilization. Nineteenth-century physics and biology developed a materialism and a radical reductionism that have proved inadequate to the problems of quantum mechanics, relativity, and information-processing neural networks. As a result, a far more sophisticated doctrine answering "How do we know?" has emerged in Karl Popper's *The Logic of Scientific Discovery* (1968), Henry Margenau's *The Nature of Physical Reality* (1950), and other twentieth-century writings in the philosophy of science. Although these books point the way toward dealing with the problem of scientific knowledge, they are known to only a small group of specialists. We have yet to benefit from the application of these philosophical outlooks to broader areas of human experience. Both of these volumes are clearly written and suitable for teacher education.

A third aspect of the problem of knowledge is the practical, everyday assessment that has allowed us to survive as a species. The knowledge necessary to provide food, shelter, and clothing is based on certain tacit assumptions about the nature of reality. This approach must have preferential status, because surviving and functioning in an everyday sense are requisites to the maintenance of a society that allows for human development in a higher sense. This practical approach has been given a more philosophical basis in C. S. Pierce's concept of *concrete reasonableness.*

Proposal

The major thrust of this chapter is the desirability of orienting the educational system to incorporate the construct of "How do we know?" into the curriculum, from kindergarten to graduate school. Educated individuals emerging from such a program should be able to approach intelligently the following types of queries with adequate conceptual devices:

1. How do we know the world is round?
2. How do we know if a television commercial is telling the truth?
3. How do we know that atoms exist?
4. How do we evaluate the claims of a charismatic religious leader?
5. How do we know if economic growth is good or bad?
6. How do we determine if surgery is necessary?
7. How do we evaluate a politician's promises?
8. How do we know if astrology has any validity?
9. How do we decide whether psychoanalysis will likely be helpful or harmful or neither?
10. How do we decide whether we should build a dam on the Stanislaus River?

Until an appreciable fraction of a civilization's population can face these types of questions by themselves with adequate techniques for developing answers, that civilization is constantly vulnerable to demagogues, propagandists, and manipulators of mass media. Only when people can individually approach such queries can we effectively and democratically begin to develop strategies for improvement and to reach toward the vision of a responsible pluralistic society.

The components of the proposed curriculum will go back, as they must, to the historical roots and will include the following:

1. Socratic inquiry as a general methodological tool
2. Logic, rules of thinking, ways of thinking

3. Empirical knowledge, verification and negation as tests of validity, and relevance of constructs
4. Practical knowledge as the core of societal existence
5. Epistemology as a deeper inquiring into the roots of knowledge

Socratic Inquiry. Socratic inquiry is not so much a specific technique as it is a general attitude that must enliven the curriculum at all levels. We must encourage and respect inquiry, and we must make every effort to respond to the students' desires to know the roots of each statement we make. Current schooling has a strong tendency to suppress questions that do not fit the established order of instruction. While this suppression is in one sense used to maintain the pace of learning, we should not allow it to thwart the spirit of inquiry. The crux of this problem lies in the attitude of the teachers and their willingness to be challenged by difficult questions. Teacher education should include those works of Plato that illustrate and record the discussions of Socrates.

Logical Rules of Thinking. We should introduce classical logic quite early in the curriculum, followed by symbolic logic. Developing the syllogism and the rules of conditional reasoning (if A, then B) provides excellent material for giving structure to thought and for allowing students to develop that structure. Truth tables and other such devices provide simple and visual approaches. An understanding of the obvious fallacies in reasoning is a first step toward more subtle modes of inquiry. In discussing syllogisms, we can talk about the notion of affirming or denying the minor premise as an empirical matter, thus laying the foundation for understanding scientific thought. The logical status of denying the consequent (*modus tollens* in classical logic) deserves special attention because of its status as a pruning device for conjectures. The material appropriate to teacher training in this area is found, for example, in *Logic and Logical Thinking* (Facione and Scherer, 1978).

Empirical Knowledge, Verification, and Negation. The character of the observed (the empirical world) needs to be thoroughly explored. The nature of sense data and the interpretation of these data are the first step. Beyond the usual discussion of this material, often carried out in elementary philosophy courses, we can introduce the nature of theoretical reasoning and its relation to observation. This will include going from sense data to constructs, operations on constructs, and return to sense data in the loop of verification. Here we note that unless a construct is vulnerable to possible rejection by observation, it is not empirically meaningful. We should also include the special role of falsification and its relationship to logic (*modus tollens*). A major task in developing the program will be fashioning this material and introducing it at the earliest possible grade level.

Practical Knowledge. Under this heading we search out those features that are primitive, common to most cultures, and revealed in what people do, not what they say they do. Here an overlap between comparative anthropology and epistemology should establish a method of exploring what is necessary for a culture to embody its survival in its thought processes.

Epistemology. The theory of knowledge as a formal subject will probably occur later in the curriculum. However, given the previous four categories, we can expect the detailed inquiry regarding how we know to follow in a natural way. We postulate that with a changed viewpoint, students will be more receptive at every grade to a level of sophistication previously deemed beyond their reach. We observed a similar result when mathematics was reoriented from arithmetic per se to a broader set-theory approach.

Implementation

A program of this magnitude requires the collaborative effort of a substantial group of philosophers, scientists, educators, curriculum writers, and others. The implementation can proceed in four steps, each of which will take about two years. Any more exact timetable will depend on the level of commitment and support. In any case, development of the program is only the first step; there will remain the difficult task of "selling" it to the educational establishment.

Study, research, and curriculum writing will involve working groups that will develop the basic ideas and communicate frequently to integrate the program. They must constantly be asking, "How do we know that this is the best approach?" This stage of the project must be creative and educationally innovative. The success of the program will depend in large measure upon recruiting dedicated and able people to transform the preliminary goals into practical approaches.

Teacher training will involve a good deal of interaction between formulators and classroom teachers and will result in a program ready for classroom testing. A field-trial program can then be taught in schools for a two-year period on an experimental basis. This aspect is somewhat open-ended, and as in any ongoing program, new approaches will be under trial at all times. Although evaluation and revision will be constantly carried out, a major rethinking of the program is mandated after the first substantial teaching period.

As a practical matter, kindergarten through fourth grade will be field tested first; sequential aspects will make it difficult to introduce the program into the upper grades without proper preparation. However, in writing the program, the entire thrust must be seen in order to develop the time sequence. Thus, the research effort is envisioned as dealing with kindergarten through undergraduate levels.

As an example of this approach, consider the teaching of high school chemistry. At present, it consists of a good deal of factual information mandated in part by achievement tests. If the course were reoriented to ask the question "How do we know that atoms exist?" then we could start out with the laws of combining proportions and develop the whole series of reasoning leading to the final arguments for atomicity that Jean Perrin made in 1913. Each student then could do the crucial experiments and could demonstrate the overall structure of scientific reasoning. Those who go on in science will acquire the factual information in college courses; they will better appreciate how science works. So too will those who do not go on in science; they will have a deeper understanding of the structure of knowledge in chemistry.

Conclusion

To attempt a strategy for teacher training in a plan of this length is to identify a problem area and briefly indicate the direction toward the solution. The strong statement we wish to make is the necessity of a shift from an authoritarian method to an inquiry method of teaching and learning in order to have the kinds of people capable of evolving a sustainable society. (It is important to draw distinctions between authoritarian and rigid and between inquiry oriented and permissive. No such identification is intended. We are talking about the intellectual spirit of education, not the specific didactic approaches to handling classroom situations.) The setting of society's goals will depend on citizens who understand its aims and the reasons for their being established. Having identified education as the first point of approach, we have stressed those technical aspects of thought that will sharpen individuals' perceptions for future planning.

In a democratic society, any attempt to devise new approaches to economic and social problems requires public support. This endorsement depends on sophisticated reasoning by the citizenry. As a first step in a strategy for an improved society, we must develop and nurture the appropriate modes of analytical thought within the educational process. This summary offers that beginning and a program for its implementation.

References

Facione, P. A., and Schrerer, D. *Logic and Logical Thinking.* New York: McGraw-Hill, 1978.

Huxley, A. *Brave New World.* New York: Harper & Row, 1946.

Jowett, B. (ed.). *The Dialogues of Plato.* Vol. 1. New York: Scribner's, 1911.

Margenau, H. *The Nature of Physical Reality: A Philosophy of Modern Physics.* New York: McGraw-Hill, 1950.

Orwell, G. *1984.* New York: New American Library, 1949.

Popper, K. R. *The Logic of Scientific Discovery.* New York: Harper & Row, 1968.

Part Three

The Moral Dimension of Teaching

In his introduction, Ernest Boyer suggested that the great teachers he has known possessed an additional characteristic thus far not discussed—an integrity and authenticity that caused students to trust them, "not for what they knew but for who they were." Boyer thereby suggested that fidelity to a set of values and an uncompromising effort to relate values professed to choices made are essential characteristics of good teaching. What then are the essential values, and how can we develop them in teacher education programs?

One of the intriguing developments in professional education during the 1980s has been the increasing attention given to the normative dimension of professional practice. This attention has manifested itself in courses, texts, teaching materials, and professional faculty members committed to professional ethics (Hastings Center, 1980). Within this movement, values are understood as moral or ethical principles (the terms are used synonymously), such as respect for persons, justice, and truth, and as precepts regulating human conduct, such as duties and obligations. The goals of ethics courses in professional fields such as medicine, business, and law include more than instruction in professional codes of conduct. Through cases and discussion, professors attempt to develop students' capacities for moral reasoning, their abilities to decide what ought to be done in particular contexts, and their skills in resolving professional moral dilemmas or conflicts.

Despite the long tradition of teaching history and philosophy in teacher education programs, the active attention to ethical issues in teaching is quite new, as illustrated by the ironic title of Reagan's (1983) paper, "Applied Ethics for Educators: Philosophy of Education as Something Else?" Only in the most recent effort to outline the knowledge base of teaching has professional ethics been explicitly introduced as fundamental to teacher preparation (Strom, 1989). However, serious and troubling questions remain. Are the moral dilemmas of teaching limited to the choices confronting teachers, or do they extend to moral dilemmas in school policy and to the content of courses and texts? What are the specific means of introducing moral and ethical discourse into the professional preparation of teachers? Can ethics, in fact, be taught (Bok, 1976), or is virtue only learned through practical experience unaided by thought or reflection?

A primary issue involves the nature of the ethics of teaching. The teacher, like any active professional, must make constant choices between means and ends in the practice of his or her craft. The choice of methods or particular content often is influenced by the teacher's values and beliefs (Grossman, Wilson, and Shulman, 1989). One perspective on this issue is to suggest that "incorrect" beliefs need to be corrected through education: "Without help in examining current beliefs and assumptions, teacher candidates are likely to maintain conventional beliefs and incorporate new information or puzzling experiences into old frameworks" (Feiman-Nemser and Buchmann, 1985, p. 29). A richer perspective is to see that beliefs involve normative dimensions, the ethical choices fundamental to practice. The choice of a particular instructional technique, form of evaluation, or subject content may therefore be argued on ethical grounds as a choice between the search for understanding and indoctrination. One particular view of such an ethics of teaching forms the underlying philosophy of *The Paideia Proposal* (Adler, 1982); it is clearly articulated in Chapter Seven of this volume. Ethical choices, however, rarely involve clear distinctions between acknowledged right and wrong but instead are usually between competing conceptions of the good. For as David Smith suggests, understanding honestly pursued shapes the way students perceive the world and ultimately affects their characters and behaviors. Thus, the dilemma confronting teachers may be between the value of improving student understanding of evolution versus respect for the autonomy of the student. The issue of what constitutes the ethics of teaching is therefore a central problem.

A second issue is the values embodied in educational settings. In his review of research on classroom instruction, Good challenged the conventional assumption that educational settings have no independent effect on learning, and he cited accumulating evidence that the culture and climate of a school may have an impact on students' ability to learn. Thus, should we limit ethical reflection to the dilemmas confronting teachers, or as Smith suggests, should we also consider the moral climate of a school by evaluating the fairness, honesty, and rationality of relevant policies? Should we be concerned with the ethics of the learning community—for example, the extent to which fidelity to persons and the quality of relationships are central to programs in teacher education (Noddings, 1984)?

A third consideration is the value content of what is taught. Recent investigations have raised troubling questions regarding the presentation of the role of religion in American history tests. Nord suggests in Chapter Nine that texts in fields such as economics routinely present to students a world in which economic rationality does not have to coexist with alternative conceptions of choice such as religious or community values. The moral principles inherent in popular education movements such as values clarification or character education are rarely subjected to serious discussion and analysis within teacher education programs. Can the ethics of teaching be more than a superficial pursuit if teachers are not made aware of the profound moral content of the subject matter they teach?

A fourth ironic point is whether teacher education programs can address the moral dimension of teaching in an ethically appropriate manner. What should be the goals of courses on the ethics of teaching, how can indoctrination be avoided, and what are the appropriate credentials for individuals who teach these courses (Hastings Center, 1980)? Fewer than 10 percent of all professional school graduates have any working knowledge of the ethical codes relevant to their respective professions (Reeck, 1982); clearly, the pedagogical issues in addressing the values essential to teaching are not trivial.

Finally, and most fundamentally, can ethics be taught? The debate over the feasibility of changing values or ethical beliefs through teaching has arisen in all professional fields. Within the field of education the question is paradoxical, since societal concern over issues such as prayer in the schools, sex education, and other curricular issues assumes that values can be altered through teaching, at least among young children. Research has been cited as supporting the relationship between analyses of moral dilemmas and gains in moral development (Strom, 1989), but use of an instrumental argument on this subject may not only be inappropriate but also may ignore a more fundamental point—that teachers confront serious ethical choices for which they are largely unprepared and that morality is a part of any reflective professional life. To leave systematic discussion of the purposes and ethics of teaching out of teacher preparation is to relegate these programs to the level of training and to miss an important opportunity to nurture the moral sense and imagination of prospective teachers in a manner that can only enrich their professional educations.

Goodlad (1984) has called for more overt attention to the moral content of education—to attempt to educate teachers who have the capacity to evoke a keener sense of humanity in students. Smith and Nord agree, arguing that the traditional moral purposes of liberal education have eroded and that the pursuit of meaningful knowledge could be an appropriate component of professional programs in teacher education. Although the ambition of this thought may seem naive in the light of the acknowledged weaknesses of existing teacher education programs, the proposal deserves some consideration. To paraphrase David Smith, since we cannot make the world as easily as we can make an argument, it may be that a serious effort to examine the moral purposes of education using the riches of the humanities is directly relevant to teacher education programs. Since teachers make and remake the world every day through their teaching, they confront immediately the emptiness of contemporary liberal education and the need to take some moral stance on what they teach and why. If course work on the moral dimension of education could be taught in an integrative, challenging manner by employing faculty members from education and from arts and sciences in active teaching that encourages teacher education students to develop the capacity to make moral choices, then there may be some hope of developing advanced professional teacher education of some challenge, scope, and meaning.

References

Adler, M. J. *The Paideia Proposal.* New York: Macmillan, 1982.

Bok, D. "Can Ethics Be Taught?" *Change,* 1976, *8,* 26–30.

Feiman-Nemser, S., and Buchmann, M. *The First Year of Teacher Preparation: Transition to Pedagogical Thinking?* Research series no. 156. East Lansing: Institute for Research on Teaching, Michigan State University, 1985.

Goodlad, J. *A Place Called School.* New York: McGraw-Hill, 1984.

Grossman, P. L., Wilson, S. M., and Shulman, L. S. "Teachers of Substance: Subject Matter Knowledge for Teaching." In M. C. Reynolds (ed.), *Knowledge Base for the Beginning Teacher.* Elmsford, N.Y.: Pergamon Press, 1989.

Hastings Center. *The Teaching of Ethics in Higher Education.* Hastings-on-Hudson, N.Y.: Hastings Center, 1980.

Noddings, N. *Caring: A Feminine Approach to Ethics and Moral Education.* Berkeley: University of California Press, 1984.

Reagan, G. M. "Applied Ethics for Educators: Philosophy of Education as Something Else?" In *Proceedings of the Thirty-Ninth Annual Meeting of the Philosophy of Education Society.* Normal, Ill.: Philosophy of Education Society, 1983.

Reeck, D. *Ethics for the Professions.* Minneapolis: Augsburg, 1982.

Strom, S. M. "The Ethical Dimension of Teaching." In M. C. Reynolds (ed.), *Knowledge Base for the Beginning Teacher.* Elmsford, N.Y.: Pergamon Press, 1989.

7

Beyond Indoctrination: The Quest for Genuine Learning

Mortimer J. Adler

Everyone knows, or certainly should know, that indoctrination is not genuine teaching and that the results of indoctrination are the very opposite of genuine learning. Yet, as a matter of fact, much that goes on in the classrooms of our schools is nothing but indoctrination. The results that are measured by our standardized tests are not products of genuine learning.

How can this have come about? How can we have so misunderstood the nature of teaching and learning that their counterfeits rather than the genuine articles are rampant in our schools?

The answer lies in the loss of three insights about the nature of teaching and learning, in consequence of which three mistakes are made:

1. It is mistakenly supposed that the activity of teachers is always the principal and sometimes the sole cause of the learning that occurs in students.
2. When it is said that all learning is either by instruction

or by discovery, it is mistakenly supposed that what students learn by instruction is something they passively receive from their teachers.

3. From the failure to distinguish genuine knowledge from mere opinion, together with the failure to distinguish impressions made on and retained by the memory from the development of understanding in the mind, arises a third mistaken supposition—that genuine knowledge can be acquired without an understanding of what is known.

These three mistaken suppositions are so integrally related to one another that if any one of them is made, the other two will be made also. It is, therefore, not surprising that all three have been made by the reigning educational establishment, with the inevitable consequence that indoctrination has been accepted as genuine teaching instead of being abominated as a vicious counterfeit.

Nor should it be surprising that the three basic insights by which the mistaken suppositions can be corrected are also so integrally related that the understanding of genuine teaching that derives from any one of these three insights will be accompanied by an understanding of genuine teaching derived from the other two. In addition, with that threefold understanding of genuine teaching will come an understanding of genuine learning as a development of the mind, not a formation of memories, and as an acquisition of knowledge and understanding, not an adoption of indoctrinated opinions.

The first of the three insights is that teaching, like farming and healing, is a cooperative, not a productive, art.

The second insight is that all learning is by discovery, either by discovery alone or by discovery aided by instruction, but never by instruction alone.

The third insight is that bits of information or matters of fact retained by the memory with no understanding of the information or the facts remembered is not knowledge, but mere opinion, no better than prejudices fostered by propaganda or other sources of indoctrination.

Let me now present a slightly more expanded statement of each of these three insights.

Teaching Is a Cooperative, Not a Productive, Art

Among the useful arts, only three are cooperative arts. All the rest are productive. The three cooperative arts are farming, healing, and teaching.

In the case of such useful arts as shoemaking, shipbuilding, and cabinetmaking, the results produced would not come into existence (certainly not in preindustrial economies) were it not for the activity of the artist or craftsman—the shoemaker, the shipwright, the carpenter. The materials out of which shoes, ships, and furniture are made, left to themselves, would not naturally tend to produce those things. Such useful products emerge only when craftsmen intervene to shape or transform raw materials into the desired objects. Here human productive activity is not only the principal, but also the sole efficient cause of the result achieved.

Now consider such things as the fruits and grains we eat, the health we possess, and the knowledge or understanding we acquire. We might call these things, respectively, the products of agriculture, of medicine, and of education.

In the case of the fruits and grains, as well as edible animal organisms, prehistoric people were hunters and gatherers. This means that the edibles they consumed were all products of nature that they merely picked or killed, in order to consume them. Farming began when human beings acquired the skill of working with nature to facilitate the production of fruits and grains and also edible animal organisms. Farming thus became the first of the cooperative arts.

Long before the art of medicine came into existence, human beings possessed health as the result of natural causes. Medicine or the art of healing emerged when humans acquired the skill of cooperating with these natural processes to preserve health or facilitate its recovery after a bout of illness. Hippocrates, whom we in the West regard as the father of medicine, wrote treatises setting forth the rules of healing as a cooperative art. They were rules for controlling the regimen of patients—the food they ate, the air they breathed, their hours of waking and sleeping, the water they drank, the exercise they engaged in, and so forth. Administering drugs, introducing foreign substances into the body, Hippocrates regarded as the least cooperative of all medical treatments. Surgery he regarded as a drastic measure to be resorted to only when all cooperative methods failed; it was, strictly speaking, an *operative* rather than a *cooperative* procedure.

Finally, we come to teaching, and here it is Socrates who first depicted teaching as a cooperative art. He did so by comparing his own style of teaching with the work of the midwife. It is the mother, not the midwife, who goes through the pains of childbirth to deliver the child. The midwife merely cooperates with the process, helping the mother in her efforts, and making childbirth a little easier and a little more hygienic. Another way of saying this is to point out that teachers, like midwives, are always dispensable. Children can be born without midwives. Knowledge and understanding can be acquired without teachers, through the purely natural operations of the human mind. If any art at all is involved in this process, it is the intellectual skill of the learner, not the art of the teacher. Teachers who regard themselves as the principal, even the sole, cause of the learning that occurs in their students simply do not understand teaching as a cooperative art. They think of themselves as producing knowledge or understanding in the minds of their students, in the same way that shoemakers produce shoes out of pliable or plastic materials. Only when teachers realize that the principal cause of the learning that occurs in a student is the activity of the student's own mind do they assume the role of cooperative artists. While the activity of the learner's mind is the principal cause of all learning, it is not the sole cause. Here the teacher steps in as a secondary and cooperative cause. Just as, in the view of Hippocrates, surgery is a departure from healing as a cooperative art, so, in the view of Socrates, didactic teaching, or teaching by lecturing or telling rather than teaching by questioning and discussion, is a departure from teaching as a cooperative art.

If, however, the lecture is always accompanied by some discussion of whatever matters are didactically presented, if there is an active interchange between teacher and students through questioning, didactic teaching can, to some slight degree, become genuine teaching of knowledge understood instead of being an indoctrination of opinions to be committed to memory, retained, regurgitated on examinations, and then largely forgotten when the tests have been passed.

Learning by Instruction and by Discovery

The distinction between these two kinds of learning is incorrectly made when it is said that all learning is either by instruction or by discovery. To suppose that that is the case is to suppose that everything we learn we learn either from a teacher or by ourselves. This false dichotomy sets up the activity of the teacher as the sole cause of learning in the case of instruction, and the activity of the learner's own mind as the sole cause of learning in the case of discovery.

If genuine teaching is a cooperative, not a productive, art, then the teacher is never the sole cause of learning. If in genuine learning, the activity of the learner's own mind is always the principal cause of learning, then all learning is by discovery.

It may be either (1) unaided discovery, when the activity of the learner's mind is not only the principal but also the sole cause of learning, or (2) aided discovery, when the activity of the learner's mind is the principal, but not the sole cause of learning. The additional cause, secondary and instrumental, is the activity of the teacher. Hence, what is miscalled learning by instruction (as if the teacher's activity were the sole cause) is really learning by teacher-aided discovery. When instruction is not accompanied by discovery, when instruction makes impressions on the memory with no act of understanding by the mind, then it is not genuine teaching, but mere indoctrination. Genuine teaching, in sharp distinction from indoctrination, always consists of activities on the part of teachers that cooperate with activities performed by the minds of students engaged in discovery.

A number of corollaries follow. Everything that ever has been learned had to be learned in the first instance by unaided discovery on the part of someone. In addition, everything that can be learned can be learned in that way—without the aid of teachers. But since there are few geniuses in any generation (such as Isaac Newton) who can learn almost everything they come to learn by unaided discovery, teachers, who, strictly speaking, are dispensable instruments in the process of education, are needed as useful aids, or cooperative causes, in most of the learning that most of us do—most, but never all. The highest praise that we can give the teachers who benefited us most is to say that they helped us to know, and to understand what we know.

Mind Versus Memory, Knowledge Versus Opinion

The Greek word for mind, *nous,* identifies it with understanding. What we do not understand at all we retain solely through memory. Memory is a by-product of sense perception; understanding, an act of the intellect. Statements that are verbally remembered and recalled should never be confused with facts understood.

Correlated with this distinction between mind and memory is the distinction between knowledge and opinion. To know something as opposed to holding a mere opinion about it is to understand it in the light of relevant reasons and supporting evidence. Students acquire knowledge by the activity of their own minds, with or without the aid of teachers. How do they come by the opinions they hold, especially those acquired in the course of schooling?

They have adopted them on the naked authority of teachers who acted as if they were productive, not cooperative, artists—teachers who indoctrinated them by didactic instruction that was not accompanied by any acts of thinking or discovery on their part. I have used the phrase *naked authority* to signify the authority teachers arrogate to themselves when they expect students to accept what they tell them simply because they are teachers. The only authority to which genuine teachers, as opposed to indoctrinators, should appeal is the authority of the relevant reasons or the evidence supporting whatever is to be learned. In the absence of such authority, teachers cannot help students acquire knowledge that is understood. They can only indoctrinate them with opinions they may or may not retain for long in their memories. Opinions adopted on the naked authority of teachers have little durability. Opinions remembered, with that memory reinforced temporarily by "boning up for tests," are opinions for the most part soon forgotten.

Much more durable are the habits of skill that are formed by the kind of teaching that is coaching, which is more cooperative than didactic teaching even when what is thus taught is illuminated by understanding through discussion. Habits are not memories. They can only be formed by coaching, never by lectures and the reading of textbooks.

Most students passing, at the end of one academic year, the standardized tests currently used, which are largely tests of memory, would probably not be able to pass them if they were given the same tests without warning at the beginning of the next academic year. But if the habitually possessed skills of students in reading and writing were measured by the level of their performance at the end of one academic year and then measured in the same way at a later time, little would be lost.

The understanding of ideas and knowledge understood, once acquired, has maximum durability. What is understood cannot be forgotten, because it is a habit of the intellect, not something remembered. Anyone who comes to understand that a truth is self-evident only if it is undeniable because its opposite is unthinkable will understand it forever. To test or measure the understanding of students, the only effective instrument is an oral examination, a probing of the mind by persistent questioning that penetrates its depths as far as possible.

Concluding Remarks

The misunderstanding of teaching and learning that prevails today has resulted in the deplorable fact, amply attested by Professor John Goodlad (1984) in *A Place Called School,* that 85 percent of all classroom time is consumed by unrelieved didactic teaching that is not genuine teaching at all, but sheer indoctrination. It results in the short-lived, mainly verbal, memory of mere opinions adopted on the naked authority assumed by indoctrinating teachers.

The conception of the teacher as one who has knowledge or information that he or she transmits to students as passive recipients violates the nature of teaching as a cooperative art. It assumes that genuine learning can occur simply by instruction, without acts of thinking and understanding that involve discovery by the minds of students.

The way in which we test or examine students and the way in which we grade them determine what teachers teach and how they teach, and what students learn and how they learn. Our present methods call for indoctrination rather than genuine teaching and for memorizing rather than genuine learning. Unless we radically change our present methods of testing and grading students, we cannot expect our teachers to become cooperative artists instead of mere indoctrinators, and we cannot expect our students to become genuine learners instead of mere memorizers. All our written tests should be open-book examinations so that students prepare for them not by boning up on what they have not adequately remembered but by trying to deepen their understanding of what they were taught or by sharpening their thinking about it. If habitual skills are to be evaluated, they should be tested by performances judged adequate or inadequate. And to measure levels of understanding, the only effective instrument is an oral examination.

Four things are needed in the training of teachers to make them cooperative artists:

1. They themselves should possess whatever knowledge students are expected to acquire through their didactic

efforts, but this by itself is never enough. They must also have an understanding of everything they know in order for them to be able to supplement their didactic performance by questioning, by answering questions, by leading discussions that will help their students acquire genuine knowledge, knowledge accompanied by understanding.

2. Teachers should have the intellectual skills they are expected to coach, and they should know how to form the habits of those skills in the students they coach.
3. They should have an understanding of the ideas and issues that they wish to help students to comprehend through discussions in a Socratically conducted seminar. For this purpose they should be trained in the art of conducting seminars by observing others conducting them, by participating themselves as students in seminars conducted by others, and by conducting seminars under the critical scrutiny of masters of this art.
4. Most important of all, they should be so prepared for the profession of teaching that they understand their own primary role as that of learners. A school should be a place where teachers learn, not just a place where students learn. A learner-teacher is one whose teaching involves genuine intellectual activity on the teacher's part as well as on the student's part, not just recitation by the teacher and memorization by the students.

Reference

Goodlad, J. *A Place Called School.* New York: McGraw-Hill, 1984.

8

Truth, Understanding, and Responsibility in Teaching

David H. Smith

In *Man for Himself,* Erich Fromm (1947) distinguishes *generative* from *reproductive* perception. His point is that persons must perceive the world in two ways. The first of these is reproductive, by which one accurately understands the world as it is. Without this capacity, persons are insane; devaluing this aspect of knowing was, I thought, a problem for students in the early seventies. On the other hand, we also must perceive the possibilities of the world; we need a vision or a sense that things could be otherwise. Without this perception of ideal possibility, we would find ourselves trapped in a particular set of institutions and practices. Fromm calls this capacity to envision alternatives generative perception. It relates centrally to the capacity that we call imagination. Many students in the 1980s fall short on this score.

I do not wish to canonize Fromm's philosophical, psychological, political, or epistemological views; I disagree with almost all of them. But Fromm was insightful to distinguish these capacities of the human mind, and I will use his distinction as a jumping-off place for the first two parts of my own analysis of the moral dimensions of teaching. There are three moral dimensions in teaching: understanding, truth, and, because of those first two, a third—responsibility.

Understanding

Public education has played an ambivalent role in the teaching of values. Universities and schools in this country radically expanded in an era when knowledge was widely thought to be "value neutral." Of course, it was not and is not. Education affects our habits and our behavior, and it does this because it alters the way we understand the world. In Sri Lanka, according to Lynn White (1973), a road must be constructed around the nest of a sacred snake, a detour that would be unthinkable in the secularized West. Education influences understanding and understanding influences behavior.

It is important for us to understand the way things happen to ourselves, in society, and in nature. Persons who know nothing about genetics, social stratification, stages of human development, or geology, and who have never reflected about the religious traditions that shape their culture, are handicapped. They are hampered by their ignorance. Teaching people to understand the way things work is a way of empowering them.

However, there are several senses in which understanding cannot be value neutral. To start with, understanding is inevitably critical: one person's understanding is not necessarily as good as another's. Some explanations are better than others: Einstein's physics offers a better hypothesis than does Newton's. And some evaluations are better than others, even in the arts or in high culture. Students should understand why Rembrandt is considered a greater painter than Andy Warhol, or Mozart a greater composer than Sting. To be sure, they may challenge these evaluations, but they need to be pushed to give reasons for their judgments and to see that the issues can be rationally discussed. The core reason the pursuit of understanding is especially important is that understanding forms our ways of comprehending, interpreting, and behaving. In effect, understanding shapes one's identity.

More important for our purposes is the fact that the way we understand the world affects or determines the kinds of persons we are. People who think everyone is out to get them have a special kind of character; people who believe everything works like a machine have another. The way we understand the world shapes our identities. Moreover, character and identity are nurtured, fragmented, or destroyed by social roles and relations. Character manifests itself in choices and style of life; we speak of a person's "integrity" when that person's life reveals a correspondence between values professed and choices made.

The decisive point is the fact that effective teaching will always alter the way students perceive the world and, in consequence, will shape a student's character. Some of these effects may be inconspicuous and subtle. Some may be long-term. Some may push students in a wrong direction. But good teaching cannot avoid entering into the moral dimension.

Truth

Fromm thought generative as well as "reproductive" perception was necessary for the good life. Just so, it is vitally important that education push students beyond the level of knowing how machines, social institutions, and bodies work to the level of questioning how they ought to work, or—as I will say—how they work in truth. The call to seek the truth is a call to imagine a world beyond the brokenness we know. Understanding is not enough; students also should embark on a search for truth. Why is this so? There are two reasons: First, our comprehension will always be imperfect, and one mark of educated persons is the humility necessary to recognize this fact. It is too easy to be smug and complacent if we lack a vision of possibility beyond the actual world we understand.

Moreover, if we learn only how to operate in the actual world, we find it too easy to accept a complete moral relativism whereby one opinion is as good as another in all things. But moral relativism, understood in its most consistent logical sense, must be false. When people are deprived of educational opportunity, selectively excluded from the professions, burned in gas chambers, or betrayed by others, it matters. These events are not simply phenomena that we must understand, although that we should certainly do. They also should be evaluated, as should alternative diagnoses of diseases, scientific hypotheses, artistic performances, and the progress of students.

Of course, a good part of education consists of moving students out of ignorance and dogmatism into awareness and appreciation of worlds they did not know, but we must make a distinction between a relativism that ultimately becomes skeptical or cynical and a pluralism that acknowledges the diverse understandings of the world that human beings have and use. On many levels of teaching, the distinction will lie in the background; a large part of our teaching consists of helping students to broaden their minds and to reach out to understand new alternatives.

Education should involve a search for an adequate perspective or hypothesis or interpretation rather than discrediting the quest altogether. Too much brilliant contemporary scholarship simply celebrates academic virtuosity, suggesting that it does not matter how we understand things so long as we offer an interesting interpretation of them, and implying that although we must make judgments, our criteria for their evaluation is strictly formal. If we could make the world as easily as we make an argument, this might be true, but we cannot, as we realize when we see death and disease, childbirth and love.

Because there is a reality with which we must come to terms, some glimmers of an absolute, we have to go beyond understanding to the quest for truth. We are unlikely to attain our goal, but I think that we will be able to identify some mistakes and some factual and moral untruths—and we should not be ashamed to label them for what they are.

Responsibility

Good teaching must support a student's quest for moral truth and should encourage wondering about the right ways to conduct familial, economic, religious, and political relations. Teachers should offer readings defending alternative viewpoints, and they should neither pontificate nor treat the quest for moral truth as too hot to handle. They should encourage the kind of inquiry they seek to foster in other aspects of the curriculum.

Because understanding is inevitably morally potent and must lead into the quest for truth, I need to say a few words about a further moral dimension of education that I will call responsibility or embodiment. Institutions and teachers must try to embody those moral values they hope the student will acquire.

This is a demand that should be made carefully. James Gustafson, the great Protestant moralist, is fond of quoting Dietrich Bonhoeffer to the effect that an ethicist cannot be expected to be the embodiment of all moral qualities. With this assertion, those of us who make our living teaching ethics will quickly agree; and if we did not, observers of our behavior would note our hypocrisy. Still, when all the caveats have been entered, it remains fair to ask that anyone committed to teaching actualize an identifiable set of praiseworthy moral values. At a minimum, this might suggest that teachers should evidence a particular commitment to the truth, to following an argument where it leads, to understanding, and to supporting other (younger and older) learners. It is the exemplary character of our teachers that we all remember, even if the example was not a good one.

But the issue is more than individual; it is institutional. No college or school can embody all moral values, and it is hopeless to expect that institutional policies will pass litmus tests of purity. But the policies of schools can be fair; they can be honest, and they can show a willingness on the part of leaders to listen to argument. Disagreement about prescriptions for social problems is appropriate, but persons who are unwilling to acknowledge legacies and patterns of racial, sexual, and religious oppression only show an inability to understand accurately the world in which we live.

To this end, it is vital that an educational institution be a community in which conversation about moral matters is frequent and sustained. A teaching community should be a community not of intimacy but of shared purposes, not of ideology but of a willingness to reason. Ultimately, at the root of this community is a sense of civic responsibility, of willingness to try to shape the common life and to win and lose discussions with grace. Trying to build such a community of understanding for the pursuit of truth is the most fundamental moral dimension of education.

A first step in this direction can be taken if schools and colleges acknowledge their responsibilities in moral education and help their faculties take those responsibilities seriously. One helpful ingredient in this process involves some study of ethics by faculty. The point of this study is not moral remediation, making saints out of sinful faculty. Nor is it a way of trying to inject philosophy, theology, or ethical theory into all courses. Certainly one should not expect faculty study of ethics to lead to faculty agreement on moral issues. But the study can provide faculty with a language of discussion, and it can help them realize that the resolution of moral problems is neither as arbitrary as we learned in the fifties nor as obvious as was supposed in the seventies.

What will the faculty talk about? The usual topics in the study of ethics include questions about the ideal world and life, discussion of the basic rights and duties of persons and the effect of professional or social roles on those rights and duties, as well as the questions of character and virtue that I have made central here. There are at least as many ways to study and teach these things as there are ways to teach first grade. Knowing the differences among us and the hurt or passion argument about them can engender, it may seem safer to ignore the moral dimension of education. This strategic attempt at a retreat from reality is understandable—but doomed to failure. Because good education always affects character, responsible faculties must get together and figure out how to affect character for the better. We must model reasonable inquiring into moral matters.

References

Fromm, E. *Man for Himself.* New York: Holt, Rinehart & Winston, 1947.

White, L. "The Historical Roots of Our Ecological Crisis." In I. Barbour (ed.), *Western Man and Environmental Ethics.* Reading, Mass.: Addison-Wesley, 1973.

9

Teaching and Morality: The Knowledge Most Worth Having

Warren A. Nord

Morality orients education: it directs, structures, sometimes constrains, and provides content for teaching. In fact, the primary purpose of education is to initiate students into an informed, critical appreciation of the moral dimension of life. This being the case, it follows that moral knowledge is the knowledge most worth having for teachers. Of course, precisely what the moral dimension of life is, and how teachers should go about initiating students into it, are neither easy to say nor uncontroversial.

We can introduce a certain amount of clarity into our discussion by distinguishing a number of different ways in which morality relates to teaching. They overlap to some considerable extent, and where I draw the lines is somewhat arbitrary. Moreover, I shall provide only the briefest schematic account of each relationship. My purpose is more to map out the moral terrain of teaching than to provide a richly nuanced picture of any particular feature of the landscape. Still, I hope that this outline will orient us morally in the world of education and establish the position of moral knowledge at the conceptual center of this world. I will conclude with a few suggestions for integrating the study of morality into teacher education.

Moral Terrain of Teaching

Professional Ethics. We are, all of us, moral beings. Simply by virtue of being persons, we have certain obligations—to tell the truth, to promote peace, and to be compassionate, for example. These are obligations that teachers, like everyone else, should act on in their professional as well as personal lives. But teachers are also members of a profession. They hold an "office" defined by special moral obligations. Some of these obligations cut across all professions—to keep up in one's field, to maintain confidentiality in professional relationships, to avoid discrimination on the basis of race or sex. Others are peculiar to the profession of teaching—to grade exams fairly, to keep parents informed, to try to understand what students say. In the National Education Association (NEA) "Code of Ethics of the Education Profession" (Soltis and Strike, 1985, pp. xiii-xv), thirteen of the sixteen principles are essentially matters of what I am calling professional ethics. For example, the teacher:

> I.7 Shall not use professional relationships with students for private advantage.
> II.2 Shall not misrepresent his/her professional qualifications.
> II.7 Shall not knowingly make false or malicious statements about a colleague [Soltis and Strike, 1985, pp. xiv-xv].

These rules are neither morally arbitrary nor simply conventional. They have moral force: it is morally good that the profession of teaching is constituted so that teachers understand themselves as having such obligations. Such codes of ethics embody a widely shared understanding of right and wrong action. This is not to say that some principles cannot be controversial or vague; some may come to be recognized as misguided. Nonetheless, to function well as a teacher, one must have knowledge of such moral principles and the moral justifications for them.

Public Policy. Professional ethics is largely internal to teaching as a profession; it guides and constrains actions within the system. Public policy questions, on the other hand, are about the shape of the system itself and about its relationships to government and to the public; often these questions come from outside the profession—from politicians or public figures. Of course, this distinction is not hard and fast: controversial matters of public policy, when resolved, often give rise to new principles of professional ethics. For example, ending racial or sexual discrimination—a policy question—gave rise to principles of nondiscrimination, which have been incorporated into professional ethics.

Any list of public policy issues relating to education will be long, but obvious ones would include the sources and extent of funding for public education, regulation of private education, teachers' unions, merit pay, accountability, competency testing, tracking, and school prayer. And, while we have settled some questions relating to discrimination, others, such as affirmative action, remain controversial.

I make two assumptions in distinguishing public policy as a domain of moral knowledge required of teachers. First, policy questions are fundamentally moral questions. We may sometimes classify them as more narrowly political—in part because answers to such questions are pursued politically—and, of course, they often have legal, even constitutional, aspects. But the root issues in many, if not most, public policy debates are moral issues that revolve around competing interests and claims about human rights and obligations, justice, and the nature of the good society. Policy issues relating to school funding require us to assess the fairness of a policy's impact on people and communities at different levels of poverty and affluence. Competency testing requires us to ask questions about the impact of tests on different groups of people and about the ways in which various forms of discrimination are morally justifiable or not justifiable.

Second, I conceive of teachers as more than technicians hired to perform clearly defined tasks. To be a professional requires one to be competent in making judgments about the institutional environment within which one acts. One of the great problems of our time is that, too often, professionals are not educated to understand and appreciate the moral and institutional contexts of their professions. The result is physicians and lawyers and business executives who pursue their narrow goals oblivious to the moral structure, relationships, and goals of professional medicine, law, and business. And so it often is with teachers and education. Teachers as teachers—as professionals rather than technicians—are obligated to have the moral knowledge necessary to participate responsibly in public debate over educational policy.

The Ethics of Teaching. The act of teaching has a particular moral structure that warrants differentiating the ethics of teaching from what I have called professional ethics. Teaching must be conducted honestly, in a way that respects the rationality of both teacher and student. This is the case for teaching any subject—at least as long as students are sufficiently mature to reason about that subject. The three NEA code of ethics principles that are not directed to professional ethics define aspects of the ethics of teaching. The teacher:

> I.1 Shall not unreasonably restrain the student from independent action in the pursuit of learning.
> I.2 Shall not unreasonably deny the student access to varying points of view.
> I.3 Shall not deliberately suppress or distort subject matter relevant to the student's progress [Soltis and Strike, 1985, p. xiv].

In effect, these principles prohibit indoctrination and, indirectly, affirm a moral context for teaching that nurtures the rationality of students.

Indoctrination is a form of dishonesty and as such is intrinsically wrong. It is wrong to withhold evidence, to use spurious arguments, to restrain attempts to follow reason, and to attempt to persuade where good reasons and sound argument are wanting. Indoctrination is also wrong because it has the effect of undercutting the moral community, which sustains intellectual inquiry. Teaching, like research, must take place in a context marked by openness, fairness, trust, respect for true authority, and reasonableness. When these principles are violated, we lose confidence that truth, rather than the vested interests of our teachers or the educational and political system, is being served.

Mortimer Adler's primary concern in Chapter Seven in this volume is with the ethics of teaching (though he does not call it that). Adler argues that teaching is a "cooperative" art, which requires the participation of the learner. The teacher is not competent to "produce" knowledge by planting it directly and didactically in the mind of the student; rather, the teacher must be the Socratic midwife, nursing the student along. But it is the student who, in the activity of learning, "discovers" the truth. This leads Adler to a rather harsh conclusion: lectures are no more than "indoctrination of opinions to be committed to memory, retained, regurgitated on examinations, and then largely forgotten when the tests have been passed"—unless, of course, they are accompanied by discussion. For students truly to know something, they must be able to place it in the context of "relevant reasons and supporting evidence" rather than simply to accept it "on the naked authority of teachers" who have "indoctrinated them by didactic instruction that was not accompanied by any acts of thinking or discovery on their part."

I believe Adler is telling us something both true and important—though I suspect he has overstated his case a little. Surely lectures unaccompanied by discussion do not automatically qualify as indoctrination; if so, to read any book is to be indoctrinated, for books do not teach by discussion. And, I can imagine Socratic discussion which, intentionally or not, is clearly indoctrinating because the reasoning is shallow or overtly ideological. The sound and tremendously important point is that knowledge always involves more than passive acceptance of facts or a point of view; it involves being able to reason about one's subject, and that is something one learns to do most effectively in discussion conducted in ways that respect the rationality of students and the authority of good reasons.

Of course, what counts as good reasons is highly controversial—and often ideologically loaded. To what extent might Adler's "relevant reasons and supporting evidence" be relative to a theoretical or cultural context? How do we define what are to count as legitimate, contending theories or schools of thought? How much background information (historical or cultural) must a student have to be able to reason responsibly about an idea or a theory? How do we know what can be accepted on authority and who the legitimate authorities are? How much is the teacher justified in acting as an authority with students? How much should the teacher guide the discussion and draw conclusions? How does the rational maturity of students at different ages weigh in the balance? These are thorny matters, for they revolve around an extremely controversial subject—what it means to be reasonable.

Many critics of the Left argue that, in fact, public education is committed to reproducing the dominant culture and sustaining the status quo by conveying it uncritically to students. The "hidden curriculum" of schooling is to keep students passive by feeding them (carefully selected) information, by not raising critical questions, and by reinforcing the idea of teacher as authority. On the other hand, some critics on the Right argue that some teachers constantly undermine authority by asking critical questions to which they allow no answers, in effect denying that there is any truth and putting everything up for grabs. For such teachers, there are no "right answers." Clearly, a teacher's ethic of teaching conveys to students an attitude toward truth, authority, right and wrong. Teachers can encourage a mindless orthodoxy or a mindless relativism, or they can encourage intellectual honesty, disciplined thinking, a respect for reasonableness, and, in effect, a Socratic concern for living the examined life. David Smith writes in his chapter in this volume a "teaching community should be a community not of intimacy but of shared purposes, not of ideology but of a willingness to reason. . . . Trying to build such a community of understanding for the pursuit of truth is the most fundamental moral dimension of education."

Moral Education. A central virtue of persons is reasonableness, a commitment to living the examined life. In teaching ethically, in nurturing our reasonableness, schools are doing moral education, but there is more to being moral than being reasonable (though it is often our reasonableness that allows us to figure out what is moral). It is commonly believed that teachers have a special responsibility for promoting the moral development and education of students more generally, and to some extent, this must happen before students reach the age of reason. Such "education" may or may not be a matter of teaching; if it is, it is often argued to be teaching of a particular kind. Such moral education is something quite different from the ethics of teaching.

One common position is that moral education is primarily a matter of what is often called *character education.* It is directed to making students honest, hardworking, fair-minded, caring, responsible, and courteous—to developing their moral characters, to instilling widely accepted moral virtues. The conventional wisdom is that the development of moral character must begin early, certainly before children are old enough to reason about morality. As such, it cannot be taught directly, but is more a matter of socialization than it is of direct teaching: students become moral by being rewarded and punished, by internalizing the values of role models, by accepting as normative the moral ambience of the school. Students become honest by being treated honestly; they learn to care by being treated in a caring way. This kind of moral education is incumbent on all teachers, for all teachers reward and punish, all teachers are potential role models, and all teachers establish a moral ambience within their classrooms. In fact, such moral education is inevitable. That being the case, the relevant questions are these: Do teachers self-consciously appreciate this aspect of their role as teachers so that they do it effectively? Is such education sufficient for moral purposes, or does it need to be supplemented in some way?

Many conservatives believe that character education should also be a matter of overt, moral (and perhaps religious) teaching; teachers should tell stories about America or the Christian tradition that reinforce and provide foundations for the moral attitudes and beliefs that educators hold to be correct, and that children must come to acquire (Bennett, 1988).

The correlative liberal position is that education, if it is not to be indoctrinating, must foster critical thinking. To be moral involves more than acting in ways that (might) happen to be moral; it requires some understanding of alternatives and some recognition of personal autonomy on the part of individuals. The two dominant models over the past several decades have been Kohlberg's (1981) model and the model developed by the values clarification movement. For Kohlberg, a developmental psychologist, children mature through a series of invariant stages of moral development. It is the teacher's responsibility to appreciate the current stages of students' development and, by employing the techniques of moral reasoning, to prompt them to ascend to higher stages in sequence.

The values clarification movement has had somewhat less ambitious goals. Ever wary of the possibility of moral indoctrination, it has had the limited goal of helping students to clarify the values they already have, rather than to propose new values. Unlike with Kohlberg, there is no assumption of stages or better and worse ways of reasoning about moral matters. Teachers are to remain neutral. In fact, the values clarification movement has been skittish about the language of morality and much prefers the more neutral term *values*. According to both Kohlberg and the values clarifiers, moral education is done overtly, through consideration of moral dilemmas or exercises that prompt students to think about their values (Kohlberg, 1981; Raths, Harmin, and Simon, 1978; Association for Supervision and Curriculum Development, 1988).

More radical critics argue that such efforts at moral (or values) education are bound to be superficial and have little effect on students. They ignore the power of the hidden curriculum to induce passivity and the power of entrenched bureaucracies to shape the curriculum ideologically; they divorce the discussion of morality from historical traditions of oppression, and they throw students on their own resources when they should be exposing the students to ideological critiques of our basic institutions and values (Giroux, 1988a).

Of course, many parents are wary of any attempt on the part of schools to engage in moral education (other than some degree of character education, which is, in any case, inevitable), suspecting that their particular understanding of morality will not be the one that wins the school day. Since the courts keep religious indoctrination out of the classroom, and since schools are often perceived as bastions of liberalism (or secular humanism), many conservative parents end up arguing for no moral education in the schools. Schools should teach just the facts and leave morality up to home and church. Correlatively, many liberal parents are suspicious of what they take to be the conservative moral and religious beliefs of teachers. Some believe that children should have the right to choose their own values. In either case, they are deeply suspicious of talk of moral education. Moreover, many teachers and educational administrators, recognizing the potential controversy connected with morally sensitive issues, try, as best they can, to ignore them. All of these factors combine to leave the state of moral education much less enlightened than it might be.

There is one kind of moral education about which there is considerable consensus, however: education for democracy. Amy Gutmann (1987) recently has argued that it is precisely in a pluralistic society in which there is deep disagreement over morality and the nature of the good life that democracy can be a point of agreement. What Gutmann calls *democratic virtue* becomes the essential characteristic of citizens. The task of schools is to teach students the virtues of democracy—tolerance, reasonableness, and nondiscrimination—and to develop in them a deliberative character that makes the open and informed discussion of moral and political issues a matter of habit. Only if citizens possess such virtue can democracy prosper.

There is remarkable agreement about the legitimacy and importance of education for democratic virtue in our society. We are unabashedly open about the goodness of democracy: we not only teach students about democracy in required courses in civics and history but we also have them practice it—albeit in rather constrained ways—in student government. The great virtue of democracy is that it embodies a set of core values that hold us together as a society and, at the same time, allow great liberty for us to act on our own understanding of the good life. Like those basic virtues of character on which most all of us agree, democratic virtue becomes a kind of moral bedrock for grounding education. Conservatives, liberals, and radicals all find something of tremendous importance in our democratic tradition, in its key texts (the Declaration of Independence, the Constitution, the *Federalist Papers,* the Gettysburg Address, and important court rulings), and in the potential of democracy for their particular vision of the good society.

Moral Content of Curriculum and Subject Matter. Overt moral education employs special problems, exercises, stories, and content for the self-conscious purpose of promoting the moral development of students. It is also the case that much of the curriculum and ordinary subject matter of schooling has an implicit moral content that contributes to the moral education of students—and that places special demands on teachers.

The heated, ongoing debates over the place of Western civilization in education and E. D. Hirsch's (1987) proposals regarding cultural literacy suggest something of the emotional power that curriculum questions can generate. Many liberals and critics on the Left argue that Hirsch and advocates of Western civilization courses support (implicitly if not explicitly) a view of the world shaped by male, white Europeans—a view that is insensitive to women and to various non-Western and minority traditions and subcultures.

On the other hand, many conservative religious thinkers have grown increasingly vocal about what they call *secular humanism*—the denigration of traditional religion and moral values—in much of modern education. For some, this is a matter of overt, ideological secularism, such as teaching evolution or sex education. For others, it is less a matter of overt secularism than it is a matter of neglect of religious ideas and values. Richard Baer (1985, p. 17), for example, argues that to emphasize math and science in the curriculum (as many of the recent reform proposals do) is to undercut traditional religion: "Math and science prepare one to be economically competent, to be successful in competing (the Latin root is the same) for the material goods and social status of this world. Bible, theology, music, poetry, and art are not considered helpful in preparing one for such competition, and they are not much emphasized. . . . [C]omputer courses will inevitably win out over classes on prayer or the devotional life in our present public schools. Physical education will take priority over spiritual formation. The concerns of the secular world will leave little room for religious concerns or things pertaining to the world to come."

Of course, most of us do not even consider including theology in the curriculum or the devotional life of the student as a proper concern of public education. There are, no doubt, good reasons for insisting that public education be secular; but the commitment to secular education undoubtedly carries with it profound implications for the moral and religious character of the students we educate.

In *A Place Called School,* John Goodlad (1984) argues that tracking has a powerful influence on the way students are treated, with devastating results. Indeed, Goodlad suggests that his findings on this matter may be the "most significant" of his report (p. 152). Many of the effects of tracking are well known, and I will just mention one that is of some importance to Goodlad. High-track courses "devoted more time to relatively high level cognitive processes—making judgments, drawing inferences, effecting syntheses, using symbolism, and so on. Low track classes devoted a much larger share of instructional time to rote learning and the application of knowledge and skills. . . . Teachers of high track English classes were more likely than others to seek in their students the more independent thinking behaviors. Teachers of low track classes much more frequently sought the more conforming types of classroom behavior" (pp. 153–154). While Goodlad does not use this language, what is at issue is the difference between two quite different models of moral character.

Often the moral implications of the curriculum go unnoticed; so it is with the treatment of potentially controversial subject matter in various courses. No one can doubt the presence of an explicit moral theology in the *New England Primers,* the *Webster Spellers,* or the *McGuffey Readers* of the eighteenth and nineteenth centuries (Spring, 1986). We make no effort, as I have suggested, to hide our moral commitment to democracy in required history and civics courses; indeed, democracy sometimes seems to be treated as a kind of civil religion. But we do not just teach generic democracy; we teach a particular, ideologically loaded version, as Francis Fitzgerald (1980) shows in fascinating detail in her study of American history and government textbooks. The lessons of history, and the goals and central values of democracy, change with the times and the powers that be.

Sometimes, the moral commitments of an author are driven underground by the need to (or at least appear to) be objective, scientific, and value free. I recently reviewed six economics textbooks and nine home economics textbooks approved for use in North Carolina high school courses. Each of these books claimed the mantle of social science and objectivity; each steered clear of moral and religious language and claims. At the same time, each provided an account of human nature, values, and decision making. The economics books portrayed persons as essentially self-interested utility maximizers; the economic world was constituted by the competition for scarce resources; decision making was to be guided by the value-free calculus of economists. None of the books explored, much less took seriously, moral or religious traditions according to which people are essentially social, with irreduceable moral obligations; none considered the possibility that society should be conceived as a community in which justice is pursued cooperatively; moral and religious knowledge had no place in this scheme of things; at best it was an externality. Whether or not one believes that the purpose of teaching economics should be to provide technical, value-free understanding to students, these books did much more: they contained accounts of human nature, values, and decision making that stand in marked tension—if not conflict—with traditional moral and religious accounts.

The home economics books each opened with at least one, often several, chapters on human nature, values, and decision making, and most went on to discuss moral issues such as dating, premarital sex, sex roles, child rearing, and sometimes abortion. They all started from a psychological analysis of human nature drawn largely, if loosely, from Abraham Maslow and Carl Rogers: our highest good is self-actualization; values are ultimately matters of free choice, and decision making is essentially a matter of acting in ways that maximize whatever it is that we most deeply value. There was no suggestion in the books that one can choose the right or wrong values; they said virtually nothing about conscience, law, tradition, religion, or even the suffering and well-being of other people, as providing standards against which one's actions must be judged. Autonomy and self-actualization are the goals. One book (Ryder, 1985, p. 75) declared that unfortunately, not all students are capable of setting up a "dependable value system for themselves" but are "dependent upon family members or social institutions to guide them."

In these books, traditional moral categories drop out of the picture, to be replaced by the categories of social science, objectivity, professionalism, and technique. Talk of values replaces talk of good and evil. Neither kind of book uses moral or religious theory in the development of an account of human nature, values, or decision making. (The economics texts do discuss Marxism and socialism, however, and in this they are much less parochial than the home economics texts, which offer no alternative theoretical frameworks for understanding their subject matter.)

Moral education is not simply a matter of role models and socialization, values clarification and moral dilemmas. To some considerable extent, students acquire their sense of who they are and how to make moral judgments from the content of texts and courses, and from the emphases of the curriculum, even when they do not seem, at first glance, to be related to morality. What students learn about economic and social behavior, for example, legitimizes ways of acting; it provides an implicit morality. Moreover, teachers will always pursue the ethics of teaching only superficially if they are not aware of the profound moral content of the subject matter they teach. If they do not recognize the implicit morality for what it is, teachers will not subject it to the kind of critical scrutiny it requires; they will not prompt discussion of how the implicit morality compares with other moral or religious theories and traditions. Indoctrination by incompetence will be the result.

Education as a Moral Enterprise

John Goodlad (1984, p. 238) has suggested that "Teachers are oriented to teaching particular things—the particular things they were taught in school. Relating these particular things to some larger purpose is not something they think about very much or have been prepared to do." What teachers actually teach in the classroom often has little to do with the morally admirable sentiments conveyed in school mission statements, and often they conceive of algebra and English as no more than the necessary steps to doing well on standardized achievement tests. Goodlad (pp. 241–242) argues that it "is difficult to be sanguine about the moral and ethical learnings accompanying many of the experiences of schooling. My perception is that the emphasis on individual performance and achievement would be more conducive to cheating than to the development of moral integrity. I have difficulty seeing how much of what goes on in classrooms would contribute to understanding and appreciating the contributions of others. I see little in the curriculum, explicit or implicit, likely to promote keen awareness of humanity." He bemoans the "paucity of vicarious experiences designed to connect students in some more passionate and compassionate way with the wholeness of human existence and especially with such existential qualities as hope, courage, and love of humankind" (p. 243).

It is worth noting that such language is relatively foreign to most of the commission reports on educational reform of the last few years. The overriding theme of these reports is the importance of education in preparing students to participate in the economy—though the prescription has typically been for a stronger education in the basics, particularly in math and science, rather than for vocational education more narrowly defined. I do not want to trivialize this point of view, but education for economic development—like education in reading, writing, and arithmetic—is, by itself, a profoundly poor substitute for what is truly important. The perennial "basics" of education and the marketplace should be recognized for what they are: necessary foundations that put students in a position where they can begin to understand, appreciate, and support themselves while they pursue that which is more fully meaningful.

My topic is the knowledge most worth having for the purpose of teacher education. Well, what is the knowledge most worth having generally? It is the knowledge, I would suggest, that gives us a sense of what makes life meaningful. And what is that? Any account will be controversial, but I suspect that I will say nothing deeply disturbing in proposing that what makes life meaningful would certainly include love; having a place in, and an identity as a member of, various communities (a family, a local community, a cultural tradition, a nation, or the community of humankind); moral purpose in one's life (caring, minimizing suffering and correcting injustice, promoting peace, living according to conscience);

religion; work that draws on one's abilities and contributes to the good of others; art; and the life of the mind.

The purpose of education should be to initiate students into an appreciation for, and a critical understanding of, what is most meaningful in life. Education should be structured so as best to realize this end, and teachers should be constantly aware of how they, through their teaching and actions, contribute to this end.

What does this have to do with morality? I want to suggest that in an important sense, what is at issue here is the moral dimension of life. Too much we conceive of morality as a matter of constraints, rules, and commandments, which hem us in by telling us what we cannot do. (People who harp constantly on what we ought not do come to be called *moralistic*—a common term of opprobrium.) Too little we think of morality as something positive, as providing students with a critical appreciation of what is meaningful in life. Morality is also a matter of caring and community, of reasonableness and ideals, of mores and morale. Morality in this broad sense empowers us by orienting us in the world, by nurturing our sense of what is meaningful, and by supporting us emotionally and intellectually in our efforts to make a life. And this is what education should do: orient us in the world, nurture our sense of what is meaningful, and emotionally and intellectually prepare us to live our lives (Purpel, 1988).

In defining education as primarily a moral enterprise, I am no doubt using the word *moral* in a somewhat expanded sense, but I know of no better word. *Spiritual* suggests a too narrowly religious conception; *moral-political-cultural-spiritual* may be more accurate, but it is much too cumbersome. Much of what I am getting at is captured in the old term *artes liberales,* but nowadays the liberal arts are much too diffuse and too removed from normative questions of meaning and morality to serve my purposes (Kimball, 1986). Moreover, the moral purposes of education are served not just through the liberal arts curriculum; they are served also through caring, through the moral ambience of schooling, and through the ethics of teaching.

Literature and history are the two subjects that have been, to a greater or lesser extent, the core subjects in education, K–12, and it is worth reflecting briefly on why this should be so. The study of literature is not primarily about learning how to read in any technical sense; nor is it about meter and plot and symbolism and characterization. These are but means to ends; this is preparatory, foundational, for what is truly important. Literature, properly taught, humanizes us by nurturing our ability to learn about the moral dimension of life: it informs our imaginations; it enables us to empathize with people different from us; it initiates us into an informed discussion of, and appreciation for, human love (its shapes and variations, its conscious and unconscious manifestations, its relationship to sexuality), the obligations and meaning of membership in families and communities, the sense of when it might be necessary to follow one's conscience rather than the law or dictates of one's community, the need for caring, and how to respond to suffering. Of course, literature is not just this; it is also art. Indeed, it is the art that, in large part, gives great literature its profound moral power. But it is the moral content of literature that makes it so important in schooling (Gardner, 1978).

Similarly, the purpose of studying history is not abstract knowledge of dates and historical events; it is through the study of history that we acquire some concrete sense of what brings about human justice and injustice, human flourishing and suffering. History provides us with some sense of our places in various traditional communities. We should study history, as Leszek Kolakowski has reminded us, to know "who we are" (1986, p. 35). Too much, modernity rips us free from the sense that we live within historical traditions. People with no sense of history are like amnesiacs: they lose their identities and any sense of what they are doing in life. The study of history orients us in the world; by telling us where we as a community (not just as individuals) have come from, it provides us with a sense of direction.

Only if teachers have some sense of the moral purposes of education, and the implications for their individual disciplines in particular, can they convey to students the significance and meaning of their subjects. Our educational system is designed to make students into certain kinds of persons—persons quite different from those created by the educational systems of the Soviet Union or Colonial America or ancient Israel. Education helps give students an identity, some sense of their places in history and the world, some sense of their responsibilities and rights, some sense of how to resolve conflicts, some sense of what is meaningful in life, and some sense of the knowledge most worth having. We cannot avoid these matters; they come with the territory. Education is inescapably moral. The problem is we do not face up to this fact; hence we do not educate well.

Teacher Education

Teacher education should always build on a solid liberal education and should take place in a context of professional and caring relationships between students and faculty. Much of the moral understanding and sensitivity we require of teachers is learned indirectly through these aspects of their education. But there is much more than this to the moral education of teachers. I will comment briefly on three aspects of teacher education in particular: ethics courses; the pedagogy of teaching ethics; and the qualifications for teaching ethics.

Ethics Courses. Considerable debate has taken place about whether ethics should be taught in special courses or integrated into the entire curriculum (Hastings Center, 1980, pp. 72–75). I have argued that moral assumptions and judgments are inextricably woven into most subject matter, and into the shape of the curriculum generally. All teachers, all faculty in schools of education, should be much more aware than they are of the implicit moral content of their courses and curriculum, and they should address that implicit morality in their teaching. But given the degree of teaching specialization and the extent of the misplaced ideological commitment to value-free scholarship and teaching, I am not optimistic about a greater emphasis on morality.

Neither am I optimistic about the possibility of adding required courses on ethics to an already full teacher training curriculum. This possibility does lend itself more readily to making a few, all-too-brief suggestions about what is most needed, however. (Much of what I propose is being done to some significant extent, with variations, in many existing courses.)

I would have all prospective teachers take at least four courses that deal explicitly with morality. First, they should take a course on those policy issues at the center of contemporary public discussion of education, for teachers are obligated to understand and to help guide the public discussion of the future of education. Second, they should take a course on moral issues in education—particularly professional ethics, the ethics of teaching, and moral education—for teachers are obligated to pursue the moral goals and to respect the moral constraints of the profession of teaching. Third, they should be introduced to the moral assumptions and judgments that inform and help shape the theories, the research methodologies, and the teaching methods employed in the particular subjects they will be teaching. And fourth, they should be required to take a course on the broad historical, cultural, and moral contexts within which the profession of teaching exists. This course should provide the foundation for the others; it should precede them, and although the others might be semester courses, this preliminary course should last a full year.

I trust that the content of the three semester-long courses is evident from what I have already said, but I need to say a little more about the content of the foundation course. Morality is controversial in our modern world (though too much can be made of this: there is, after all, much morality on which people agree). To be educated morally is not simply to be given the moral truth; it is to be initiated into a critical discussion about morality. This, of course, was Adler's point about education generally. Morally educated persons, and certainly morally educated teachers, must understand what the various voices in the ongoing discussion about morality are saying; they must have a critically informed understanding of morality.

Hence, all teachers should be required to take a yearlong course in those "live" cultural and philosophical traditions (to use William James's language) that shape modern debates over morality and education (James, 1977, pp. 717-718). This course would not be simply a course in educational foundations or the philosophy of education; those are already much too narrow. Nor would it be a course only in formal theories in philosophical ethics (though that would be a part of it) for that focus also is too narrow. My course would explore competing traditions for conceptualizing human nature, society, and morality—traditions that are sometimes explicit, but often implicit within the academic and public discourse of our time: utilitarianism and cost-benefit analysis; Freudian, behavioral, and humanistic psychology; conservative and liberal religious traditions; Kantian (and Kohlbergian) accounts of moral autonomy and reason; recent feminist accounts of an ethic of caring; and individualistic and communitarian views of persons and society.

Education is not an autonomous discipline; it is entwined within a larger cultural and philosophical context, and the goal of my course would be to establish the shape of the larger discussion and its implications for education. We understand what words mean only in the context of sentences and paragraphs; we understand historical figures only in the context of their times; and we understand our own values and the conflicts in which we are engaged only when we can place them in the context of various cultural and philosophical movements and traditions. The philosophical theories embodied in these movements provide us with guidance, with resources for developing our positions. In fact, we are often unaware of the controversial nature of our moral positions until we can place them in the context of a larger debate. Most important, we appreciate the strengths and weaknesses of our positions only if we have an understanding of competing traditions and are open to their implications.

Moral Pedagogy. A good course on ethics must promote four somewhat different, if integrated, kinds of learning—all of which are likely to be necessary if sound moral judgment is to be the result.

First, ethics courses must nurture moral feelings and the moral imagination. The relationship between feeling and reason in ethics is complex and controversial, but certainly morality is grounded to some considerable extent in the moral feelings—compassion, guilt, hope, despair, dignity, mercy, and love, for example. When ethics is stripped of its emotional dimension, it becomes artificial, abstract, and lifeless. In some ways, the moral imagination is just the imagination applied to moral matters, so we must be able to understand imaginatively what life would be like if various actions were taken, or policies adopted. The peculiarly moral aspect of imagination involves being able to understand and feel how the lives of people other than us—particularly people who are very much unlike us—would be affected by various actions and policies. We must be able to imagine ourselves as them—with their feelings, their hopes, their suffering, their values, and their traditions. The ability to do this does not come easily. To do it well we must do it self-consciously, for we are likely to assume uncritically either that people are just like us or that they fit some easily understood stereotype. Moral imagination must be informed by a great deal of personal, cultural, and historical understanding.

Second, decision making is always guided by moral principles, theories, and traditions, no matter how implicit they might be in our thinking and feeling. I do not mean to suggest that we have access to any neat and systematic body of moral principles, but we do have some often vague sense of what generally makes for rightness and wrongness in our actions. Few of us are so creative as to be able to invent moral principles, theories, and traditions on our own; we inherit or acquire them from the various historical communities of which we are a part. To become moral is, in part, to learn the moral principles, theories, and traditions of these communities.

But third, no matter how clear and helpful our moral principles and theories may be, our decisions and our actions always take place in particular situations and affect particular individuals. If it is often clear what we are obligated to do, it is also often unclear. Situations are muddied by conflicting obligations or by conflicting rights, by the hopes and expectations of people who do not share our values, by the necessarily uncertain consequences of our actions, or by misunderstandings of the motivations of other actors in the situation. Ethics is always contextual, and the analytical and imaginative skills needed to sort out particular situations are often considerable. We need a great deal of practice.

Fourth and finally, there is philosophical ethics. Many conflicting moral principles, theories, and traditions are parts of various historical and ideological communities. If we are not to abdicate our responsibility to think responsibly about how to live our lives and practice our professions, we must self-consciously explore the merits of these differing traditions. Indeed, to some considerable extent, morality requires us constantly to reflect on, test, and organize our moral feelings so that our considered moral judgment is the result of more than accident of birth in a particular culture. How one sorts out, confirms, or falsifies moral principles and theories is the subject of philosophical ethics.

Whether there is such a thing as moral knowledge at all is, I suppose, the fundamental question of philosophical ethics, and it is a question no teacher can ignore. Much recent discussion in education has focused on this question because it is at the heart of Allan Bloom's (1987) critique of American education. And, arguably, much hangs on our response to the question. Is morality the will of God, inherent in the laws of nature, right reason, cultural tradition, the interests of power elites, or is it the free, existential choice of each individual? How we answer this question will inevitably shape our confidence in dealing with moral issues in the classroom and how we teach students about morality. Of course, an inescapable part of modern life is that there will be no consensus answer; the pluralism of our culture has led to the proliferation of private moral languages. Indeed, it is difficult to carry on a conversation about moral issues even with people we know well, for we mean such different things with moral language; we talk at cross-purposes, reasoning about moral issues is frustrated, and political and legal solutions to moral problems become necessary. This itself becomes a profound moral problem: how, morally, do we live and teach in a world divided by deep moral disagreement (Adams, 1969, 1975; Bellah and others, 1985)?

Moral feelings and the imagination are nourished through biography and autobiography, through anthropological studies and film, but especially through imaginative literature, which better than any other medium takes us inside the hearts and minds of people. We can learn moral principles, theories, and traditions in relatively straightforward ways through moral, religious, and other cultural texts. Case studies force the application of general moral principles and traditions to real-life problems; they inevitably reveal the complexity and richness of life and, often, the moral ambiguity of particular situations. And, through the study of philosophy and philosophical ethics, we can learn something about sorting out and critically assessing conflicting principles, theories, and traditions. A good ethics course will draw on all of these sources to prepare teachers for their task as moral agents. To focus on any one or two of these will oversimplify and distort the workings of the moral enterprise.

It is worth mentioning that the use of primary source material in courses that deal with ethics is itself a moral requirement of teaching. We do not take people and their intellectual and cultural traditions seriously if we do not try to understand them as they understand themselves. This means reading their own accounts of what they believe and how they pursue the good life—not settling for a description strained through the conceptual net of an observer (no matter how objective that observer tries to be). And it goes without saying that whatever the text, we use it to inform critical, reasoned discussion—not rote learning.

Qualifications for Teaching Ethics. Faculty in schools of education (like all faculty) should have the knowledge most worth having. They should be liberally educated and morally informed, and they should model the ethics of teaching. Only faculty who have done significant academic work in ethics should teach the courses that deal primarily with ethics. I do not deny that one can be admirably moral in his or her personal life without ever studying ethics, but I am highly dubious of the claim that anyone can teach the kinds of courses, using the kind of pedagogy I have suggested, without some serious academic study of ethics. The authors of the Hastings Center (1980) report on *The Teaching of Ethics in Higher Education* argue, quite reasonably, that professional school faculty who teach professional ethics should have at least a year of academic study in ethics. It is also true, of course, that turning these courses over to the philosophy or religious studies department may prove counterproductive, for faculty there may be as ignorant of the study of education as faculty in schools of education may be of the study of ethics. Team teaching, when feasible, is a happy solution to the problem; certainly much more interdisciplinary work is needed all around.

Conclusion

Teachers are more than technicians, conveyers of formal, inert knowledge, whose every move is structured by a precise curriculum and narrowly defined authority. I conceive of teachers much as Henry Giroux does when he argues that they should be "transformative intellectuals" (Giroux, 1988b). It is their task to make their students sensitive to and knowledgeable about the moral contours of life. This is as true for faculty in schools of education as it is for teachers, K–12. This is no small responsibility for teachers to bear. It is not just another responsibility tacked on to an already burdensome list of responsibilities; it is the central responsibility of teachers. Everything else is preparation for this. That is why moral knowledge is, for teachers, the knowledge most worth having.

References

Adams, E. M. "Ethics and the Aims of Education." In W. T. Blackstone and G. L. Newsome (eds.), *Education and Ethics.* Athens: University of Georgia Press, 1969.

Adams, E. M. *Philosophy and the Modern Mind.* Chapel Hill: University of North Carolina Press, 1975.

Association for Supervision and Curriculum Development. *Moral Education in the Life of the School.* Alexandria, Va.: Association for Supervision and Curriculum Development, 1988.

Baer, R. *Censorship and the Public Schools.* Milwaukee, Wis.: Catholic League for Religious and Civil Rights, 1985.

Bellah, R., and others. *Habits of the Heart: Individualism and Community in American Life.* Berkeley: University of California Press, 1985.

Bennett, W. *Our Children and Our Country.* New York: Simon & Schuster, 1988.

Bloom, A. *The Closing of the American Mind.* New York: Simon & Schuster, 1987.

Fitzgerald, F. *America Revised.* New York: Vintage Books, 1980.

Gardner, J. *On Moral Fiction.* New York: Basic Books, 1978.

Giroux, H. *Schooling and the Struggle for Public Life.* Minneapolis: University of Minnesota Press, 1988a.

Giroux, H. *Teachers as Intellectuals.* Granby, Mass.: Bergin & Garvey, 1988b.

Goodlad, J. *A Place Called School.* New York: McGraw-Hill, 1984.

Gutmann, A. *Democratic Education.* Princeton, N.J.: Princeton University Press, 1987.

Hastings Center. *The Teaching of Ethics in Higher Education.* Hastings-on-Hudson, N.Y.: Hastings Center, 1980.

Hirsch, E. D. *Cultural Literacy.* Boston: Houghton Mifflin, 1987.

James, W. "The Will to Believe." In J. J. McDermott (ed.), *The Writings of William James.* Chicago: University of Chicago Press, 1977.

Kimball, B. A. *Orators and Philosophers: A History of the Idea of Liberal Education.* New York: Teachers College Press, 1986.

Kohlberg, L. *The Philosophy of Moral Development.* New York: Harper & Row, 1981.

Kolakowski, L. "The Idolatry of Politics." *New Republic,* June 16, 1986, pp. 29–36.

Purpel, D. *The Moral and Spiritual Crisis in Education.* Granby, Mass.: Bergin & Garvey, 1988.

Raths, L., Harmin, M., and Simon, S. *Values and Teaching.* Columbus, Ohio: Charles E. Merrill, 1978.

Ryder, V. *Contemporary Living.* South Holland, Ill.: Goodheart-Willcox, 1985.

Soltis, J., and Strike, K. *The Ethics of Teaching.* New York: Teachers College Press, 1985.

Spring, J. *The American School: 1642–1985.* New York: Longman, 1986.

Part Four

Toward a Reform of Teaching

There have been many waves of reform in American education, but the current effort has some unique dimensions. Previous reform efforts in the twentieth century have focused on introducing curricular or organizational innovations into the schools. The distinctive component of the reform movement of the 1980s has been its focus on reform of the teaching profession itself, primarily through attention to the knowledge base of teaching.

The remarkable report by the Carnegie Task Force on Teaching as a Profession (1986) has led to a National Board for Professional Teaching Standards, which will begin offering national certification based upon "high and rigorous standards" by 1993 (Graves, 1989, p. 1). The research and experimentation undergirding this effort have led to an unprecedented national dialogue on what teachers should know, believe, and have the capacity to do. The Educational Testing Service has similarly announced a major redesign of the National Teacher Examination (NTE) to be implemented by 1991 ("California Students, Teachers to Test Revised Licensing Exam," 1989). The NTE change will also reflect the developing knowledge base for teaching and new assessment techniques. Finally, the work of the Holmes Group (1989) has ineluctably turned to concentrate on the knowledge base and curriculum for teacher education. This collective reform effort is thus particularly noteworthy for its national scope and persistence. But the implications and impacts of the effort are still quite difficult to predict. In this concluding part, we turn from the effort of articulating the knowledge, skills, and values essential to teaching to a review of the implications of this reform for the educational settings critical to the teaching profession—the schools themselves and the professional schools that prepare the teachers.

Griffin (1989) argues that there will be a need for substantial changes in the features of schools whose teachers share the common understanding suggested by the emerging knowledge base of teaching. But introducing the concept of teacher professionalism into schools that have been modeled after mass production factories with hierarchical authority structures and limited discretion for those providing the service will be difficult at best (Callahan, 1975). First, we need a fuller understanding of the implications of the Carnegie Task Force (1986) recommendations for the way teaching will actually be practiced in the schools. Second, we need to think creatively about the structural reforms necessary to create a more professional setting in the schools. How, for example, can we increase the frequency of teacher interaction, discussion, and professional interchange, and by what mechanisms can we encourage teachers to exercise the skills of coaching and the professional judgment of decision makers? Finally, the articulation of a knowledge base suggests that teachers will need to learn more and to learn continuously, as do the members of other professions. How can the organization and conduct of school settings provide support for this type of professional behavior?

Because schools of education are a primary source for the production of knowledge about teaching, and because teacher education programs attempt to put this knowledge into action, the arguments from this collection have particular bite for the design of these settings. But change will not be simple; universities are by nature conservative institutions. Schools of education, however, are unique professional schools, with missions and structures that vary substantially from more successful professional schools such as those of medicine, law, and business (Dill, 1980). It is unlikely that we can reform the knowledge base for teacher education without influencing the underlying strategy and structure of the professional schools of education. Achieving organizational integration would be a key element of such reform. How can the various factions and programs within schools of education be coordinated to provide the quality and intensity of professional education suggested by the authors of this volume? What forms of integration are feasible in a Janus-faced organization that must look toward the disciplines in the arts and sciences and, at the same time, toward mentor teachers in the schools? What types of curricular and pedagogical reforms are needed within schools of education to prepare teachers who have the sophistication of understanding, the value commitments, and the levels of skill suggested by the authors of this collection?

In the concluding chapters, Albert Shanker, a participant-observer in the current reform movement, and David Dill summarize and explore the implications of this volume for the reform of these critical educational settings.

References

"California Students, Teachers to Test Revised Licensing Exam." *Educational Daily,* May 19, 1989, pp. 1–2.

Callahan, R. *Education and the Cult of Efficiency.* Chicago: University of Chicago Press, 1975.

Carnegie Task Force on Teaching as a Profession. *A Nation Prepared: Teachers for the 21st Century.* Washington, D.C.: Carnegie Forum on Education and the Economy, 1986.

Dill, D. D. "Schools of Education as Complex Organizations." In D. E. Griffiths and D. J. McCarty (eds.), *The Dilemma of the Deanship.* Danville, Ill.: Interstate, 1980.

Graves, B. "Hunt's Board Outlines National Teacher Certification Plan." *Raleigh News and Observer,* July 18, 1989, pp. 1, 4.

Griffin, G. A. "Coda: The Knowledge-Driven School." In M. C. Reynolds (ed.), *Knowledge Base for the Beginning Teacher.* Elmsford, N.Y.: Pergamon Press, 1989.

Holmes Group. *Work in Progress: The Holmes Group One Year On.* East Lansing: Michigan State University, 1989.

10

Restructuring the Teaching Profession and Our Schools

Albert Shanker

Many people working in public education did not exactly welcome the wave of school reform that began with the release of *A Nation at Risk* (National Commission for Excellence in Education, 1983). They had grown accustomed to periodic attacks in newspapers, in magazines, and on television alleging all sorts of shortcomings in their performance and in the institutions for which they worked. When the reform reports appeared, the first impulse of those in public education was to start fighting back by pointing to the inaccuracies and exaggerations that many reports contained. That was my first inclination as well. One could honestly take issue with a great deal in the reports, although much was right on the mark. Fortunately, a number of us resisted our first impulses and did not immediately engage in a vitriolic debate. Instead, we began a serious assessment of the state of our schools.

For most of our history, the public schools were held in high regard. They were viewed as a means of providing opportunity for wave after wave of immigrants. Public education was an inspiring success story. Moreover, prior to the expansion of higher education in the 1960s, schoolteachers were likely to be among the most educated people in their communities and, as such, among the most respected. But by the time the reform reports began coming out in the early 1980s, we had reached a point in our society at which our teachers were not much more educated than the large mass of citizens. Whether or not schools were better or worse than they had been in the past, criticism of them accelerated as more and more Americans felt educated enough themselves to pass judgments on their educational institutions.

Polls showed that throughout the 1970s, more and more people were giving the schools lower and lower grades. The schools had less and less of a political constituency because, aside from the people who work in the schools, only the direct "customers"—the mothers and fathers of the students—were very involved. Although every citizen should be concerned, people who have children are more directly interested. Regardless of the social consequences, it is all too easy to become apathetic about other people's children. We went, in a short period of time, from a society that had up to 60 percent of the voting population in some communities with children in the schools (a powerful constituency for any politician) down to the level in 1986 of about 22 percent.

In addition, in the late seventies and early eighties, our society moved to other agendas—reindustrialization and rebuilding our infrastructure and defense capabilities at a time of stagnant economy. It was clear that our schools were going to be squeezed out by this other set of priorities. At this time, tuition tax credits and vouchers gained great popularity—and not exclusively among those groups who wanted tuition for the children they were sending to private schools. Polls over the last six years show that about 50 percent of the American population have, in effect, given up on the public schools as the major delivery system. "The schools are too rigid; they're too bureaucratic," they say. "They're not successful enough. Why not create competition in a market system? Why not give parents the right to pull their children out of public school?"

Despite all their criticism, the reform reports are in essential agreement on giving our public schools the opportunity to retool. Each of the thirty reports prepared by commissions made up of top business and political leaders in this country rejected, either implicitly or explicitly, the option of private schools as an alternative to public education. They all talked about strengthening public education—even the commission appointed by the Reagan administration, which was committed to vouchers and tax credits. All this was a plus.

Another plus was that for the first time, members of the business community in this country, at least those involved in preparing the reports, came to realize that an investment in people is just as important as rebuilding industry or rebuilding the infrastructure. These committees, which have generally fought to keep taxes down, still want them kept down. But they have come to recognize that an investment in education pays off on the bottom line. This conviction has been translated into action. In California, the Business Round Table came up with a reform plan with a two-year price tag of $2.6 billion and sent it to the newly elected governor, George Deukmejian; and they used their muscle to see that it was enacted. In Texas, H. Ross Perot, hardly a flaming liberal, chaired a special education committee for Governor Mark White and managed to get $2.8 billion of his proposed $5 billion increase incorporated into the state education budget. Perot acted from the conviction that the only way the state could invest money in Texas and have some reasonable assurance of a decent economy was to invest in people, in the talent that would attract business and industry.

This conviction has gained strength across the country. There has been some additional investment and some additional support for public education by the business community. But the changes brought about—minimum standards for teachers, testing for students, and a more defined curriculum—are mainly efforts to get rid of some of the excesses of the 1960s. And I am somewhat amused by the kinds of laws passed in state after state, some running to 150 pages, telling teachers how many minutes to teach a particular subject or mandating what text or test to use. Such laws, if passed for business, would be called overregulation, but in education they are called reform.

Teacher Supply

Since many local education agencies did not do the job themselves, unfortunately, they did have to be reformed. But now there is a growing awareness that the whole education reform movement is being threatened by what is about to happen with the supply of teachers. In the next seven years, America will lose one-half of its public school teachers—1.1 million out of 2.2 million will leave. To compound the problem, we no longer can rely on the usual sources of supply from which the schools of this country were staffed in the past. We once had the benefit of many outstanding people who went into teaching because of the Great Depression of the 1930s. At the time, because of high levels of unemployment, our schools could pick almost anybody they wanted. Most of those people are now retired. Later, the schools could choose from among many capable men who chose to serve in our urban schools for a draft exemption rather than serve in Korea or Vietnam. But the draft is gone, and we no longer get those men. Then, of course, the schools were once staffed by large numbers of talented women and minorities to whom other doors were closed. But with the expansion of other opportunities—in finance, medicine, or law, for example—the number of women entering teaching in recent years has plummeted.

This is wonderful for women and minorities—a great example of the rich opportunity of American society. But it is a disaster for education, which has lost a once-deep reservoir of talent. The figures graphically illustrate how teaching has declined as a profession of choice. In 1973, 24 percent of college undergraduates said they wanted to be teachers. In 1983, the figure had declined to 4.5 percent. In 1988, even with all the reform initiatives, the figure went up to only 6 percent, and all too many of those were heavily clustered in the bottom quartiles of their classes, based on SAT results and on all other indicators.

You can see vivid evidence of the decline in quality in California and Florida, where from 30 to 45 percent of the candidates could not pass a sixth-grade arithmetic entry-level exam for teachers. And not long ago, the city of Baltimore gave its new teachers a basic competency test in literacy and numerical skills. About 35 percent failed, but when the opening of school came around, those applicants who failed received telegrams asking them to report for duty immediately because of a shortage of teachers. And these newly anointed teachers, who instructed young people during the day, were required to go to school at night to learn to read and write. The education authorities in Texas must have seen the handwriting on the wall, because they issued a directive explaining how to retain a teacher who fails the statewide examination, if no replacement is available.

So far in the school reform movement, we have had a substantially increased investment in education on the part of the states (but not by the federal government, whose contribution has declined), and we have had a substantial increase in investment and in interest by the business community around the country. But, along with these positive developments, we are probably going to have to embark on the disastrous course of dipping deeper into the available talent pool and hiring teachers who are far poorer than those who now staff our schools. This will certainly mean that schools will resort to systems of management that undermine the morale of the more able people and drive them out of the profession. Inevitably, hiring people with marginal competence demands more and more supervision. You have to keep an eye on those whose abilities are suspect. But in our public schools, you cannot just watch those you think are incompetent. That would be discriminatory, particularly where you have a good union. Management has to look at everyone very carefully, and when they do that, they start driving out those better people who should be free to exercise their professional judgment.

This eventuality will set the stage for a violent backlash against the reform movement. A sharp decline in teacher effectiveness will send a clear message to taxpayers about the futility of all the states' initiatives—salary increases, career ladders, new rules and regulations. This backlash will most likely lead to greater support for vouchers and tuition tax credits for private education.

Teacher Recruitment

Some simple arithmetic shows the magnitude of the recruiting problem our schools face. Simply to replace the teachers who will be leaving, our schools would need to hire 24 percent of all the college graduates in the country in the next ten years. Let us assume that, since we want quality personnel, we are not going to draw from the bottom quartile, but will only consider candidates from the top half of each class. This is not a lofty standard when we consider quality of college graduates and the singular importance of the teaching profession. But is it reasonable for a society like ours to say that one-half of the talent in the top half of our colleges will be devoted to one industry? Do we not also need people in other professions and occupations? Do we really think that share of the talent in our country will go into the public elementary and secondary schools? Whenever there is talk about the problems of teacher recruitment, you are bound to hear some old, familiar slogans. But what might have made sense in the past can seem rather foolish in the light of current realities. Nevertheless, some of these simple, time-honored battle cries certainly have kernels of truth to them.

To some observers, the solution to a teacher shortage is simple. You have to have salaries that are substantially greater than they are now and that are competitive with other professions. It is a cut-and-dried problem of the marketplace. You set your standards and pay what you have to to get the talent you want. But when you think about what this will cost in a mass industry of 2.2 million people, you will begin to get an idea of just how difficult it will be to implement. The average teacher salary is now around $24,000. A $1,000 salary increase for each teacher would cost $2.2 billion, not counting Social Security and other fringe benefits. Obviously $1,000, while it would probably be welcomed by everybody, would not do much to change the market. Probably you would have to offer a 50 percent increase, to about $35,000, to get the talent that now goes into other fields. Then other employers would raise salaries to keep the people they have. So, if you want to get any shift in the schools' share of talent, you will have to do something dramatic. The tab for that will be about $30 billion, without fringes. It is not very likely to happen. And even if you did all that, you still would not get people in math and science because they hardly exist, and the private industries who need the few available will just meet the market price and up the salary ante in those fields, so even a vast expenditure will solve only some of our schools' recruitment problems.

Another difficulty has to do with the whole question of the intrinsic satisfaction a teacher receives. Most people did not go into teaching because they thought they were going to get rich. They knew what it was like, and they went into teaching because perhaps they had some outstanding teacher, and they wanted to do for children what someone had done for them. Good teachers know that education is not just getting kids to do well on a multiple-choice test. What they are trying to do is to teach their students to write, to express themselves, to weigh alternatives, to exercise judgment, and to persuade—not just to be able to choose A, B, or C on an examination.

How does one get children to develop these skills? Theodore Sizer (1984) puts it quite well in *Horace's Compromise.* Students need to do a lot of writing and have frequent practice in organizing their thoughts, but this means that the teacher has to spend time reading many essays and coaching each student, talking to Johnny about whether what he wrote is the best way to express his thoughts and whether his second point logically follows his first. By this constant coaching, a student does eventually get to develop these skills. But can you do this if you are a secondary school teacher with thirty students in a class, five classes a day—150 students? If it takes you ten minutes to mark the paper and discuss it with the student, you have twenty-five hours for one set of papers. If you do not do it, you know you are not doing your job, and you get no satisfaction. If you do it, you are driving yourself beyond any point that is realistic.

Another popular recruitment slogan is "Let's improve working conditions! Reduce class size." If we cut registration by 20 percent, we won't have thirty students per class; we will have twenty-four. Instead of taking twenty-five hours, grading one class set of compositions will take only twenty hours. Life will be wonderful for teachers! If you reduce class size by 20 percent, you need more teachers. But there is a shortage of teachers, and if you have a shortage, you have to hire more teachers. Guess which teachers you are going to hire. You have to dig deeper and lower into the talent barrel. The more you hire, the lower you have to go. Therefore, to improve working conditions even marginally, you have to bring in more people who are not really qualified to teach.

I have not even begun to discuss the money required for this rather modest reform, which offers little relief for teachers. So, reducing class size, although it is still a great slogan, really does not do much to alter the overall picture.

A third popular slogan addresses the problem of ending teacher isolation and promoting collegial relationships. Being locked up in a room all day with only children for almost all of your working life is not exactly the sort of thing that a sane adult would want to do. And the truth is that vast numbers do not. In every city I visit, I hear someone call to me, "Hi, Al." I turn around to see if I recognize the face. Usually the person says, "You don't know me, but I used to be a teacher." After a while, it occurred to me that it would be a good idea to retire as president of the American Federation of Teachers and start an organization that has the possibility of being ten times as large—the American Federation of Ex-Teachers.

We do not have vast numbers of former doctors, former lawyers, former engineers, and so on. So why are there so many former teachers? Substandard salaries and oversized classes are part of the answer. But, more important, the narrowness of the teacher's world denies the possibility of satisfying exchanges with other adults and the sense that one is part of a thoughtful community of professionals. Again, the solution is simple. Decrease the teaching load—four periods a day instead of five, for example. But how many teachers would we have to hire to do this? We will need 1.1 million just to maintain current staff levels, and we are not likely to get those. So, if we attempt to reduce class size, we will need 1.4 million. And if we want to reduce the teaching periods, we will need 1.7 million. So, we will get to the point where we need more than 24 percent of college graduates; we will need 35, 36, or 37 percent.

These are not outlandish or unrepresentative figures. This is essentially the premise on which arguments of the Carnegie report *A Nation Prepared* (Carnegie Task Force on Teaching as a Profession, 1986) are based. It all seems hopeless. We can forget about it. We can lie to teachers, repeat the old slogans about salaries and working conditions, and make them believe that things are going to get better—and know they are not. Or we can wait for things to get worse and keep our fingers crossed.

Structure of Schools

What about the students' side of the story? This is a very important perspective, one that is often ignored in most discussions of education reform. Suppose, for the sake of argument, we put all of the recommendations of the last three years into effect. What would the schools look like? They would look like what they were in 1945. We would test teachers, get the kids to take required courses, and deny them diplomas if they did not measure up to rigorous standards. Back in 1945, 75 percent of the students dropped out of school, and it was not considered a disaster. A high school dropout could always work in an auto plant and make more than a teacher. But the job market has changed, and now a 25 percent dropout rate is a disaster.

If all the traditional reforms took hold, we would still face not only the problem of recruiting and retaining sufficient teachers but also the problem of engaging large numbers of students we now lose. Goodlad (1984) has shown that teachers spend about 85 percent of their time lecturing to kids and imparting information, a method that is simply ineffective for many students.

I do not think that any person in his or her right mind would organize an institution in which kids come at nine in the morning and sit still until three in the afternoon to listen to someone lecture; and no intelligent adult would want to be in the room with kids for all that time. With so many students in a class, a teacher is not really talking to the whole group. Some already know what the teacher is saying; they're bored. Another third are lost and nowhere near the teacher. It is a very inefficient system. Besides, we now have videocassettes, slides, films, audiocassettes, computers, and all sorts of other educational tools. What makes us assume that a lecture by a teacher about how Indians or Eskimos live in Alaska is necessarily more effective than a series of other experiences that are now easily and cheaply available?

Another example: A child comes to school when it opens in September. Like many other human beings, knowing that the payoff is not until next June when the report card comes, he delays getting down to serious work. After all, the day of judgment is a long way down the road, and he has plenty of catch-up time. A lot of kids do that, and by the time they get to mid October, they find that they are hopelessly behind. So what is the rational thing to do if you are hopelessly behind in October or November? The rational thing to do is to drop out, one way or another. Why sit there if you do not know what is going on and when you know you cannot catch up? If you drop out, when is the next time that you can drop back in? Next September. But by next September, all your friends have gone on ahead, and you have been out in the world and have had a good time for a year, hanging out in the streets or watching daytime television; there is a strong temptation not to go back at all.

Given our present school structure, the chances of getting back on track are very poor. But what if school were not organized on an annual basis? Suppose there were four-week "semesters" instead? If a student fell behind and failed a four-week course, it would be easier to make up that time than to make up a whole year's work. Besides, for some students, the prospect of a final grade after four weeks would offer a more immediate reward and would be a more effective incentive than would a distant reckoning four or more months down the road. Schools with such flexibility do exist. Do they really retain more students and have a different pace of instruction and intensity and commitment? They certainly do. Why do not more schools do this? Well, administratively it is easier to do things the way we do now.

Rigidity creates other problems. As things are now, all students are required to begin classes the day schools open; otherwise, they miss a whole learning sequence or two. Though school districts have cutoff birthday dates for entrance eligibility, there are significant age differences among the students on each level. A few months, particularly in the lower grades, can mean great differences in maturity, readiness, and physical size.

Research tells us a great deal about the effect of these age differences. Those who are a year older do much better in the same class than those who are a year younger. A year makes a lot of difference at the age of five or six. So, quite early, the older students get the message that they are a lot smarter and more powerful, and the younger ones get the message that they are a lot dumber and much weaker. That message tends to persist throughout life; it is a very hard lesson to overcome. But if we had semesters start at a different time, and if we had a more flexible system, we could avoid or mitigate this sort of problem.

Essentially, the Carnegie report is unique in that it set our sights beyond reform, beyond tinkering here and there to make modest adjustments in the prevailing system. It asked if there were ways in which the fundamental structure of schools and of the teaching profession could be changed so that they could function more effectively.

Proposals of the Carnegie Report

Specifically, the Carnegie report says that we have to do for teaching what has been done at various times for other professions. For example, medicine was not always the kind of career it is today. We have examples from the not-too-distant past of fathers' letters to their sons at Harvard threatening to cut them off without a cent if they went into medicine, because it was a field that was held in such poor esteem. Law and business administration were also not always the high-prestige fields they are today. We have within our own history and in living memory examples of careers that went from being fairly poorly paid, with low status and poor training, to professions that are now widely respected and richly rewarded. Implementation of the Carnegie recommendations would mean that teaching would have the characteristics of all other professions. The teaching field would be based on a significant body of knowledge, and its practitioners would act on the basis of accepted procedure consistent with that knowledge.

Another aspect of professionalism is the question of empowerment. The problem with most existing education legislation and all too much of the new reform regulations is that they essentially tell teachers what to do. If something like this were done to any other profession, it would be called legislative malpractice. But when it comes to education, legislators think nothing of writing bills telling teachers what to do in complex situations in which a professional practitioner should have the freedom to analyze the facts and exercise his or her judgment. A legislative mandate prevents the professional from exercising judgment and, therefore, from taking the proper steps.

There is an element of this issue of professionalization that is tied in with the approaches of Japanese management and modern management companies. By and large, American schools have employed teachers whom the authorities did not hold in very high esteem. As a result, schools were structured very much along the lines of an industrial-factory model.

The modest credentials of most teachers once may have justified such an approach. For many years, teachers in our public schools were graduates of one-year training schools, and the principal was the only one on the school staff with a college degree. Therefore, the teachers were viewed as "hired hands" who had to be closely supervised by the far-more-qualified "foreman." Between the principal and the teaching staff was a palpable educational distance and an authority relationship. This relationship has remained, although teachers are much more educated than they once were. But the financial structure of the schools still reflects this old hierarchical relationship. In operating budgets across the country today, only about thirty-six cents of every dollar go to teachers' salaries.

I will give the example of New York City to dramatize my point, but if you analyze your own community, you will most likely come up with something similar. The operating budget includes $5,000 for each child. Since the fiscal crisis, each class has at least thirty children—sometimes more than thirty. For a class of thirty children, New York is spending $150,000 in each classroom. The teacher's salary, at the top, is $40,000, and if you add pension and other benefits, maybe the teacher is getting $50,000. Now where is the other $100,000?

In reality, most of the remaining money goes into support staff to help teachers, although, by and large, the average rank-and-file teacher would be hard-pressed to identify exactly what sort of help he or she is getting. In any other industry, if you had an institution that was thought not to be doing very well, and if only about one-third of the money were up front in the productive process and two-thirds were somewhere back there with supervisors and administrators, coordinators, and all sorts of other people, you would ask some hard questions.

Although the Carnegie report is a complex document that defies easy summary, I want to underline an important point that almost every journalistic account misses. We tend to focus on some of the more daring proposals—the professional-level salaries and the professional-certification board, for example. These things are there, and they are the easiest to write about and argue about, so they appear on almost everyone's agenda. But what will not be on the agenda is something that can't be summarized in two or three sentences—the report's assumption that the structure of the schools of the future will differ radically from the points of view of the professionals and the students.

The Carnegie report assumes that we will get away from highly structured classrooms and group instruction, and, for want of a better analogy, we will move toward a model that is much closer to what the Boy Scouts and Girl Scouts do. That is, each student will have a prescribed curriculum. Every student is to accomplish and master certain tasks, but not through lectures. The job of the school will be to provide a series of experiences, whatever those experiences may be, to get the student to master whatever has to be mastered. Similarly, in the Boy Scouts, the scoutmaster never gives a lecture on how to tie nine knots. Some kids are past knots; some are still involved in other things and are not ready for knots on a particular day. Whoever is ready gets a book and a piece of rope and encouragement to try to do it on his own by copying. If that does not work, the scouts try to learn from samples of the actual knots. If that does not work, they try some peer tutoring with another scout who is a whiz at knot tying.

The job of education is connecting the student to a series of illuminating experiences, and the job of the teacher is one of thinking out and planning strategies and games, evaluating materials, evaluating the videotapes, and training some of the people for tutorial functions.

In a school where students are actively engaged in learning by going through a series of prescribed tasks (not necessarily in order, but all of them required), teachers will have the time for a fuller professional life; they will have time for collegial relations, to share their experiences and ideas with other teachers; they will have time to mark papers and coach students individually, because they will no longer be locked into four or five hours of daily lecturing. The old slogans about improving working conditions can become reality only if teachers are free from what they do most of the time, from what most of the literature says they should not do and do not do very well, and from what the kids are not getting much out of in the first place.

The Carnegie report deals with that issue—with how we can liberate teachers from the rigidity of our present classroom structure, so they can think about what experiences and technology will best serve their students. The report suggests that other people can help in the school, whether they are volunteers or retirees; it suggests new approaches to the training of new teachers, so that a large number of interns and residents can be parts of the instructional process, both to enhance their own experiences as future teachers and to help run the schools.

The Carnegie report advocates not only a restructured teaching profession but also a completely redesigned school system. This proposal will be extremely controversial and will mean an administration much leaner than we now have. Understandably, the principals are already up in arms. No principals or school board members were on the task force that produced the report, and to many, it will look like some radical plot by teachers to overthrow the "upper classes." Of course, it is not. It is really very much like a model management people are talking about for private industry.

Politics of Reform

The greatest problem, however, may well be how teachers themselves will react. Most of them are dissatisfied with what society thinks of them, how they are being rewarded, and what they are able and not able to do in schools. Many of them have great dreams of what teaching could be like. However, major change is not something that most of us take to very well, even if we are fairly miserable in our present condition. What the Carnegie report advocates will never be imposed on teachers. We will never force teachers to take responsibility for making educational decisions regarding the training of other adults or regarding the running of the schools as senior partners do in a law firm or as faculty members do in a college. Nobody can force a group of people to do that if they choose not to. If huge numbers of teachers in the country say, "This is not what I want. Making decisions is the principal's job. Leave me alone. Just give me my money and, if you can, reduce my class size," then the offer that is on the table in the Carnegie report will be removed, and we are unlikely to see another that is equally promising for a long time. A negative teacher response would be disastrous. The issues are complex. They require much more than minor patching up or minor changes in the way we educate our children; they require the ability to envision an entirely new system.

Let us think about the current system for a minute. We have school board people. They are very nice people, and they want to do something for education. They get elected; most of them serve without remuneration. But what happens? They want to be reelected. They are not usually elected through any political parties. The only way they can be reelected is through name recognition. The more they find out what is wrong in the schools and the more they publicize it, the more their names become known. The poor school superintendent is the only chief executive officer in the country who has to meet with his board of directors in a public meeting every week or two—a meeting at which the major game of the board of directors is to bring up every embarrassing event that has occurred in the institution since they last met. Now, the superintendent is also a nice person, usually someone who rose from the ranks on the basis of talent. But when faced with the constant carping of the local school board, the message goes out to middle management that, although creativity is appreciated and all that, what is really most important is "no more grief from board members."

So, doing something positive is not the top priority of the schools; preventing anything negative from happening is. Institutions that are devoted to that goal generally are not very good. The price of preventing anything negative from happening is preventing anything good from happening.

The principals then turn to the teachers and say the kids are out in the hall too much and making too much noise or too much of a disturbance, and that is a sign of lack of control, and it could mean that someone gets injured. That is all the board has to hear! So, teachers know that they are really judged on routines and rituals, not on the performance of students and certainly not on any great innovation. Get your plan book and reports in on time; make sure all the kids are sitting in the classroom. The great commandment is, "Thou shalt not make waves."

The public school is an institution that stresses control. The superintendent develops a big, fat book of rules. If anything goes wrong, he or she can prove in black and white that it was not his or her fault. (Some incompetent just violated rule number 167.) That is how a superintendent protects himself or herself against criticism—by showing that he or she thought about all contingencies before, but some stupid underling just had not read the whole manual recently.

The question is this: Is it possible to turn this situation around and to make the school an organization that everyone buys into? Right now, every teacher locked in a room with a bunch of kids has to be a multitalented superstar. He or she has to be an excellent lecturer, a disciplinarian, and a diagnostician of multitudinous student problems. Above all, he or she has to have a personality that meshes with all sorts of students. Not many people are built that way, and certainly not many people with all those qualities will stay in an institution like this. If you open up the system, and the children can move around to different adults, and adults can move around to other adults, you can essentially exercise the strengths that all these adults have. If someone happens to be a brilliant lecturer, let that person give a lecture several times a week. There is nothing wrong with a lecture. The cruel thing is to get two million people who cannot do it very well and tell them that it is the only way they can teach, or to tell the students who do not learn very well that way, but who might learn very well other ways, that it is the only way they are entitled to learn, and that if they do not learn that way, they are going to be considered disruptive or stupid. That is where the system is now.

Conclusion

What are the consequences if we do not do something? The stakes are high. There is no way we can continue with the current system. Unless we can create a different scenario regarding the talent (or the lack of it) that is about to enter the system—a scenario not so closely tied to the current reward system, the current structure, or the current demographic and economic facts of life—then indeed the current system will get worse. There is really only one place that this leads; more and more people who are now committed to public education will give up. Although they will probably continue to believe in the public schools in the abstract, they will be unwilling to sacrifice their children to a failed ideal.

The consequences for the country are very great. One of the most dramatic and frightening statistics is one that Harold Hodgkinson (1985) came up with a few years ago. When the first person retired on Social Security, there were seventeen people in the work force to support that person. Ten years from now, when I retire on Social Security, only three people will be working to support me. One of those will be a black or Hispanic, and some will be whites who did not make it in school. We may be getting very close to a society in which, instead of seventeen people supporting one person, we will have two people working, one of them supporting someone on Social Security and the other supporting someone who cannot work because that person did not get the educational background that would equip him or her for a job. What does that do to our standard of living? If the standard of living dips dramatically, what does that do to the faith of citizens in a democratic society? Clearly, many will start looking for alternatives. If we lose faith in public education, what types of schools will we have if we seek alternatives? There is no question. We will have Catholic schools, Protestant schools, Jewish schools, fundamentalist schools,

Lyndon Larouche and Farrakhan academies, left-wing learning centers, and many foreign language and ethnic schools.

This problem is unique to our country. In Japan, everybody is Japanese. If you come from somewhere else, no one will ever attempt to turn you into a Japanese. In Germany, a large influx of Turks as guest workers have been living there for such a long time that many no longer speak Turkish. But, even though some were born in Germany and speak German, they will never be Germans. As a matter of fact, Germany is offering them money to go back to Turkey because the government does not want to have a problem with ethnic friction. Nowhere in Germany is there the ideal that people who go there and live there for generations will become Germans. The same is true in France.

But this country is different. We all came from different ethnic backgrounds, and somebody 200 years ago would not have given us great odds that we would survive, because the history of most other societies of people who came from different places, different religions, and different races shows that people have a nasty tendency to try to kill each other. That is the experience the world has had. Perhaps the only great exception to this is the United States. I like to think that some of our success is because we do not send little children off to separate schools to develop the identities that they get at home anyway. We believe that people do become Americans and are Americanized most effectively in our schools. I think the question is not whether we will have a public education system in the future. We will always have kids in public schools, because there will always be students the private schools will not want. But public schools could come to resemble charity wards in hospitals, with patients nobody else will take.

The choices that we now make in education will have very great consequences for our society. I hope that all concerned citizens will study the Carnegie report. It is a package, not a shopping list that one can choose from. It might be wise to develop several other models and visions of overall changes that would be alternatives to the one the report presents. The alternatives should not, however, nitpick at this report, nor should the successful alternative emerge out of attempts to make minor changes in the current system. Other major revolutionary visions and transformations may be better than this one, or equally good, or valid as points of discussion. But I do think the Carnegie report does something necessary at this point in history. It looks at the basic structure of the school from the point of view of both students and adults. It does this in terms of economics and in terms of demography. It does it in terms of the technological developments that most schools have ignored. It is an exciting report. I recommend it to you, and I hope it becomes the basis for discussion everywhere.

All of us can play an important role in the next few years. I have indicated that one group of people could kill the Carnegie report. I would not mind it if they killed it after sober and informed reflection. But I am worried that American Federation of Teachers members will get the AFT version of it, and that National Education Association members will get the NEA version of it, and that people will march to the tune of whatever their leaders say. I think that would be a terrible thing on either side. I hope that those in other communities, whether school administrators or university professors, will create opportunities for educators throughout our entire public school system to go into these recommendations in great detail, so that whatever conclusions they arrive at are based on informed judgment and not on the red flags or slogans used by leaders on one side or the other. The stakes are far too high for this effort to be defeated by factionalism.

References

Carnegie Task Force on Teaching as a Profession. *A Nation Prepared: Teachers for the 21st Century*. Washington, D.C.: Carnegie Forum on Education and the Economy, 1986.

Goodlad, J. *A Place Called School*. New York: McGraw-Hill, 1984.

Hodgkinson, H. L. *All One System: Demographics of Education, Kindergarten Through Graduate School.* Washington, D.C.: Institute for Educational Leadership, 1985.

National Commission for Excellence in Education. *A Nation at Risk.* Washington, D.C.: National Institute of Education, 1983.

Sizer, T. R. *Horace's Compromise.* Boston: Houghton Mifflin, 1984.

11

Transforming Schools of Education into Schools of Teaching

David D. Dill

What is the mission of schools of education in major research universities, and how should this mission be implemented? Clarity of purpose is a necessary condition for long-term commitment and meaningful contribution. Reports on schools of education consistently emphasize their confusion of goals, conflicting objectives, and lack of cohesion (Clifford and Guthrie, 1988; Holmes Group, 1989). Some portion of the low esteem of teaching can be traced to the failure of the faculties in schools of education to find in the education of teachers a sufficiently compelling calling, to commit themselves to this calling for the long haul, and thereby to contribute to the knowledge base of teaching, the authority of teachers, and the pride of the teaching profession.

In his remarkable foreword to *Orators and Philosophers: A History of the Idea of Liberal Education* (Kimball, 1986), Joseph Featherstone argues that what has been lost in contemporary liberal education is the sense of a community of learning. Such a community provides a connection with a tradition of knowledge, emphasizes the public expression and testing of that tradition, and applies the knowledge in actions that make a difference in the world. Featherstone's concept of a community of learning offers a valuable metaphor for clarifying the mission and structure of a professional school of education. In the sections that follow, I will explore this metaphor by comparing the singular irony of the mission of schools of education with other, more unified professional schools and by suggesting what the emerging knowledge, skills, and values of teaching imply for the staffing, research efforts, organization, and pedagogical forms of a professional school of education.

Singular Irony of Schools of Education

Recent critiques of schools of education in major universities (Bok, 1987; Clifford and Guthrie, 1988) have made comparable points about their failure to contribute significantly to the profession of education. Schools of education have been too enamored of the prestige of the arts and sciences. They have appointed social scientists with little commitment to or experience in education, and they have placed a disproportionate emphasis on the Ph.D. degree (as opposed to truly professional degrees). They have ignored and avoided the public schools, increasingly selecting students and designing programs for nonschool markets such as higher education, business and industry, or consulting. The research the faculties of these schools have produced has been superficial, enraptured with methodology, and, in many cases, irrelevant to the practice of teaching in the schools. In short, these critiques conclude that schools of education must redefine their mission and commit themselves to preparing educational professionals for the schools. (One assumes the emphasis should be on public schools, but this is frequently left ambiguous.)

This critique of schools of education in major universities generally results in strong support from arts and science faculty from within these institutions, agreement from school personnel, and strongly negative reactions from many faculties of education. The critique, however, sustains rather than confronts the singular irony of the mission of schools of education, a mission that restrains the contribution a school of education could make to the profession of teaching. One is tempted to ask these critics whether they would similarly charge the school of business at their universities to prepare professionals only for the banking industry, or the medical school to prepare professionals only for public health hospitals, or the law school to prepare professionals only for the courts. In short, why can more respected professional schools pursue the clear mission of educating individuals to join a particular profession, to be practiced without regard to institutional context, while schools of education must prepare professionals for a particular institutional setting? Although the attempt to align the mission of schools of education more closely with the schools appears to clarify the education schools' purpose, it fails to do so. The consequence of this strategy becomes more clear when one explores the meaning of the plural term *professionals,* as used in respect to schools of education.

Bok (1987), for example, suggests that the school of education at Harvard focus on the preparation of various types of professionals involved with the nation's schools—schoolteachers, of course, as well as planners and policy analysts, educational administrators, college faculty members, researchers in the field of education, and "the more amorphous group of specialists who contribute to the contemporary school system" (p. 54). (Former Secretary of Education Bennett often referred to this latter group, inelegantly, as "the blob"—that group of nonteaching support personnel who constitute over two-thirds of the cost of schooling [Bok, 1987, p. 14].) Bok's criteria for selecting this collection of professionals are interesting: (1) They can make a positive impact on the quality of education. (2) Jobs are sufficiently plentiful and attractive for the profession to ensure an adequate applicant pool. (3) The career attracts degree candidates who are interesting to teach. (4) The professional roles require the kinds of knowledge and skills faculty members can teach effectively and with satisfaction.

These criteria, while more limited than those previously employed by the Harvard University Graduate School of Education, still result in a school whose mission is less coherent and whose knowledge base is less integrated than those of its sister schools of business, medicine, and law. The problem is similar at major public schools of education where graduate programs and advanced credentials for fields other than teaching have proliferated, often under the imposition of state education officials.

This failure to see that the emperor has no clothes is pervasive. Clifford and Guthrie's (1988) stinging analysis of the history of schools of education reveals that these schools were seduced away from their original mission as schools of pedagogy by a desire for male students over female students, by attraction to higher-paying, more influential careers (for example, principals and superintendents rather than teachers), and by the prestige and status of conducting social science research rather than professionally oriented field research. They nonetheless conclude their critique by defining as the proper mission for schools of education "the preparation of *educators,* the study of *the educative process* and the study of *schooling* as a social institution" (p. 349, emphasis added). Conspicuously absent are the simpler and clearer respective terms *teachers, teaching,* and *the teaching profession.*

The singular irony in the mission and strategy of schools of education is that there is not one major university in the United States today that has a professional school dedicated to the teaching profession in the same sense that those universities have schools dedicated to the professions of law, medicine, business, and theology. Instead, all schools of education are holding companies for professional programs of different types—programs that share no common base of knowledge (Dill, 1984). In medicine, law, and business, all professional students must pass through a basic professional curriculum that socializes them to the core knowledge of the field. (In many schools of business, Ph.D. students who have not received an M.B.A. are often required to complete essential M.B.A. courses as part of their doctoral programs.) Most, if not all, faculty members in these schools teach in the basic professional curriculum. In schools of education, this is not the case. Thus, schools of education are riven by debates over who must teach in the teacher education program and over whether any knowledge base exists for all students in the school.

In short, a community of learning is not possible within schools of education, given their current missions. The effort given over to the development, public debate, and implementation of the knowledge base for teaching within these schools is marginal rather than central to their activity. There is no distinguished "lighthouse" professional school of teaching whose stature and reputation signal a model professional school curriculum as do the Harvard School of Business, the Yale School of Law, or the Stanford School of Medicine for their respective fields. While the influence and impact of a professional school on the stature of its profession should not be overstated, there is every reason to believe that the failure of American schools of education to adopt the education of teachers as their central mission has diminished the teaching profession and has retarded the development of its knowledge base.

The first step in the design of a community of learning in a school of education must be the adoption of the profession of teaching as the school's primary calling. The second step is to adapt the form of the school to this essential function. In the following sections, I explore the organizational implications of the knowledge base of teaching suggested in the preceding chapters.

Staffing

The discussion of the knowledge base for teaching throughout this volume emphasizes the teacher as an active decision maker, with a deep conceptual understanding of content, strong interpersonal and presentation skills, and a capacity to instruct and assess students through carefully honed discussion and questioning skills grounded in knowledge of subject matter. This description suggests a sophistication of understanding and level of behavioral skill that can only be developed under close supervision, coaching, and discussion-centered teaching.

By contrast, many teacher education programs are treated as so-called cash cows by their parent universities. Student-faculty ratios are high, and lectures are the predominant mode of instruction. Developing teacher education programs of the quality suggested by the authors of this volume will require a student-faculty ratio lower than is now common. To some extent, this lower ratio can be accomplished by reallocating faculty resources within schools of education in accord with the previously suggested reorientation of mission in schools of education. Many faculty resources in schools of education are currently committed to doctoral programs and advanced professional programs for educational professionals other than teachers, and the staffing ratios of these programs are frequently more favorable than those in teacher education programs.

But staffing changes will also require a mix of talents different from the current practice. The centrality of content knowledge emphasized by Good, Sigel, Lloyd-Jones, Hilton, and Morowitz and the arguments in support of the moral dimension of teaching by Smith and Nord suggest that schools of education need to develop their faculty resources in relevant disciplinary fields, including those areas in the humanities that can shed light on moral and ethical issues in teaching. But the appointment of content specialists in each content field tends to further fractionalize already segmented schools of education. Instead, staffing patterns should emphasize contracting for subject matter expertise and humanistic instruction from the basic arts and sciences departments, using joint appointments where appropriate. (Instruction in content-related areas should also involve clinical master teachers as discussed below.) This type of staffing would not only increase the knowledge base of the school in content areas and in the humanities but would also provide an organizational rationale for the close interaction between the school of education and the arts and sciences disciplines, which will be needed in any event. This staffing pattern could actually increase the sense of cohesion among the core faculty members within schools of education, because much current factionalism plays itself out along disciplinary lines.

Most critical to the staffing of schools of education is the adoption of a clinical faculty model characteristic of medical schools. Both Adler and Evertson call for the use of master teachers in teacher education programs. Several schools of education—notably New Mexico, Colorado, and North Carolina—have pioneered in appointing experienced teachers as clinical professors in their schools of education. These clinical master teachers can supervise student teachers, help coach and mentor in teaching laboratories, and plan and instruct content-oriented courses in pedagogy. The inclusion of experienced, practicing teachers as a separate but significant force within schools of education means that tenure-track, research-oriented faculty can be selected on grounds other than practical teaching experience and thus have the potential for surviving in a university culture. Furthermore, the inclusion of clinical teaching faculty better connects teacher education programs to the wisdom of practice, and it provides needed role models for students. It also provides for needed creative conflict within schools of education—conflict between experienced proponents of professional practice and the traditional faculty oriented to increasing the knowledge base of teaching.

The current reform efforts to introduce career ladders and master teacher programs in many school districts have generally not capitalized on the creative solution of identifying master teachers through clinical appointments to schools of education. This process could involve not only teachers who are appointed to university schools of education full time for specified periods but also joint appointments and adjunct appointments whereby full-time schoolteachers may help teach a single course in the afternoon or evening, during vacation periods, or during the summer. This type of clinical affiliation would respond to the need for a clear distinction between the role and responsibilities of master teachers and traditional teachers; it would provide an alternative means of increasing the pay of master teachers, and it would more efficiently use the financial resources of schools of education to increase the size and relevant experience of the faculty involved in teacher education. Finally, the public debate over the criteria for identifying such master teachers and over the assessment and selection of candidates would be a powerful enactment of the concept of a community of learning engaged in the knowledge base for teaching.

Research Efforts

Good has called for increased effort in research on teaching and teacher education, and substantial new efforts are under way in conjunction with the new National Board of Teaching Standards, supported in part by the Carnegie Corporation (L. S. Shulman, 1987). However, the development of the knowledge base of teaching is so central to the function of schools of education in research universities that means for enhancing such research should be part of the design of such schools. This might include creation of a center for research on teaching, developing a program of case-based research on teaching, and establishing resource centers for research on international curricula.

One means of conceptualizing the role of a professional school in a research university is through the process of technology transfer. Schools of education thereby discover basic knowledge on teaching; develop this knowledge into articles, texts, learning experiences, and curriculum materials; and disseminate (frequently market) this knowledge through their teaching programs, continuing professional education, and publications. Central to the effectiveness of this process are organizational mechanisms—usually called research centers or institutes—for conducting, developing, and disseminating this research. It is likely not a coincidence that many of the leaders of the current effort to articulate the knowledge base of teaching are or have been affiliated with Michigan State, or that M.S.U. serves as the center of the Holmes Group, because that university houses one of the best-known research centers in the field, the Institute for Research on Teaching.

Shulman (1986) has suggested that the accumulated wisdom of practice is as important to guiding professionals as are empirically derived principles. He recommends active programs of research to identify a body of case knowledge that can inform the professional literature and teacher education programs. Shulman has argued that case knowledge is not reductionist, but essential to theoretical understanding. Recent work with teachers in the field has suggested the potential richness of this approach (J. Shulman, 1987). It is worth noting that the respected Harvard School of Business, one of the most professionally oriented of major business schools, for decades has conducted and aggressively supported case-based business research by its faculty as a means of developing knowledge to advance the field of business (Christensen, 1987). As Harvard economist John T. Dunlop once observed, the goal of professional education should be not rigor with as much relevance as possible but relevance with as much rigor as possible. Therefore, case-based research into teaching provides a creative means of more effectively tying schools of education to the professional field of practice.

A third important focus for research is curricular knowledge (Shulman, 1986). The curriculum and its associated materials represent the treatments available to teachers in addressing the varying capacities of student achievement. Teachers need to understand well and to be skilled in applying the alternative materials for teaching particular subjects and topics at a given level. Curriculum and instruction courses have been staples of teacher education programs, but only recently has the true potential for research on curricular knowledge been tapped.

For example, the University of Chicago School Mathematics Project has developed an International Mathematics Education Resource Center as a research facility on mathematics curricula ("Learning from Other Countries," 1989). The center houses translated textbooks, workbooks, and teacher manuals from educationally advanced countries including Japan and the Soviet Union. The center also houses translations of outstanding Soviet research in the psychology of learning and teaching mathematics. This project suggests the potential richness of research on curricular knowledge, if understood in its universal context. Many fields taught in

American schools, including mathematics, geography, science, foreign languages, and, of course, English, are also taught in advanced countries throughout the world. These countries have developed extensive curricular materials for students of all abilities. Research on these materials and the ways in which they are taught, as well as the provision of these curricular alternatives in schools of education, offers a potentially important focus on teaching that literally makes a difference in the world.

The development of research centers on teaching that can bring together faculty members from within the school, as well as teachers in the field, to pursue research on the knowledge base of teaching is a critical mechanism for creating a community of learning.

Organization

A major problem in academic organizations—particularly in schools of education, which must bridge the traditional arts and sciences with the schools—is discovering organizational mechanisms for integration. Three areas in which increased integration would improve the knowledge base for teacher education are general education, subject content knowledge, and pedagogical content knowledge.

Adler, Smith, and Nord each argue that teachers' general knowledge is critical for assisting students in achieving conceptual understanding. But programs of general or liberal education frequently lack the definition or focus necessary to provide the type of integrative education helpful to teachers. Recent efforts to improve the quality of undergraduate education are employing outcomes assessments that use various planning and evaluation techniques to clarify the purposes and outcomes of an academic program (Ewell, 1988). One cardinal principle of quality control in any organization is specification of quality standards for critical inputs and enforcement of those standards at the point at which critical inputs enter the organization. Because of their perceived status relative to the traditional arts and sciences, few schools of education have had the courage or vision to attempt to define the type of general knowledge appropriate to their students in teacher education or to assess incoming students by oral or written assessment techniques. At best, schools of education have relied upon existing requirements in the arts and sciences and the general education battery of the National Teacher Exam. The process of defining and assessing the general education component of teacher education—a project that could be carried out in conjunction with faculty members in arts and sciences and experienced teachers—would be one organizational mechanism for further integrating arts and sciences knowledge with pedagogical knowledge.

A variant of this approach would focus on integrating content in the teaching specialties. Hilton, Lloyd-Jones, and Morowitz provided arguments for the content knowledge appropriate to their respective fields of mathematics, English, and science. But each also suggested that this preparation would vary from existing majors or minors in each field—although they argued that the knowledge appropriate for teachers would be the best knowledge to require of all—and would have to be reconciled to the different content expectations of teaching at the school level. One means of accomplishing this reconciliation would be to assign the task of defining appropriate content knowledge in each specialty to project teams consisting of faculty members from arts and sciences, relevant faculty members in education, and relevant experienced teachers from the schools. Each project group also would be responsible for designing written and oral assessment procedures for assuring that each student achieved, by the conclusion of his or her program, the requisite conceptual understanding and skills of the content specialty. Preparation for such an assessment could be the responsibility of each student, guided by recommended course selections, by suggested readings, and by other related components of the teacher education program.

A third device for integration would focus on pedagogical content knowledge (Shulman, 1986). Good and Sigel both emphasize the importance of integrating content and pedagogy with active teaching, especially through the use of questioning, discussion, and careful assessment of student level of understanding. However, schools of education frequently teach courses on classroom management and presentation skills without reference to the content specialty; and traditional methods courses, which ostensibly combine content and pedagogy, have come under heavy criticism (Doyle, 1988). One integrating innovation would be to develop case-study-oriented seminars focused on pedagogical content knowledge and planned by teams of experienced teachers and faculty members from arts and sciences. The cases could be developed as part of a content-oriented curriculum to examine means of representing ideas, understandings of what makes learning of specific topics easy or difficult for certain students, and techniques of assessing students' understandings. These cases should be taught in the form of grand rounds in medicine, with several mentor teachers from the content specialty leading discussions of cases or simulated situations with students from that specialty. Thus, experienced, knowledgeable teachers, in an active situation, could impart the skill of thinking with pedagogical content knowledge.

The underlying logic of each of these integrating mechanisms is similar—to bring together individuals representing different stages of the complex technology transfer process of teaching (that is, arts and sciences faculty, education faculty, and experienced teachers), to ask them to define the knowledge essential to teaching, and then to implement that knowledge through active learning experiences and through clearly articulated assessment procedures that provide an opportunity for integration and assimilation. Consistent with the idea of a community of learning, these organizational mechanisms would allow academic organizations publicly to articulate and debate the knowledge base of teaching and then to translate it into action.

Pedagogical Forms

Ironically, one of the primary implications of the many suggestions in this volume is for changes in the ways schools of education conduct teaching and learning. Each of the authors has argued for a more active conception of teaching, with teachers as decision makers and teaching as thought in action. Good, Sigel, and Evertson emphasize teaching as a behavioral skill, practiced continuously on stage. The discussion of the moral dimension of teaching also suggests an active process, one of reflection and choice among competing ethical claims. How can we cultivate these active skills? The authors imply two primary tools—active analysis of cases and dilemmas and carefully designed clinical experiences.

The Harvard Business School bases its case-study approach on a clear conception of the manager as decision maker, and it assumes that the most effective means to prepare professional managers is to provide them the opportunity to make choices and decisions by confronting them with richly detailed case studies of actual business situations that require decisions. The philosophy of the method is precisely captured in a quotation journalist Fred Friendly once saw on a grade school blackboard: "Our job is not to make up anyone's mind. Our job is to make the agony of decision making so intense that you escape only by thinking" (Wagner, 1989).

Shulman (1986) has argued that case instruction, carefully conducted, also has the potential for better connecting schools of education to the field by codifying and conveying the wisdom of practice. Recent materials on discussion-centered and case-method teaching have made the techniques more broadly available (Christensen, 1987; Weiss, 1987). Case materials are now also becoming available on the ethics of teaching (Strike and Soltis, 1985). Discussion-centered teaching, case studies, and other forms of decision-oriented simulations are needed pedagogical innovations for schools of education, and they are consistent with the essential knowledge and skills of teaching.

Evertson's critique of the practice of teaching observation reveals one of the difficulties of developing the essential skills of teaching. That is, students are not always coached with the appropriate feedback and reinforcement necessary for learning the skill of observing. Nor do they learn the relationship between observing and acting—or their combined role in the process of teaching. In short, current clinical experience in observation is neither skill based nor directly relevant to active teaching.

As Evertson suggests, we need to place more emphasis on developing individual skills in inquiry and decision making relevant to active teaching through a process of active learning. In this view, students may best learn teaching skills through guided, on-campus clinical experience. In a controlled, risk-free environment with appropriate coaching, students could learn the skills of observation, reflection, and action. The implementation of teaching laboratories could immensely aid the development of these skills by providing students with microteaching experiences, role play, extensive feedback, and assistance in self-analysis. The support and involvement of clinical master teachers would further enhance such skill development.

Schools of education have long been the homes of programs in school psychology, clinical psychology, and counseling psychology, which employ sophisticated behavioral skill development as part of their training programs. Many of these skills and most of these methods are directly applicable to teacher education programs. Clearly, the development of appropriate teaching laboratories and skill assessment centers is a needed reform in teacher education programs.

Conclusion

Schools of education are the most incoherent of all major professional schools. Clifford and Guthrie (1988, pp. 152–153) pointed to the steady retreat of schools of education from the professional preparation of teachers to graduate programs for those leaving teaching: "The prevailing curricular approach . . . [made] a virtue of near anarchy in the name of individualization. This meant designing a program of studies that accepted each student's *prior* preparation (itself highly varied, unlike that of medical or engineering school graduates, for example), professional experience, and personal ambition. This reduced the strain on the institution's diminished capacity to agree upon the desiderata of competence and knowledge in professional education and on how to achieve them. However, this also made it every year more difficult to obtain some national consensus on what an advanced degree in education stood for in the programmatic sense. In this regard, too, schools of education bore scant resemblance to the law or medical school *ideal.*"

The task of defining the knowledge, skills, and values essential to teaching must be central to schools of education. But it can become so only if these schools honestly confront their fundamental mission. They must clarify their primary calling to be schools of teaching (Dill, 1984). Only if they take this simple, but most difficult to implement, step can schools of education make the transition from their current confused status as social science research institutes and training conglomerates to true professional schools.

If they can make that transition, they can create a community of learning united in its commitment to a common calling, actively engaged in defining and debating a shared professional tradition, and dedicated to applying that tradition in the education of future professionals. Intrinsic to that community will be the question "What are the knowledge, skills, and values essential to good teaching?"

References

Bok, D. "The Challenge to Schools of Education." *Harvard Magazine,* May–June 1987, pp. 47–57, 79–80.

Christensen, C. R. *Teaching and the Case Method.* Boston: Harvard Business School, 1987.

Clifford, G. J., and Guthrie, J. W. *Ed School.* Chicago: University of Chicago Press, 1988.

Dill, D. D. "New Strategies for Schools of Education Ought to Include Schools of Teaching." *Chronicle of Higher Education,* Jan. 18, 1984, p. 80.

Doyle, W. "Curriculum in Teacher Education." Paper presented at the annual meeting of the American Educational Research Association, New Orleans, Apr. 1988.

Ewell, P. T. "Outcomes, Assessment, and Academic Improvement: In Search of Usable Knowledge." In J. Smart (ed.), *Higher Education: Handbook of Theory and Research*. Vol. 4. New York: Agathon Press, 1988.

Holmes Group. *Work in Progress: The Holmes Group One Year On*. East Lansing: Michigan State University, 1989.

Kimball, B. A. *Orators and Philosophers: A History of the Idea of Liberal Education*. New York: Teachers College Press, 1986.

"Learning from Other Countries." *UCSSMP Newsletter*, Spring 1989, no. 5, p. 3.

Shulman, J. "Cases as Catalysts for Cases." Paper presented at the annual meeting of the American Educational Research Association, Washington, D.C., Apr. 1987.

Shulman, L. S. "Those Who Understand: Knowledge Growth in Teaching." *Educational Researcher*, 1986, *15* (2), 4–14.

Shulman, L. S. "Knowledge and Teaching: Foundations of the New Reform." *Harvard Educational Review*, 1987, *57*, 1–22.

Strike, K. A., and Soltis, J. F. *The Ethics of Teaching*. New York: Teachers College Press, 1985.

Wagner, M. T. "No Easy Answers from 'Ethics in America.' " *Center Piece*, Jan. 1989.

Weiss, P. F. *Program Guide: A Seminar Approach to Teaching and Learning*. Chicago: Encyclopaedia Britannica, 1987.

Index